Logic Programming
and Knowledge
Engineering

D1474282

INTERNATIONAL COMPUTER SCIENCE SERIES

Consulting editors   **A D McGettrick**   University of Strathclyde
                         J van Leeuwen   University of Utrecht

OTHER TITLES IN THE SERIES

Programming in Ada (2nd Edn.)   *J G P Barnes*

Software Engineering (2nd Edn.)   *I Sommerville*

An Introduction to Numerical Methods with Pascal   *L V Atkinson and P J Harley*

The UNIX System   *S R Bourne*

Handbook of Algorithms and Data Structures   *G H Gonnet*

Microcomputers in Engineering and Science   *J F Craine and G R Martin*

UNIX for Super-Users   *E Foxley*

Software Specification Techniques   *N Gehani and A D McGettrick* (eds.)

Introduction to Expert Systems   *P Jackson*

Data Communications for Programmers   *M Purser*

Local Area Network Design   *A Hopper, S Temple and R C Williamson*

Modula-2: Discipline & Design   *A H J Sale*

The UNIX System V Environment   *S R Bourne*

Prolog Programming for Artificial Intelligence   *I Bratko*

Prolog   *F Giannesini, H Kanoui, R Pasero and M van Caneghem*

Programming Language Translation: A Practical Approach   *P D Terry*

Data Abstraction in Programming Languages   *J M Bishop*

System Simulation: Programming Styles and Languages   *W Kreutzer*

The Craft of Software Engineering   *A Macro and J Buxton*

UNIX System Programming   *K F Haviland and B Salama*

An Introduction to Programming with Modula-2   *P D Terry*

Pop-11 Programming for Artificial Intelligence   *A M Burton and N R Shadbolt*

The Specification of Computer Programs   *W M Turski and T S E Maibaum*

Software Development with Ada   *I Sommerville and R Morrison*

UNIX^{TM} is a trademark of AT & T.

Logic Programming and Knowledge Engineering

Tore Amble

ADDISON-WESLEY
PUBLISHING
COMPANY

Wokingham, England · Reading, Massachusetts · Menlo Park, California
New York · Don Mills, Ontario · Amsterdam · Bonn · Sydney
Singapore · Tokyo · Madrid · Bogota · Santiago · San Juan

The programs in this book have been included for their instructional value. They have been tested with care but are not guaranteed for any particular purpose. The publisher does not offer any warranties or representations, nor does it accept any liabilities with respect to the programs.

Cover graphic by Laurence M. Gartel.
Typeset by Columns of Reading.
Printed and bound in Great Britain by T J Press (Padstow) Ltd, Cornwall.

First printed 1987.

British Library Cataloguing in Publication Data

Amble, Tore
    Logic programming and knowledge engineering.
    —(International computer science series).
    1. Expert systems (Computer science)
    2. Electronic digital computers—
    Programming   3. Logic, symbolic and
    mathematical
    I. Title   II. Series
    005.13'1   QA76.76.E95

    ISBN 0–201–18043–X

Library of Congress Cataloging in Publication Data

Amble, Tore, 1945–
    Logic programming and knowledge engineering.

    (International computer science series)
    Bibliography: p.
    Includes index.
    1. Logic programming.   2. Expert systems (Computer
science)   I. Title.   II. Series.
    QA76.6.A464   1987   005.1   87–13556
    ISBN 0–201–18043–X

Preface

Pioneering research in computer science in the 1970s has led to a revolution in information technology this decade. Two of the most important new directions in software engineering are logic programming and knowledge engineering. They both embody the basic change in computing – a move away from program-controlled computing to computing derived by deduction and reasoning.

The key idea behind logic programming is to replace programming and computation by a logical description of a problem and an automatic proof mechanism for deducing the answers.

The basis of knowledge engineering is to make intelligent, problem-solving expert systems knowledge-based by finding and applying the rules and heuristics that govern experts' problem-solving processes. Knowledge-based systems differ from traditional programs in that they are derived directly from these rules, with no intervening programming.

The combination of these two ideas will change the future of software engineering and replace ideas that have become too formalized, inflexible and problematic. Computer technology will adapt itself to support this development.

This book is written for students and professionals with an interest in engineering, who need a theoretical as well as practical introduction to logic programming and how it can be used to build knowledge-based systems. It is suitable for an undergraduate course at third or fourth year level. For complete understanding, it requires two years of programming experience with some knowledge of Pascal, but parts of the book should be comprehensible to a wider readership.

The book falls roughly into two parts: an introduction to logic programming; and applications of logic programming. The first part introduces predicate logic, resolution and the programming language Prolog. It looks in detail at a subset of the language, list processing in Prolog and advanced programming techniques, with the emphasis on meta-level logic programming. The second part of the book looks at the application of Prolog for formula manipulation, including program verification, and as a sophisticated query language for relational databases. It also describes how to process formal languages, including compiler writing; how to process an interesting and useful subset of natural language; and how to apply knowledge for problem-solving. In addition, it describes an expert system shell in Prolog, with several applications, and gives a short overview of a knowledge engineering project using these ideas.

The appendix contains a collection of useful Prolog predicates.

The language used for the programming examples will be a subset of the Edinburgh Prolog, specifically the C-Prolog VAX version (Pereira, 1984) under the VMS operating systems. The language subset is kept simple, so that the ideas of logic programming are easier to follow. This text, therefore, is not intended to be a reference manual of the fast, user-friendly Prolog system.

Acknowledgements

This book about logic programming and knowledge engineering is a result of 12 years of research and teaching at the University of Trondheim's RUNIT Computing Centre and Division of Computing Science. It is a sequel to an earlier version (Amble, 1984). Many of my colleagues deserve to be mentioned for their help with that version, but I must confine the list to those who have been particularly helpful with the current volume.

First, I am grateful to my colleague Haakon Styri for his encouragement and good advice, based on his impressive knowledge of all aspects of logic programming.

I was fortunate enough to have the opportunity of working on two different projects, both applying logic programming for knowledge engineering. The first was an expert system for diagnosing and teaching television repair; in this field, Roger Eide is an enthusiastic expert and teacher. The other project was to make an expert system for designing welding processes. On this project, I had the pleasure of working with Bjarte H. Nes, who is co-author of the chapter on knowledge engineering. Both projects confirm that the idea of applying logic programming for knowledge engineering works.

Among the people who have scrutinized the manuscripts at various stages, Arild Waaler and Catherine Churchill deserve thanks for their helpful corrections and comments.

A draft version of the book was used for a logic programming course at the University of Trondheim in the fall of 1986. I gained invaluable feedback from the class.

Finally, my bad conscience leads me to express my gratitude towards my wife and children: young children's parents shouldn't really write books.

Contents

Preface   v

Chapter 1   Introduction   1

   1.1   Make specifications, not programs   1
   1.2   Symbolic processing language   2
   1.3   Fifth generation computer systems   3
   1.4   History of logic programming   4
      1.4.1   Aristotelian logic   4
      1.4.2   Symbolic logic   5
      1.4.3   Logic programming   7
   1.5   Artificial intelligence   8
      1.5.1   The limits of mind   9
      1.5.2   Knowledge-based systems   9
      1.5.3   Expert systems   10
      1.5.4   Knowledge engineering   11

Chapter 2   Introduction to Logic   12

   2.1   Elements of logic   12
   2.2   Propositional calculus   13
      2.2.1   The elimination rule   15
      2.2.2   Clausal form   16
      2.2.3   Refutation proofs   17
   2.3   First order predicate logic   20
      2.3.1   Predicates and arguments   21
      2.3.2   Quantifier-free notation   22
      2.3.3   Formalizing queries and contradictions   22
      2.3.4   Horn clause resolution   23
      2.3.5   Alternative proof strategies   24
      2.3.6   Functions in predicate logic   25
      2.3.7   Unification of functional terms   26
      2.3.8   Logic programming   26

Chapter 3   Resolution   29

   3.1   Some logical concepts   29
   3.2   Quantifiers   31
      3.2.1   Examples of quantifiers   32
      3.2.2   Second order logic concepts   32
   3.3   First order predicate calculus   33
      3.3.1   Skolem functions   34

	3.3.2	From predicate logic to clausal form	35
	3.3.3	Clause normalization algorithm	36
	3.3.4	The complete unification algorithm	38
3.4	The resolution proof method		39
	3.4.1	Resolution step	39
	3.4.2	Resolution proof	40
	3.4.3	Resolution proof search strategies	41

Chapter 4   Predicate Logic as a Programming Language   44

4.1	Syntax		44
	4.1.1	Basic syntax	44
	4.1.2	Functions	45
	4.1.3	Clause syntax	45
	4.1.4	Program structure	45
	4.1.5	Describing predicates	46
	4.1.6	Input/output and comments	46
4.2	The semantics of Prolog		46
4.3	Search tree		48
4.4	Recursion		48
4.5	On variable bindings		50
	4.5.1	Anonymous variables	51
	4.5.2	Renaming variables	51
	4.5.3	Occur check	52
4.6	Symmetry properties		53
	4.6.1	Symmetry of sequence of conclusions	53
	4.6.2	Symmetry of sequence of conditions	53
	4.6.3	Test-or-generate symmetry	54
	4.6.4	Input/output parameter symmetry	54
4.7	Cutting the search tree		54
4.8	Using the cut operator, !		56
	4.8.1	Negation as failure	56
	4.8.2	Cut unnecessary search	58
	4.8.3	Cut destroys symmetry	58
	4.8.4	Variable conditions	59
	4.8.5	Equality and inequality	60

Chapter 5   Programming in Prolog   62

5.1	Predicate library		62
5.2	Interactive Prolog		63
5.3	Basic input and output		65
5.4	Built-in operators in Prolog		66
5.5	Evaluation of expressions		67
5.6	Query processing		68
5.7	Manipulating the database		69
	5.7.1	Assert	69
	5.7.2	Retract	70
5.8	Operator declarations		71

5.8.1   Extralogical features   75

Chapter 6   List Processing   78

6.1   List processing   78
6.2   S-expression   78
6.3   The empty node   79
6.4   List notation   80
      6.4.1   Transforming list notation to dot notation   82
      6.4.2   Transforming dot notation to list notation   83
      6.4.3   Extension to Prolog S-expression   83
6.5   Elementary list predicates   84
      6.5.1   The cons predicate   84
      6.5.2   The member predicate   85
      6.5.3   The append predicate   86
      6.5.4   The delete predicate   87
      6.5.5   Naive reverse   88
      6.5.6   Smart reverse   88
6.6   Lists and sets   89
      6.6.1   Representing information as lists or as facts   91
      6.6.2   The unexpected nature of the built-in setof   92
      6.6.3   Set construction without databases   94
6.7   D-lists   95
      6.7.1   D-list manipulation   96
      6.7.2   Limitations of Prolog list structures   97
6.8   An application: sorting   97
      6.8.1   Mergesort   97
      6.8.2   Quicksort   98
6.9   Alternative list syntax   99
      6.9.1   Strings   99
      6.9.2   Round lists   100
      6.9.3   List processing with round lists   101

Chapter 7   Logic Programming Techniques   104

7.1   Constructing recursive programs   105
      7.1.1   A closer look at recursion   105
      7.1.2   Path problems   106
      7.1.3   Finding the path   107
7.2   Constructing iterative programs   108
7.3   Possible implications   112
      7.3.1   An application: Mastermind   112
7.4   The cut operator considered harmful   114
      7.4.1   Examples of hazardous cuts   115
      7.4.2   Structured use of cut   115
7.5   Resolution preprocessing   116
7.6   Inversion   117
7.7   Non-Horn logic programming   119
7.8   Meta-programming   121

      7.8.1   Element by element application   122
      7.8.2   Aggregate functions   123
  7.9 Meta-logic   124
      7.9.1   Explaining facility in meta-level logic   126

Chapter 8   Formula Manipulation   130

  8.1 Symbolic differentiation   130
  8.2 Manipulation   131
  8.3 Anatomy of operator expressions   131
  8.4 Formula evaluation   133
  8.5 Algebraic simplification   135
      8.5.1   Common subexpressions   137
  8.6 Integration   138
  8.7 Program verification   139
      8.7.1   Program verification in Prolog   141
      8.7.2   A verification condition generator   141

Chapter 9   Logic and Databases   146

  9.1 Relational databases   146
      9.1.1   A relational example   147
      9.1.2   Binary relations   148
      9.1.3   Composite keys   148
  9.2 Database retrieval   149
      9.2.1   Efficient retrieval   149
      9.2.2   Virtual tables   150
      9.2.3   Symbolic naming   151
  9.3 Database updating   153
  9.4 Data modelling   154
      9.4.1   Normal forms   155
      9.4.2   Relational normal forms   155
  9.5 Beyond the relational model   158
  9.6 Semantic nets   158
      9.6.1   The class concept   159
  9.7 The course model   163
      9.7.1   Coupling semantic nets to tables   164
      9.7.2   Typical questions   165

Chapter 10   Logic Programming and Compiler Writing   167

  10.1 Language processing   167
  10.2 Lexical analysis   167
  10.3 Syntax analysis   170
      10.3.1   Clause grammar   173
      10.3.2   Table-driven parsing   175
      10.3.3   Constructing a syntax tree   177
      10.3.4   Prettyprinting a syntax tree   177
  10.4 Semantics and production   178

10.5   Advanced grammar formalisms   182
       10.5.1   Two-level grammars   182
       10.5.2   Attribute grammars   183

Chapter 11   Natural Language Processing   188

11.1   What is natural language?   188
11.2   Applied natural language   188
11.3   Natural language systems in Prolog   189
       11.3.1   Definite clause grammars   190
       11.3.2   Natural language is ambiguous   190
11.4   Soft Systems   194
       11.4.1   The Soft Systems language   194
       11.4.2   Sample questions   196
       11.4.3   The dialogue context   196
       11.4.4   The reference model   197
       11.4.5   Lexical analysis   198
       11.4.6   Syntax analysis   200
       11.4.7   A short attribute grammar for de-verbed
                language   200
       11.4.8   Semantic analysis with semantic nets   202
       11.4.9   Query processing   203
11.5   Pure natural language   204
       11.5.1   A logic for commonsense knowledge   204
       11.5.2   Why do we do what we do?   205
       11.5.3   A Prolog program for a room situation   206
11.6   Natural language processing in the future   207

Chapter 12   Logic for Problem Solving   209

12.1   What is the problem?   209
12.2   Generalized function application   209
12.3   Algorithmic versus search problems   210
12.4   Knowledge for problem solving   211
       12.4.1   Generate-and-test   213
       12.4.2   Generate-or-test   214
12.5   A meta-problem solver   216
12.6   Robot planning   218
       12.6.1   Kowalski's formulation   218
       12.6.2   Linear planning   222
12.7   Using estimates to guide searches   222
       12.7.1   Stepwise increasing length of solution   223
       12.7.2   Finding short paths   224
       12.7.3   Making a plan before execution   226

Chapter 13   Expert Systems   229

13.1   Expert systems   229
13.2   Expert systems in Prolog   230

13.3   Principles of the EXPLAIN expert system shell   231
        13.3.1   Why and how – explanation   231
13.4   An example of use of EXPLAIN: television repair   232
13.5   The structure of EXPLAIN   235
        13.5.1   Important predicates   235
        13.5.2   EXPLAIN program skeleton   236
        13.5.3   Handling of negation   237
        13.5.4   Opening the closed world   237
        13.5.5   Storage versus recomputation   238
13.6   EXPLAIN reference manual   239
        13.6.1   Rules   239
        13.6.2   Base variables and equality   240
        13.6.3   Coupling to relational tables   241
13.7   EXPLAIN user guide   242
        13.7.1   Expert system components   242
        13.7.2   Calling EXPLAIN   243
        13.7.3   Summary of commands   243
        13.7.4   The EXPLAIN dialogue explained   244
13.8   Another example of EXPLAIN: pollution detection   245
        13.8.1   The pollution detection knowledge base   245
        13.8.2   Sample dialogue   248
        13.8.3   The structure of the pollution knowledge base   249
13.9   EXPLAIN expert system shell listing   250
13.10   Non-exact reasoning   254
        13.10.1 Multivalued logic   254
        13.10.2 Uncertain logic   255
        13.10.3 Uncertainties in EXPLAIN   257

Chapter 14   Knowledge Engineering   261

14.1   A knowledge engineering example   261
        14.1.1   The problem   263
        14.1.2   The project   263
        14.1.3   Knowledge acquisition   264
        14.1.4   Knowledge base statistics   265
        14.1.5   Performance   266
        14.1.6   User reactions   266
        14.1.7   Sample dialogue for a welding consultation   267
14.2   Comparison with traditional system development   268

Appendix   Predicate Library   269

             Bibliography   274

             Index   279

Chapter 1
Introduction

Make rules,
not programs!

1.1 Make specifications, not programs

The first computers were built to alleviate the burden of numerical computation. The computer could with little effort be programmed to perform any sequence of operations, and such was people's confidence in the machines that some engineers predicted that only a few computers would ever be needed for all the world's data processing.

Every day, computer applications once regarded as an unthinkable misuse of costly laboratory instruments are being developed. In fact, so many new applications are appearing that programming itself is losing its status as an art or handicraft, and is becoming more like traditional engineering. To cope with problems in large scale programming, the computer languages that control the computers have become more and more high level and standardized so that programmers can now exchange programs between systems.

To increase the level of programming, users have to specify what a program should do, but not how it should be done. However, as computing machinery became faster and cheaper, economics allowed more details to be automated by advanced computer software.

It is amusing today to read old arguments explaining why the computer should translate mathematical formulae, as in FORTRAN, instead of letting them be programmed more efficiently by skilled assembly language programmers (Backus, 1958). Few programmers today realize that FORTRAN formulae were once regarded as high-level mathematical specifications of a problem, rather than as programs themselves.

The tendency towards making specifications rather than programs is never ending. The ultimate goal would seem to be natural language specifications, therefore. However, natural language is imprecise, ambiguous and sensitive to context, and precision cannot be compromised. A formalism that approximates to precise natural language descriptions is logic. The ideal specification language of the future may well be some

1

kind of symbolic logic, leaving natural language for communication through the user interface.

Logic programming is the use of logic to define computer programs. The most notable programming language for logic programming is Prolog, an acronym for PROgramming in LOGic. What makes Prolog not just another programming language is its emphasis on the specifications of a problem. Rather than defining the algorithm for solving the problem, Prolog solves problems by systematically searching for a solution. Thus, Prolog is a significant step towards automatic programming.

Since the conception of Prolog in the early 1970s, the number of Prolog programmers has been doubling every year, which has created a market for fast and intelligent implementations of the language.

1.2 Symbolic processing language

Prolog is a language for processing symbolic information, that is, for processing general dynamic symbolic data structures and creating new structures during run-time. This is also a dominant feature of the programming language LISP (Winston and Horn, 1981). In symbolic processing languages, **identifiers** represent *themselves* rather than being names of storage locations as in languages such as Pascal. Prolog is also a **declarative** language. Programmers describe what they know in a precise manner, and leave the rest to the Prolog interpreter.

For example, a programmer wants to say that Harold is the father of Robin. In Pascal, he or she could imagine a linked list of name-records with pointers representing the father relations:

```
TYPE
  person = RECORD
         name : PACKED ARRAY [1..12] OF CHAR;
         father :^person ;
         next :^person ;
      END
var a,b:^person
   .
   .
   .
   a^.name :='HAROLD ';
   b^.name :='ROBIN ';
   b^.father := a ;
   .
   .
   .
```

In addition, separate programs must be written in Pascal before any information can be obtained.

In Prolog, this symbolic information can be expressed much more directly as

father(harold,robin),

which Prolog accepts as a true statement. If Prolog gets the query

?–father(X,robin),

it will respond with the answer

X=harold;

The query

?–father(harold,Y).

will give the answer

Y=robin;

while the query

?–father(X,Y).

will elicit the answer

X=harold
Y=robin;

1.3   Fifth generation computer systems

Prolog is now a generic name for various languages and dialects around a logic programming paradigm, and has gained great enthusiasm among an increasing number of programmers. This enthusiasm was boosted by the announcement of the Japanese Fifth Generation Computing Systems Programme (Moto-Oka, 1982), which adopted Prolog as the kernel language (Fifth Generation Kernel Language, FGKL) of the new type of computers called knowledge information processing systems (KIPS).

The fifth generation computer project aims to develop a completely new type of computer that can communicate in everyday language, reason intelligently and bring an enormous amount of stored knowledge to help solve any problem that the user may have. The machines will be cheap and reliable, and so widespread in offices, factories and homes that society itself may be changed by the huge fund of expertise made available.

The fifth generation computer will have three main components:

- an intelligent man machine interface (natural language, written or spoken, graphical);
- problem solving (with logic and statistical reasoning);
- a knowledge base facility able to store and retrieve vast amounts of data, and also give judgements and advice.

The programme's detailed plans promise to make incredibly fast Prolog machines for the 1990s; with a reasoning capacity of up to a billion logic inferences per second (one gigalips), and with associated memory storage of hundreds of gigabytes.

By 1986, the Japanese were already producing high performance Prolog workstations as a tool to accelerate their own development. Needless to say, recent achievements in the Japanese high-technology industries have conditioned us to expect a new success.

In light of this, logic programming, and Prolog in particular, is becoming very important.

1.4   History of logic programming

1.4.1   Aristotelian logic

Logic programming is based on logic, so the right place to start is with the origin of logic, which has its roots with the philosopher Aristotle (382–324 BC). He had an enormous influence on scientific thinking, but some of his ideas did not deserve much reverence. For example, Aristotle said that horses had more teeth than men, without counting them, and that the brain was an organ for cooling the blood, which is only true metaphorically. However, he will be remembered forever for his classic work *Organon*, where he summarized the laws of correct systematic thinking. According to Aristotle, correct reasoning proceeds by the application of strict rules of inference called **syllogisms**. A small example is:

Premise 1:   All humans are mortal.
Premise 2:   All Greeks are humans.
Premise 3:   Socrates is Greek.

Conclusion: Socrates is mortal.

The conclusion that Socrates is mortal in this example can be proved by the application of two such logical inferences.
From Premise 1 and 2:

> *Lemma*:   All Greeks are mortal.

From Lemma and Premise 3, we get

> *Conclusion*:   Socrates is mortal.

Alternatively, the same conclusion may be reached using the same information in a different order. From Premise 2 and Premise 3 conclude:

> *Lemma*:   Socrates is human.

From Premise 1 and Lemma:

> *Conclusion*:   Socrates is mortal.

1.4.2 Symbolic logic

In passing through history, consider Leibnitz (1646–1716). Although he did not study logic, he put forward the idea of a universal calculus of reasoning. One of his ideas was to represent primary concepts as prime numbers, and more complex concepts as products of these. In this way, Leibnitz was among the first to propose a method for formally representing knowledge and a method for solving disputes, by calculating the answers from these representations.

The first account on formal logic was by George Boole (1815–1864) who let **truth values** be denoted by **identifiers**, and devised an algebra for calculating new truth values for expressions with the **logical operators** AND, OR and NOT. Boole gave his work the name 'Investigations of the Laws of Thought' (1854).

Somewhat later, the German mathematician Gottlob Frege (1848–1925) was working with the foundations of mathematics, preparing the ground for a formal symbolic logic called **predicate logic** (Frege, 1879). He also laid down the rules of inference in this formalism, and showed that we can replace logical inference by **symbolic manipulation**. With this formalism, our little example would look like:

		% Informal comments:
1	$\forall x(\textbf{Human}(x) \Rightarrow \textbf{Mortal}(x)).$	% for all x, if x is human % then x is mortal.
2	$\forall x(\textbf{Greek}(x) \Rightarrow \textbf{Human}(x)).$	% For all x, if x is Greek % then x is human

    3   Greek(Socrates).   % Socrates is Greek.
    Conclusion: Mortal(Socrates).

With the introduction of computers, it became possible to handle symbolic information such as formulae in symbolic logic, and to mechanize the proof procedures. An important milestone in this endeavour was reached by the **Resolution Method** (Robinson, 1965).

The resolution method has several properties: it is correct, simple, uniform and easily mechanized. In addition it is complete, that is, it is able to prove everything that is actually true.

Actually, Robinson's work was predated by 30 years when J. Herbrand (1930) devised the original basis for proving the resolution theorem. The reason why Herband's work was not considered so important at the time was the sheer amount of work necessary to achieve a proof of his version of the theorem. This is in sharp contrast to the grand simplicity of Robinson's version.

The problem with a theorem is finding a proof, which is essentially a search problem. However, the cost of completeness is combinatorial explosions, i.e. searches among many alternatives to find combinations that lead to a proof. Thus, the completeness property may only be of theoretical interest if the search problems are not solved. Therefore, considerable research effort has been made to make smart strategies for the resolution proof procedures, so that searches are efficient, and the property of completeness is preserved. One of the methods is the so-called **linear resolution** developed by Kowalski and Kuehner (1971) and others.

With these methods, researchers tried to represent and prove difficult mathematical theorems, because this task was deemed an important part of artificial intelligence (AI). AI is an attempt to mechanize processes supposed to need human intelligence. However, there are two important points to consider here:

- automatic proof of interesting theorems is difficult to achieve autonomously, without aid and advice from mathematicians;
- the theorems could be formulated in such a way that the proofs produced answers to questions formulated in predicate logic.

The same techniques for proving a theorem, when applied to non-mathematical areas, gives deductive question-answering systems. Green (1969) was one of the researchers to recognize and exploit this **answer extraction** property, and he should be reckoned among the pioneers of logic programming. In retrospect, the application of resolution to prove mathematical theorems may turn out to be a small, but very important stepping stone.

1.4.3 Logic programming

At the University of Marseilles, a research group led by Alain Colmerauer was working with the difficult problem of natural language processing. Colmerauer became interested in Kowalski's linear search strategies for resolution. After a period of co-operation between the two, a radical solution was put forward: to use one single, very specialized search strategy for finding proofs. This strategy was fast and took up little space, but it was not complete, and it put much of the responsibility for success on the way the problem was written. Using the answer extraction property, this logic system could be used as a programming language. The new programming language was called Prolog by the Marseilles group, which made the first interpreter in 1972 (Roussell, 1975). This interpreter is the ancestor of most of the Prolog systems of today.

The most influential of these Prolog implementations was the DEC–10 Prolog compiler written by Warren *et al.* (1979). This system implicitly defined a *de facto* standard Prolog syntax, and its efficiency proved that Prolog, besides being an interesting high-level language, could also be a very powerful programming language.

The main idea in Prolog is to formulate a set of rules and facts in predicate logic together with a problem for which a solution is sought. Here is a small example, although not in the original syntax:

mortal(*x*) if human(*x*).	% *x* is mortal if *x* is human
human(*x*) if greek(*x*).	% *x* is human if *x* is Greek
Greek(Socrates).	% Socrates is Greek
answer(*x*) if mortal(*x*).	% *x* is an answer if *x* is mortal
⇒ **Socrates.**	% this is an answer

The idea of logic programming had its main advocate in Kowalski, who in 1974 presented his landmark paper *Predicate Logic as a Programming Language* (Kowalski, 1974a). The idea was presented with short, well known examples. For instance, the factorial function, **Factorial(*n*)**, is traditionally defined recursively as:

Factorial(*n*) := if n = 0 then 1
else *n* ∗ Factorial(*n* − 1) ;

If instead, a recursive **predicate** is defined:

Factorial(m,n)

it is true whenever *n* is the factorial of *m*. This predicate is defined by

logical clauses, where Plus and Times are predicates for addition and multiplication.

> Factorial(0,1).
> Factorial(s,u) if Plus($x,1,s$) and
>   Factorial(x,v) and
>   Times(s,v,u).
>
> answer(s) if Factorial(4,s).
>
> ⇒ **24**

This definition could be given a procedural interpretation, i.e., the deductions could be used to simulate computation, an idea also advocated by Hayes (1973). However, the fundamental idea of logic programming is one step ahead: computation is deduction.

1.5 Artificial intelligence

Artificial intelligence (AI) is a phrase coined early in the 1950s to draw parallels between the human brain and the electronic brain. The field must, however, be considered as two subfields, with the same name but different paradigms:

(1) Pure artificial intelligence, which tries to make computers achieve human-like intelligence. The key question is whether this is possible.

(2) Applied artificial intelligence, which makes computers perform tasks that are assumed to require human intelligence. The key question is whether this is useful.

Another metaphor can be used to explain the difference. A farmer's tractor can be viewed as an artificial horse, because it solves problems that require horse-power. But this doesn't mean that a tractor is an attempt to mimic a real horse.

Pure artificial intelligence is closely related to **cognitive psychology**. Psychologists build AI programs to test theories of how the human mind works, and cast light on human cognitive processes. This view of artificial intelligence is the most popular, because people are attracted by the wording. This view is also implicit in Alan Turing's definition with the so-called Turing test:

> If a person communicating through a neutral communications medium to both a computer and a human cannot distinguish between the two, then the computer is said to have artificial intelligence.

This idea is not very constructive, however, because the modelling of human fallibility becomes as important as that of human achievement.

1.5.1   The limits of mind

Philosophically, the view of human intelligence is divided into two main groups: those who consider the human mind to be infinite in some deep sense, and those who think the human mind is finite.

A famous result from mathematical logic (Gödel, 1931) states that, for any finite consistent logical system capable of defining arithmetic, there must necessarily exist mathematical theorems which can neither be proved nor disproved in the system. This is not because of capacity problems, but due to self-referential paradoxes, such as the sentence: 'This sentence cannot be proven.'

Applied to computing, which is concerned with finite logic systems, the result implies that for each program designed to solve general problems, there exists a problem that cannot be solved, regardless of any resources used.

If humans were like programmed computers, such limitations would apply to them as well. According to some schools of thought, it is unthinkable that humans should not be able to transcend such a restriction; humans should be able to solve all problems. On the other hand, a corollary to Gödel is that a finite system stating that it can solve all problems is inconsistent. So, the question is unanswered.

In applied AI, in contrast to the human mind, there are definitely no transcendental sources of intelligence. All intelligent behaviour is built up by non-intelligent basic mechanisms.

1.5.2   Knowledge-based systems

Research effort in AI has led to the development of useful languages, programs and methods for advanced problem solving. The early endeavours that let the computer try difficult problems on its own – to give it help was considered cheating – met with little success. On the other hand, computer-aided problem solving in specific areas produced systems that performed well, and gradually became a source of real help to users. The key to this success was found to be the knowledge that was put into the system by experts, and not some general problem solving ability to any large degree.

Programs that solve problems at expert level are called **expert systems**. When a program is written to solve a class of problems, this program represents the knowledge necessary to solve the problems in a very specialized way. However, when the knowledge can be represented explicitly in terms of its non-algorithmic content, and the program acts upon this by deduction and reasoning, instead of computation, it is called a **knowledge-based system** or **knowledge system**.

It is important to distinguish the concept of an expert system, which classifies performance, from a knowledge-based system, which is a method of implementing systems. However, knowledge systems are popularly called expert systems, even though only advanced knowledge systems that can solve difficult problems deserve that name. Knowledge-based systems are a better technology for handling the complexity of these problems.

It is said that intelligence is the ability to solve new problems based on previous experience, e.g. to learn from mistakes. Although today's expert systems can solve a variety of problems without being reprogrammed, they are not intelligent in this sense – the knowledge base is a substitute for intelligence. A better name is 'artificial expertise', whose ultimate goal is to make expert systems that are better and cheaper than any known expertise. However, less ambitious goals are also worthwhile, i.e. when expert systems save money, or are just better or cheaper or more available than the available expertise.

1.5.3 Expert systems

The field of expert systems is now becoming commercial, and a number of expert systems are manufactured under various trade marks. Already today, there are some spectacular successes

- DENDRAL is a necessary tool for mass spectrometry analysis in many universities;

- PROSPECTOR is a mineral prospecting expert system which has found a deposit worth $100M;

- CADUCEUS knows more of internal medicine than any human, and has passed an arranged students exam;

- MACSYMA is a large formula-manipulation package, which outperforms most non-professional mathematicians; it is used extensively by physicists;

- BELLE is a chess program that plays at chess club championship level;

- XCON configures VAX computers. It is reported to have saved millions of dollars for the manufacturing company, the Digital Equipment Corporation.

- TAUM-METEO is a natural language system that automatically translates Canadian weather forecasts from French to English and vice versa.

In the last few years, hundreds of new expert systems have come into practical use. Also, many new books have arrived to introduce the field, for example Hayes-Roth *et al.* (1983), Waterman (1985), Harmon and King (1985) and Jackson (1986).

1.5.4 Knowledge engineering

Feigenbaum (Feigenbaum and McCorduck, 1984) is one of the pioneers of expert systems, and coined the phrase **knowledge engineering** to describe the process of transferring knowledge from the experts to the computer (the people in charge of that process are called *knowledge engineers*). The specialized computers that run knowledge-based systems are sometimes called **knowledge processors**, or **knowledge information processing systems** (KIPS) as the Japanese call their fifth generation computers. A picture of tomorrow's computer vocabulary can be imagined, if all the words containing 'data' or 'information' are replaced by the word 'knowledge'.

Feigenbaum has emphasized the importance of knowledge engineering technology very strongly by the statement: 'This is not only the second computer revolution – it is the important one'. Logic programming will play an important part in this revolution.

EXERCISES

1.1 Many text books and articles contain definitions or descriptions of artificial intelligence (AI). Collect as many of these as you encounter, and discuss them. Try to classify these according to the distinctions pure AI and applied AI made in the introduction.

1.2 What are the similarities between AI and Alchemy?

Chapter 2
Introduction to Logic

Was sich überhaubt sagen lasst,
lasst sich mit predikat-logik sagen;
und wovon man nicht reden kann,
darüber muss man schweigen.

Freely from Wittgenstein

2.1 Elements of logic

Logic is the science of correct thinking, not the science of the truth of this world. Even though all that is allowed to be said within logic is supposed to be true by the subject stating it, it may be false in the real world. Sentences may actually be right or wrong, and new sentences may be deduced correctly or incorrectly. The following examples are inspired by the play *Erasmus Montanus* (Holberg, 1730).

Erasmus, after returning from Copenhagen where he was studying logic, starts by saying to his mother:

A stone cannot fly.
Little mother cannot fly.
Therefore, little mother is a stone.

This example of illegal use of logic based on correct assumptions causes little mother to weep. So Erasmus comforts her by saying.

A stone cannot weep.
Little mother can weep.
Therefore, little mother is not a stone.

This example is correct, both in premises and deductions. For completeness the other combinations are as follows:

A woman cannot fly.
Little mother cannot fly.
Therefore, little mother is a woman.

This is not a valid use of logic (it is called **abduction**), even though the conclusion happens to be true.

> All stones can fly.
> Little mother is a stone.
> Therefore, little mother can fly.

This example is logically correct, but absurd in the real world.

It is stated by wise philosophers that in order to understand what is really happening in the world, we must understand what is not happening, i.e. the invariant properties of things. With this in mind, students of logic should consider sets of statements as logical when they are descriptions of matters that can be assigned the property of being true or false, independent of the time and place of the statement. This book covers the rules for correctly deriving new logical statements from other logical statements.

Following is some of the Aristotelian logic covered earlier, but displayed using a formal symbolic notation; a general principle called **resolution** is derived, which actually unifies the Aristotelian logic into one formalism.

2.2   Propositional calculus

The simplest logic formalism is **propositional calculus** or **propositional logic**, which is another name for **Boolean algebra**.

An example of formulae in this calculus:

$$A \lor (B \land \text{TRUE} \lor \sim D)$$

> It rains.
> I am wet $\Leftarrow$ it rains $\land$ I am outside.
> I am outside.

The basic units are the logic constants TRUE and FALSE, and identifiers denoting whole sentences or propositions, which may be either TRUE or FALSE.

The sentences are combined by the logical operators $\land$ (AND), $\lor$ (OR), $\sim$ (NOT), $\Rightarrow$ (IMPLIES), $\Leftarrow$ (IF), and some others. Since the objects of our discourse have only two values, the logical operators may be completely defined by a so-called **truth table** (Table 2.1).

The logic formalism itself does not know any meaning of the identifiers of a formula. There are two levels of meaning:

- **informal meaning**, which relates the statements to an external world through our interpretation of the words;
- **formal meaning**, which relates the identifiers to a set of truth values.

Table 2.1 Truth table.

A	B	$\sim A$	$A \wedge B$	$A \vee B$	$A \Rightarrow B$	$A \Leftarrow B$	$A \Leftrightarrow B$
TRUE	TRUE	FALSE	TRUE	TRUE	TRUE	TRUE	TRUE
TRUE	FALSE	FALSE	FALSE	TRUE	FALSE	TRUE	FALSE
FALSE	TRUE	TRUE	FALSE	TRUE	TRUE	FALSE	FALSE
FALSE	FALSE	TRUE	FALSE	FALSE	TRUE	TRUE	TRUE

The informal meaning is outside the scope of logic. Therefore, all that is true initially must be given as **logic axioms**, i.e. they must be true without proof.

The formal meaning is called an **interpretation**, which for propositional calculus means assignment of truth values to identifiers. Special formulae called **valid formulae** are of particular interest: for these formulae the truth value will be TRUE for any interpretation.

Here is a valid formula:

$$A \vee \sim A$$

There are principally two different ways of determining whether or not a formula is valid:

- either by trying all interpretations, using the truth table to verify a formula;
- or by using algebraic methods and reducing the formula to the constant TRUE.

For the algebraic approach, the following important equalities are easily verified:

- Exclusive law: $A \wedge \sim A = $ FALSE
- Inclusive law: $A \vee \sim A = $ TRUE
- Idempotency laws: $A \vee A = A$
  $A \wedge A = A$
- Reversive law: $\sim \sim A = A$

- Associative laws:

$$(A \land B) \land C = A \land (B \land C) = A \land B \land C$$
$$(A \lor B) \lor C = A \lor (B \lor C) = A \lor B \lor C$$

- Commutative laws:

$$A \land B = B \land A$$
$$A \lor B = B \lor A$$

- Distributive laws:

$$(A \land B) \lor (A \land C) = A \land (B \lor C)$$
$$A \lor (B \land C) = (A \lor B) \land (A \lor C)$$

- De Morgan laws:

$$\sim(A \land B) = (\sim A) \lor (\sim B)$$
$$\sim(A \lor B) = (\sim A) \land (\sim B)$$

- Derived rules:

$$(A \Leftrightarrow B) = (A \Leftarrow B) \land (A \Rightarrow B)$$
$$(A \Leftarrow B) = (B \Rightarrow A)$$

$$(A \Leftarrow B) = A \lor (\sim B)$$
$$(A \Leftarrow (B \land C)) = A \lor \sim (B \land C) = A \lor (\sim B) \lor (\sim C)$$

$$\sim(A \Leftarrow B) = B \land (\sim A)$$

$$(A \Leftarrow \text{TRUE}) = A$$
$$(\text{FALSE} \Leftarrow A) = \sim A$$
$$(\text{TRUE} \Leftarrow A) = \text{TRUE}$$
$$(A \Leftarrow \text{FALSE}) = \text{TRUE}$$

A formula with an implication sign has a dual reading: $F \Rightarrow G$ means first that $F \Rightarrow G$ is true, which happens when G is true or when F is false. It can also be used on a 'meta-level' to deduce a new formula, G, so that whenever F is true, G must also be true. The two implications are equivalent, so there is no need to use different notations.

2.2.1 The elimination rule

A special rule of this kind will play an important role in the resolution method. It is called the **elimination rule**, In its basic form, it says:

$$((A \lor B) \land (\sim A \lor C)) \Rightarrow (B \lor C)$$

which is easily verified (see the exercises). It is called the elimination rule because if there are two formulae:

$$A \lor B$$
$$\sim A \lor C$$

it allows a new formula to be derived

$$B \lor C$$

which is true, regardless of the truth value of A. The elimination rule is generic, and appears in numerous variants of which the following are examples:

$$(A \lor B \lor C) \land (\sim A \lor D) \Rightarrow (B \lor C \lor D)$$
$$(A \lor \text{FALSE}) \land (\sim A \lor C) \Rightarrow (\text{FALSE} \lor C)$$
$$A \land (\sim A \lor B) \Rightarrow B$$
$$((A \Leftarrow B) \land (\sim A)) \Rightarrow (\sim B)$$

2.2.2 Clausal form

When language is used to describe something, everything cannot be stated in one sentence; it must be broken up into several sentences, and it must be assumed that all the sentences are true, and that the conjunction of the sentences is true.

It is a consequence of the laws of propositional calculus that all formulae can be transformed into **conjunctive normal form**, which is a **conjunction** ($\land$) of a set of **clauses** which are **disjunctions** ($\lor$) of basic expressions in the form of either A or $\sim A$. For example:

$$D \Leftarrow ((A \lor B) \land (\sim A \lor C)) =$$
$$D \lor \sim ((A \lor B) \land (\sim A \lor C)) =$$
$$D \lor \sim (A \lor B) \lor \sim (\sim A \lor C)) =$$
$$D \lor (\sim A \land \sim B) \lor (A \land \sim C) =$$
$$(D \lor \sim A \lor A) \land$$
$$\quad (D \lor \sim A \lor \sim C) \land$$
$$\quad (D \lor \sim B \lor A) \land$$
$$\quad (D \lor \sim B \lor \sim C)$$

The conjunctive normal form is particularly important for resolution, which essentially proves any valid formula in conjunctive normal form by using only the elimination rule on conjunctive clauses.

A shorthand notation of conjunctive normal form was defined by Kowalski (1974), called (Kowalski) **clausal form**:

Define: $A_1, A_2, \ldots, A_m \leftarrow B_1, \ldots, B_n$
to be: $A_1 \lor \ldots \lor A_m \lor \sim B_1 \lor \ldots \lor \sim B_n$.

The motivation for the notation follows from the derivations:

$$A_1 \vee \ldots \vee A_m \vee \sim B_1 \vee \ldots \vee \sim B_n =$$
$$(A_1 \vee \ldots \vee A_m) \vee \sim (B_1 \wedge \ldots \wedge B_n) =$$
$$(A_1 \vee \ldots \vee A_m) \Leftarrow (B_1 \wedge \ldots \wedge B_n)$$

The As are **conclusions**.
The Bs are **conditions**.
A common name for both As and Bs is **literals**.
In this notation, our little example becomes:

$$D,A \leftarrow A$$
$$D \leftarrow A,C$$
$$D,A \leftarrow B$$
$$D \leftarrow B,C$$

We have the following special cases:

$m > 1$	The conclusions are **indefinite**, i.e., there are other conclusions.
$m \leqslant 1$	Such clauses are called **Horn clauses** (Horn, 1951).
$m = 1, n > 0$	$A \leftarrow B_1,\ldots,B_n$ **Definite clause**, i.e. there is one definite conclusion.
$m = 1, n = 0$	$A \leftarrow$ **Unconditional definite clause**, fact. Sometimes, the $\leftarrow$ is dropped, as in 'A'.
$m = 0, n > 0$	$\leftarrow B_1,\ldots,B_n$ Pure negation of $B_1,\ldots,B_m$.
$m = 0, n = 0$	$\leftarrow$ The empty clause.

For example:

It rains $\leftarrow$
I am wet $\leftarrow$ it rains, I am outside
I am outside $\leftarrow$
$\leftarrow$ I am wet

2.2.3 Refutation proofs

If P is a set of axioms, and Q is a clause that has to be proven, logic rules can be applied and the clause Q derived. For technical reasons, to prove that $P \Rightarrow Q$ is TRUE, it may instead be proven that $P \wedge \sim Q$ is FALSE by deriving a contradiction. To prove that something is false is called a **refutation**.

Such proofs are called *reductio ad absurdum*, and are generally easier to perform than straight proofs, because more may be assumed during the proof.

The duality of proving a formula in clausal form and proving that its negation leads to a contradiction is reconciled by a simple formal trick. To prove a proposition, Q, for example, we make the clause: $\leftarrow Q$, and try to derive the empty clause $\leftarrow$, which in effect represents the truth value FALSE. In this context, the proposition Q is called a **goal**.

Propositional formulae in Horn clause form are called propositional Horn clauses (PHC). It can be shown that any PHC formula can be proven by using one simple deduction operation called a **PHC resolution**. A set of basic deduction steps is listed below. They are all special cases of the elimination rule in clausal form.

- Pattern 1:
$$P \leftarrow Q,R \qquad \text{P if Q and R}$$
$$\leftarrow P \qquad \text{P is false}$$

$$\leftarrow Q,R \qquad \text{(Q and R) is false, i.e. not both true}$$

- Pattern 2:
$$P \leftarrow \qquad \text{P is true}$$
$$\leftarrow P,Q \qquad \text{(P and Q) is false}$$

$$\leftarrow Q \qquad \text{Q is false}$$

- Pattern 3:
$$P \leftarrow \qquad \text{P is true}$$
$$\leftarrow P \qquad \text{P is false}$$

$$\leftarrow \qquad \text{Contradiction}$$

Pattern 3 demonstrates that '$\leftarrow$' represents the contradiction, since it is derived from contradictory propositions, and no others.

The general version of a PHC resolution step is as follows:

$$A_1 \leftarrow B_1,\dots,B_n$$
$$\leftarrow A_1,\dots,A_m$$

$$\leftarrow B_1,\dots,B_n, A_2,\dots,A_m$$

Here is an example of a proof using PHC resolution:

(1) It rains ←
(2) I am wet ← it rains, I am outside
(3) I am outside ←
(4) ← I am wet   % negated goal

A proof of the contradiction is as follows:

(5) ← it rains, I am outside   % (2,4) Pattern 1
(6) ← I am outside   % (1,5) Pattern 2
(7) ←   % (3,6) Pattern 3

The equivalence of proving a goal and refuting its negation is crucial, but very obvious. When a goal is proven, it is reduced to subproblems, where '←' represents 'no problem'. When something is refuted, a contradiction is deduced (represented by '←').

This proof is particularly simple, since there is actually only one way to combine the clauses: using the PHC resolution. In general, there is a search for the candidate clauses to be combined, in order to arrive at ←.

For example:

(1) $P \leftarrow A , B$
(2) $P \leftarrow C , D$
(3) $A \leftarrow$
(4) $C \leftarrow E$
(5) $E \leftarrow$
(6) $D \leftarrow$
(7) $\leftarrow P$

The proof is as follows:

(8) $\leftarrow A , B$ % (1,7) The goal P can match two conclusions, tried the first
(9) $\leftarrow B$ % (3,8)

However, there is no conclusion to match condition B here, so this clause must be forgotten and another alternative found.

(10) $\leftarrow C , D$ % (2,7)
(11) $\leftarrow E , D$ % (4,10)

$(12) \leftarrow D$ % (5,11)

$(13) \leftarrow$ % (6,12)

2.3 First order predicate logic

Propositional calculus is a subset of a more general logic system called first order predicate logic, or first order predicate calculus. For its introduction, consider again the examples from Aristotle, but the topic is changed slightly. Consider the statements:

> *Premise 1*: All mammals are animals.
> *Premise 2*: All elephants are mammals.
> *Premise 3*: Clyde is an elephant.
> *Premise 4*: All sharks are animals.
> *Premise 5*: Bonnie is a shark.
>
> *Conclusion 6*: Clyde is an animal.
> *Conclusion 7*: Bonnie is an animal.

According to the Aristotelian principle of contradiction 'a thing cannot both be true and not true at the same time', so if someone says 'Clyde is not an elephant', this directly contradicts Premise 3. If on the other hand someone says 'There are no animals', there is no direct contradiction, but a contradiction can be deduced or inferred.

> There are no mammals $\% \leftarrow 1$
> There are no elephants $\% \leftarrow 2$
> Clyde is not an elephant   % for example
> Contradiction ! $\% \leftarrow 3$

In other words, if the premises are taken as axioms, i.e. true by definition, we can prove the following sentence:

> There is an animal

by a *reductio ad absurdum* proof.

In information processing, logic refutation is not the primary objective. However, logic rules govern information retrieval as in the query:

> What animals are there?

This can be solved stepwise by application of the rules:

What mammals are there?   % ← 1
What elephants are there? % ← 2
Clyde is an answer   % ← 3
What sharks are there?   % ← 4
Bonnie is an answer   % ← 5

There is a close parallel between a **refutation** and **question answering**. In logic, an information retrieval query is often regarded as a refutation of the existence of a solution. By asking the logic interpreter to find a contradiction in the refutation statement, it is forced to find a counter example, which is a solution to the problem. This is an informal version of the answer extraction property described earlier.

2.3.1 Predicates and arguments

In the sentence 'Clyde is an elephant', something is said (being an elephant) about something (Clyde). 'Being an elephant' is a **predicate**, while that being talked about is called an **argument**.

In symbolic logic, the standard is to write the simple predicates as identifiers, followed by the arguments enclosed in parentheses. Mathematically, a predicate is a function delivering only truth values; for example:

elephant(Clyde)

A predicate with arguments is called a **literal**.
To make a predicate-argument of the rule:

All elephants are mammals.

a logical variable, x, is introduced which may represent any argument.

For all things x,
  x is a mammal if x is an elephant.

This sentence may be viewed as a logical procedure to test a property of all things in the world, or as a conjunction of all the individual sentences that arise when the x is **instantiated** to a thing.
For instance, let x be Clyde:

Clyde is a mammal if Clyde is an elephant.

This makes perfect sense. If 'Clyde is an elephant' is true, in our world, it may be concluded that Clyde is a mammal.

On the other hand, if x is Norway, then the sentence states:

Norway is a mammal if Norway is an elephant.

which also makes sense, because the sentence as a whole is true when the condition 'Norway is an elephant' is not fulfilled; it does not matter if the conclusion in isolation (Norway is a mammal) is false; (FALSE ⇐ FALSE) = TRUE. In formal notation, we may write:

$\forall x$ (mammal(x) ← elephant(x))

The symbol $\forall$ is called a logical **quantifier**. $\forall$ is followed by a list of logical variables and a logical formula, which is supposed to hold for all possible values of the variables. The logical variables are only defined inside the logical clause, which is the **scope** of the logical variables.

In contrast to the logical variable, a **constant identifier** is used to denote an atomic entity or concept. It cannot be substituted by any other term and it will have the same interpretation in all clauses or any derivations of them. The constant identifier cannot, however, be divided into parts. Two different constant identifiers will be regarded as necessarily different. This is known as **unique name assumption**.

2.3.2 Quantifier-free notation

In computer systems based on predicate logic, universally-quantified clauses are often needed, but to write the quantifiers all the time is a nuisance. This introduces the problem of distinguishing logical variables, such as x above, from constants such as Clyde. In this chapter about logic, the standard conventions of symbolic logic will be followed, and logical variables will be single, late-alphabet, lower-case letters, such as x. However, when Prolog programs are written, the convention is different.

Any clause formula containing logical variables is supposed to be true for all possible values of the variables in the formula. Quantifier-free notation is used with clausal form as in the example:

mammal(x) ← elephant(x)

2.3.3 Formalizing queries and contradictions

As with propositional Horn clauses, questions are formalized as negated statements that must be refuted.

← animal(x). % For all x it is not true that x is an animal

With these conventions in mind, our animals example becomes:

animal(x) ← mammal(x)
mammal(x) ← elephant(x)
elephant(Clyde) ←
animal(x) ← shark(x)
shark(Bonnie) ←
← animal(x)

2.3.4 Horn clause resolution

By introducing logic variables, **first order predicate logic** or **first order predicate calculus** is entered.

A clause with logical variables is supposedly true for every set of values of the variables. This is called the **axiom of general specification**. By using the general specification systematically, two clauses can be instantiated so that the elimination rule can be applied. This generalizes the PHC resolution into Horn clause resolution (HCR).

For example:

(1) $p(\text{TA})$
(2) $q(x) \leftarrow p(x)$
(3) $\leftarrow q(\text{TA})$

The proof of $q(\text{TA})$ is as follows. The conclusion $q(x)$ of clause 2, and the condition of clause 3 are different. But clause 2 contains the variable x, which can be specialized to the constant TA.

(2′) $q(\text{TA}) \leftarrow p(\text{TA})$ $(x = \text{TA})$

Using this special version of clause 2 follows the same pattern as in PHC resolution, which generates the following:

(4) (2′,3) $\leftarrow p(\text{TA})$
(5) (1,4) ←

The specialization of clause 2 was by no means an accident. On the contrary, the conclusion in 2 was purposely made identical with the condition in 3 by proper substitutions. This process is called **unification**, and plays a crucial part in the resolution method.

In short, resolution is combining unification and elimination in one operation. We say that we **resolve** two clauses, and produce a **resolvent**.

To continue with the animal example:

(1) animal(x) ← mammal(x)
(2) mammal(x) ← elephant(x)
(3) elephant(Clyde) ←
(4) animal(x) ← shark(x)
(5) shark(Bonnie) ←
(6) ← animal(x)

Here, clause 6 can be combined with 1 and 4. If there is no other information there is no better choice than to try one before the other.
    Unifying 1 and 6 gives

(7) ← mammal(x)

Unifying 2 and 7 gives

(8) ← elephant(x)

Letting x = Clyde allows resolution with clause 3.

(9) ←

i.e. x = Clyde is one answer. However, as explained, clause 6 could also resolve with 4:

(10) ← shark(x)

and then by letting x = Bonnie,

(11) ←

i.e. x = Bonnie is the other answer. This example shows how logic could be used to find an answer to the query:

    What animals are there?

2.3.5 Alternative proof strategies

Logic can be used to answer questions, by applying a special strategy for finding the resolvents. Recollecting the variable bindings extracts the answers. This strategy is called **top down**: it starts with a goal, and reduces this goal into subgoals, until there is only an empty subgoal. These are only examples of resolutions for the first literals of each clause. However, the same logic clauses can be used in any other direction. For instance, if facts are combined with rules, the strategy is **bottom up**. In the animals example, combining fact 3 with rule 2 gives a new fact:

(7) mammal(Clyde) ←

This fact can be combined with rule 1:

(8) animal(Clyde) ←

Similarly, starting with 4 and 5:

(9) animal(Bonnie) ←

Rules can also be combined with other rules, to generate more specialized rules. Combining 1 and 2, for example, gives an equally valid rule:

animal(x) ← elephant(x)

which on applying fact 3 gives the answer

animal(Clyde) ←

2.3.6 Functions in predicate logic

Until now arguments have been either variables or constant identifiers. However, in first order predicate logic **functional terms** may be used – these are functions applied to arguments:
For example:

sin(PI)
max(2,A)
tree(root,left,right)

Functional terms have the same syntax as literals, although their purposes are different. They can be nested indefinitely by having functional terms appear as arguments, for instance:

tree(2,tree(nil,1,nil),tree(nil,3,nil))

The function name (e.g. tree) is called a **functor**, and the number of arguments (e.g. 3) is called its **arity**.
What the functional terms denote depends on the interpretations. However, logic is primarily interested in properties that are independent of interpretations, which means that functional terms are unevaluated. Instead, the effects of the functions with various arguments are defined axiomatically by clauses. In logic, a functional term only denotes the existence of some value which is uniquely dependent on its arguments.

Strangely enough, terms play the role of data structures when it comes to programming in logic.

2.3.7   Unification of functional terms

Since evaluation is not considered, functional terms are equal only if they coincide both in functor, and each of their arguments.

max(1,3) is different from max(3,1)

even though an interpretation of max as a maximum function would make the values identical.

Since constant identifiers are unique, different constants cannot be unified. The only way to unify functional terms is by substituting variables. Assuming A and B are constant identifiers:

$f(A)$ and $f(A)$ may be unified (they are identical)
$f(x)$ and $f(A)$ may be unified by letting $x = A$
$f(x)$ and $g(x)$ may not be unified
$f(A)$ and $f(B)$ may not be unified
$p(x,x)$ and $p(A,B)$ may not be unified
$p(x,\text{John})$ and $p(\text{Mary},y)$ may be unified ($x = \text{Mary}, y = \text{John}$)
$q(x,z,x)$ and $q(y,y,B)$ may be unified ($x = B, y = B, z = B$)
$r(x,f(y))$ and $r(A,z)$ may be unified ($x = A, z = f(y)$)
$r(x,x)$ and $r(y,f(y))$ may not be unified

A more thorough treatment is given in the next chapter.

2.3.8   Logic programming

Formal logic usually defines some knowledge. From a logical point of view, this is a declaration of things that are held to be true. It represents the set of all facts that are stated, or can be deduced. This is the **declarative interpretation** of clausal logic. On the other hand, when the same clauses are combined with the top-down proof procedure, this gives a procedure that solves problems. This is the **procedural interpretation** of clausal logic. Usually, instances of the logical variables that made the proof possible must be collected, because these are the solutions. An elegant trick is to have a special answer-predicate, as a condition holding a variable. When only the answer-condition remains, the variable holds a solution.

In the following example, clause 4 can be combined with both 1 and 2.

(1) parent(x,y) ← father(x,y)
(2) parent(x,y) ← mother(x,y)
(3) mother(Catherine,Halvard)
(4) ← parent(z,Halvard),answer(z)

If there is no other information there is no better choice than to try one before the other.

Programmers must first unify 1,4 by specializing 1 ($x = z$, y = Halvard):

(1′) parent(z,Halvard) ← father(z,Halvard)

Then the following clauses become:

(5) (1′,4) ← father(z,Halvard),answer(z) % dead end, try the other parent
(6) (2,4) ← mother(z,Halvard),answer(z)
(7) (3,6) by specializing z = Catherine in 6 (in *both* conditions) ← answer(Catherine)

This example shows how logic can be used to find an answer to the query:

Which x is a parent of Halvard?

Clausal logic is a specification language of **universal expressivity**, with an automatic deductive mechanism for solving any problems specified. The property of being both a very powerful specification language, and at the same time a very high level programming language makes clausal logic a very strong formalism. The procedural interpretation of clausal logic makes it into one of the most powerful programming languages ever conceived.

The use of predicate logic as a programming language is called **logic programming**. The key idea underlying logic programming is programming by description (Genesereth and Ginsberg, 1985). A traditional program consists of a sequence of operations to be performed in solving a problem. The assumptions on which the program is based are left implicit. In logic programming, these assumptions are made explicit in logic, while the sequence of operation is implicit.

EXERCISES

2.1   Formulate the invalid rule of inference that Erasmus is apparently applying to show that his mother is a stone. Show its invalidity.

2.2   Prove that the elimination rule

$$(A \lor B) \land (\sim A \lor C) \Rightarrow B \lor C$$

is a valid formula by using two different methods: (i) by a truth table method showing that the truth value is TRUE for all interpretations of A, B and C; (ii) by algebraic simplification to TRUE.

2.3   Convert the following sentences to Kowalski clausal form:

All birds are animals.
All carnivores and ungulates are mammals.
Cheetahs and tigers are carnivores while giraffes and zebras are ungulates.
Ostriches, penguins and albatrosses are birds.
All ungulates have hooves.
Ostriches have black and white colours.
Giraffes and ostriches have long necks and long legs.
All birds except penguins and ostriches can fly.
No birds except penguins can swim.

Chapter 3
Resolution

Like processes programmed in logic,
the universe is moving
towards unknown goal.

But history is not at all
a hopeless search for proving,
it is the proof.

3.1 Some logical concepts

Though this is not a book on the foundations of logic programming (see Lloyd, 1984), a number of logical concepts are important, and are used throughout the sections on logic programming, so the more important definitions are given here, illustrated with short examples.

Definition A **logic system** is a set of rules for writing well-formed formulae of logic, and rules to derive formulae.

Definition An **interpretation** of a formula is defined by a **domain** of values, and assignment of values to the identifiers in the formula.

This means that constant identifiers are mapped into constant values, while functors are mapped into functions on this domain and predicates are mapped into relations on this domain.

For example, if the formula is $A \lor B$, then one interpretation is $A = \text{FALSE}$ and $B = \text{TRUE}$. Let the formula be $ge(\max(x,y),y)$. Then what follows is an interpretation:

$\max(x,y)$ is the function maximum of x and y;
$ge(x,y)$ is the predicate $x \geq y$.

Definition A formula is **satisfiable** or **consistent** if there is an interpretation which makes the formula true. The formula is said to be **satisfied** by the interpretation.

In the earlier formula, $A \lor B$ is satisfiable because the interpretation above makes the formula true. (Note that there are other interpretations.)

Definition   An interpretation of a formula that makes it true is called a **model** of the formula.

Thus, in the example, $A = $ FALSE and $B = $ TRUE is a model for $(A \lor B)$. The given interpretation of $ge(max(x,y),y)$ is also a model.

Definition   A formula F is said to be **valid** if it is true for all interpretations of the identifiers in F.

So $A \lor B$ is *not* a valid formula, because the interpretation $A = $ FALSE and $B = $ FALSE makes it FALSE. However, $B \lor \sim B$ is valid.

Definition   To **prove** a formula is to show that it is valid.

Informally, a set of axioms (A) is sometimes taken for granted, and then a formula B is 'proven'. Formally, it is proven that $A \Rightarrow B$ is valid.

Definition   A formula F is **inconsistent** or **unsatisfiable** if it is false for all interpretations of the identifiers in F, i.e. it has no model.

For example, $B \land \sim B$ is inconsistent (and invalid).

Definition   To **refute** a formula is to show that it is inconsistent.

Definition   A formula F **logically implies** a formula G if all models for F are also models for G (that is all interpretations that make F true also make G true).

This rather general definition of logical implication is impossible to use directly, since it deals with the intractable set of all interpretations. Instead, the notion of proof method is introduced.

Definition   A **proof method** is a method used to prove a goal clause by iteratively deriving new clauses until the goal is derived.

Definition   A proof method is **correct** or **sound** if all derived clauses are logically implied by the initial formula, and it is **complete** if all clauses logically implied by the initial formula may be derived from the initial formula by the proof method.

If the proof method is correct and complete, **provability** can be used as a synonym for logic implication.

Definition   A logic system is **decidable** if for every formula it can be proven valid or invalid. Propositional calculus is decidable, because the set of all interpretations of a formula is finite – the truth table of a formula is finite.

The more general first order predicate logic is not decidable, however. This means that an attempt to prove a formula may go on forever, but there will be no indication of when to stop without sacrificing formulae that can be proven.

First order predicate logic is complete; it has a complete proof procedure.

This section closes with a comment on notations commonly used for logic implication and provability.

If a formula, F, is valid in a logic system, M, of axioms and inference rules, it is written:

$$M \models F$$

If a formula, F, is provable in the logic system, M, it is written:

$$M \vdash F$$

The correctness and completeness of first order predicate logic can then be summarized by a master equation:

$$\models \; \equiv \; \vdash$$

This has been chosen as the logo of the *Logic Programming Newsletter* (1982).

3.2 Quantifiers

The concept of predicate logic has already been introduced formally. To be a little bit more formal, the phrase:

all x are P

is formalized as $\forall x\ P(x)$.

The quantifier $\forall$ means 'for all', or 'for any'. If it precedes a formula as in:

$$\forall x \ P(x)$$

then it may be interpreted as:

$$P(a_1) \wedge P(a_2) \wedge P(a_3) \wedge \ ... \ \wedge P(a_N)$$

for all possible individuals a_1, ..., a_N. In other words, the 'all' quantifier behaves as a generalized $\wedge$ operator.

Similarly, the phrase:

some x are P

is formalized as:

$$\exists x \ P(x)$$

and is equivalent to the possibly infinite formula:

$$P(a_1) \vee P(a_2) \vee P(a_3) \vee \ ... \ \vee P(a_N)$$

Thus $\exists$ acts as a generalized $\vee$ operator.

3.2.1   Examples of quantifiers

To show how powerful predicate logic is for representing knowledge, here are a number of examples where a meaning represented in natural language is transformed into predicate logic.

God loves everybody:

$\forall x \ \text{loves}(\text{God},x)$

In every crowd, there is a fool:

$\forall x \ (\text{crowd}(x) \Rightarrow \exists y \ (\text{member}(y,x) \wedge \text{fool}(y))$

In every class there is a student who knows the answer to all questions:

$\forall x \ (\text{class}(x) \Rightarrow \exists s \ (\text{student}(s) \wedge \text{member}(s,x) \wedge$
$\forall q,r \ (\text{question}(q) \wedge \text{answer}(q,r) \Rightarrow \text{knows}(s,r))))$

3.2.2   Second order logic concepts

First order predicate logic is called first order logic because the quantifiers range over the simple constants. Second order logic allows quantification over predicates and functions. A good example of second order logic is the induction axiom for integers, where P denotes any one place predicate defined on non-negative integers:

$$\forall P \ [\forall N(P(N)) \ \Leftrightarrow \ (P(0) \ \wedge \ (\forall x \ (P(x) \ \Rightarrow \ P(x + 1))))]$$

Another example is the equality axiom, actually originating from Leibnitz, which stated that two entities are equal if there are no one-place predicates to distinguish between them:

$$x = y \ \Leftrightarrow \ \forall P \ (P(x) \ \Leftrightarrow \ P(y))$$

Even higher order logics, including set theory and number theory, are not complete. This means that there are valid formulae in mathematics that cannot be proven.

3.3 First order predicate calculus

First order predicate calculus (FOPC) is a formal version of first order predicate logic without functions. A well-formed formula (WFF) in FOPC may be defined recursively by the composition rules. A well-formed formula is completely defined as follows:

- The logic constants, TRUE and FALSE, are WFF.
- If P is an n-place predicate, and w_1, ..., w_n are constants or logical variables then
  $P(w_1,...,w_n)$ is a WFF;
- If X,Y are WFF, then
  $X \wedge Y$ is a WFF
  $X \vee Y$ is a WFF
  $\sim X$ is a WFF
- If P is a well-formed formula, then
  $\exists v_1,...,v_n \ P$ is a WFF
  $\forall v_1,...,v_n \ P$ is a WFF

In first order predicate calculus, there are rules to transform these formulae into equivalent formulae. The propositional rules were covered earlier, so this section concentrates on the rules for the quantifiers.

If $P(x)$ is a general WFF containing x, and
    $P(y)$ is the same WFF, but with x replaced by y
    then:

$$\exists x \ P(x) \Leftrightarrow \exists y \ P(y)$$
$$\forall x \ P(x) \Leftrightarrow \forall y \ P(y)$$

$$\exists x \ \sim P(x) \Leftrightarrow \sim \forall x \ P(x)$$
$$\forall x \ \sim P(x) \Leftrightarrow \sim \exists x \ P(x)$$

$$\forall x \ \forall y \ P(x,y) \Leftrightarrow \forall y \ \forall x \ P(x,y) \Leftrightarrow \forall x,y \ P(x,y)$$
$$\exists x \ \exists y \ P(x,y) \Leftrightarrow \exists y \ \exists x \ P(x,y) \Leftrightarrow \exists x,y \ P(x,y)$$

$$\exists x \ (P(x) \lor Q(x)) \Leftrightarrow \exists x \ P(x) \lor \exists x \ Q(x)$$
$$\forall x \ (P(x) \land Q(x)) \Leftrightarrow \forall x \ P(x) \land \forall x \ Q(x)$$

Finally, there are some rules which are not equivalences:

$$\exists x \ (P(x) \land Q(x)) \Rightarrow \exists x \ P(x) \land \exists x \ Q(x)$$
$$\forall x \ (P(x) \lor Q(x)) \Leftarrow \forall x \ P(x) \lor \forall x \ Q(x)$$

3.3.1 Skolem functions

The manipulation of all combinations of the operators $\land$, $\lor$, $\sim$, $\forall$ and $\exists$, has been described, except for adjacent combinations of $\forall$ and $\exists$. In the following example, for every integer x there is an integer y which is greater (G) than x:

$$\forall x \exists y \ G(y,x)$$

In other words, for each x, the existence of a y is postulated such that $G(y,x)$. However, how to find this y for a given x is not explicitly described. The existence of y is *a priori* quite non-procedural, and the same x may give a different y at different times.

However, a unique function f may also be postulated such that for each x, a unique y greater than x is computed. It is not necessary to give this function any interpretation, just a name $f(x)$. Thus the $\exists$ operator and the y variable are no longer needed.

$$G(f(x),x)$$

Such a function is called a **Skolem function** after the Norwegian logician Thoralf Skolem, who proved that the validity of a formula was preserved by this simplification.

This transformation is called **Skolemization**, where all existential quantifiers are removed and all occurrences of existentially quantified variables are replaced by Skolem functions. These take as arguments all the universally quantified variables 'global' to the existential variables, as in this example:

$$\forall x,y \ (\exists z(\forall u,v(\exists w \ P(w,z))))$$

is transformed, replacing z with $f(x,y)$, into:

$$\forall x,y(\forall u,v\ (\exists w\ P(w,f(x,y))))$$

and, by replacing w with $g(x,y,u,v)$ to

$$\forall x,y(\forall u,v\ P(g(a,y,u,v),f(x,y)))$$

A special case occurs when the $\exists$ is placed at the outermost level, i.e. not inside the scope of any universally quantified variable. Then the Skolem function becomes a zero argument function, or a constant. Such a constant is called a **Skolem constant** and formally, it should be written with empty parentheses. For example, there exists a country Utopia where all inhabitants are happy:

$$\forall x\ (\text{inhabitant}(x,\text{Utopia}) \Rightarrow \text{happy}(x))$$

3.3.2 From predicate logic to clausal form

The resolution method requires the predicate logical formulae to be put in a standard form, called clausal form. It assumes that the assertion to be proven is negated, and included together with the axioms, and that the derivation of a contradiction will be the task.

The transformation of a general WFF to clausal form is quite mechanical, and it will be demonstrated on a sentence that is initially contradictory. The student reader is advised to try to follow the transformations, and to assign meanings to the formulae.

> There is a highest prime number and
> there is no highest prime number.

This may be represented in predicate logic:

$P(x)$ means prime x
$G(y,x)$ means $y > x$
$\exists x\ (P(x) \wedge \forall y\ (P(y) \Rightarrow \sim G(y,x)))$
$\wedge$
$\sim\exists x\ (P(x) \wedge \forall y\ (P(y) \Rightarrow \sim G(y,x)))$

In fact, the sentence is only one possible interpretation of the formula, while the formal proof of contradiction is quite independent of this or any other interpretation.

3.3.3 Clause normalization algorithm

(1) **Remove the implication symbols**. All occurrences of $A \Rightarrow B$ are then replaced by $\sim A \lor B$

$$\exists x \; (P(x) \land \forall y \; (\sim P(y) \lor \sim G(y,x)))$$
$$\land$$
$$\sim \exists x \; (P(x) \land \forall y \; (\sim P(y) \lor \sim G(y,x)))$$

(2) **Reduce the scope of the negation symbols**. The rules involving negation must be applied in the direction where the negation sign has smaller operands, i.e. the negation sign must be pushed inwards. On the second conjunct this happens as follows:

$$\sim \exists x \; (P(x) \land \forall y \; (\sim P(y) \lor \sim G(y,x)))$$
$$\forall x \; \sim (P(x) \land \forall y \; (\sim P(y) \lor \sim G(y,x)))$$
$$\forall x \; (\sim P(x) \lor \sim \forall y \; (\sim P(y) \lor \sim G(y,x)))$$
$$\forall x \; (\sim P(x) \lor \exists y \; \sim (\sim P(y) \lor \sim G(y,x)))$$
$$\forall x \; (\sim P(x) \lor \exists y \; (\sim \sim P(y) \land \sim \sim G(y,x)))$$
$$\forall x \; (\sim P(x) \lor \exists y \; (P(y) \land G(y,x)))$$

The result on the whole formula is:

$$\exists x \; (P(x) \land (\forall y \; \sim P(y) \lor \sim G(y,x)))$$
$$\land$$
$$\forall x \; (\sim P(x) \lor \exists y \; (P(y) \land G(y,x)))$$

(3) **Standardize the variables**. There must be no confusion with variables names when the quantifiers are removed. Since variables are only dummy names, they can be changed so that all different variables get different names.

$$\exists u \; (P(u) \land (\forall v \; \sim P(v) \lor \sim G(v,u)))$$
$$\land$$
$$\forall x \; (\sim P(x) \lor \exists y \; (P(y) \land G(y,x))).$$

(4) **Skolemize the formula**. H now represents a postulated highest prime number; $f(x)$ represents the next prime above x.

$$P(H) \land \forall v \; (\sim P(v) \lor \sim G(v,H))$$
$$\land$$
$$\forall x \; (\sim P(x) \lor (P(f(x)) \land G(f(x),x)))$$

(5) **Convert to prenex form**. All universal quantification is put at the front.

$\forall x \forall v$
$P(H) \wedge (\sim P(v) \vee \sim G(v,H))$
$\wedge$
$\sim P(x) \vee (P(f(x)) \wedge G(f(x),x))$

(6) **Remove universal quantifiers**. The order of the universal quantifiers is immaterial. So assuming variables are distinguished by conventions of notation, the quantifiers are redundant.

$P(H) \wedge (\sim P(v) \vee \sim G(v,H))$
$\wedge$
$\sim P(x) \vee (P(f(x)) \wedge G(f(x),x))$

(7) **Convert the formula to the conjunctive normal form.** This means there is a conjunction of disjunctions:

$P(H)$
$\wedge$
$\sim P(v) \vee \sim G(v,H)$
$\wedge$
$\sim P(x) \vee P(f(x))$
$\wedge$
$\sim P(x) \vee G(f(x),x)$

(8) **Eliminate the AND operators**. The collection of clauses signifies their conjunction:

$P(H)$
$\sim P(v) \vee \sim G(v,H)$
$\sim P(x) \vee P(f(x))$
$\sim P(x) \vee G(f(x),x)$

(9) **Convert the formula to clausal form**:

$P(H) \leftarrow$
$\leftarrow P(v),G(v,H)$
$P(f(x)) \leftarrow P(x)$
$G(f(x),x) \leftarrow P(x)$

The formula is now in standard form, and it is finished. This formula, incidentally, is in Horn clause form, although the algorithm works as well for non-Horn clauses. It may be proven that this clause set is inconsistent. However, that involves the unification of functional terms, which should be defined properly first.

3.3.4 The complete unification algorithm

The unification algorithm, which is part of the resolution method, not only finds a set of substitutions, but finds a **minimal set of substitutions** that is most general, i.e. it has no unnecessary specifications. The unification algorithm here is an adaptation of the original version by Robinson (1965). The idea is that when a variable is substituted with a term, the variable is immediately replaced in all its occurrences in the clauses where it occurs. Unification may then be explained by the following iterative process. It is assumed that all predicates and functions have the same number of arguments.

The unification algorithm is as follows:

- rename all variables, so that the variables in the two literals are initially disjoint;
- match the identifiers of the two literals until there are two different identifiers, or the end is reached;
- if the end of the literal has been reached, return with success;
- otherwise, if none are variables, return with fail;
- otherwise, assuming one of the identifiers is a variable, substitute all occurrences of this variable in both literals with the term at the corresponding place in the other literal;
- continue scanning.

Follow the pair of literals C and D through the following series of iterations:

(1) C $DQ(p(x,p(z,y)),z,p(x,y))$
$\downarrow$

    D $DQ(p(p(A,u),u),B,v)$

(2) C $DQ(p(p(A,u),p(z,y)),z,p(p(A,u),y))$
$\uparrow$

    D $DQ(p(p(A,u),u),B,v)$

(3) C $DQ(p(p(A,p(z,y)),p(z,y)),z,p(p(A,p(z,y)),y))$
$\downarrow$

    D $DQ(p(p(A,p(z,y)),p(z,y)),B,v)$

(4) C $DQ(p(p(A,p(B,y)),p(B,y)),B,p(p(A,p(B,y)),y))$
$\uparrow$

    D $DQ(p(p(A,p(B,y)),p(B,y)),B,v)$

(5) C $DQ(p(p(A,p(B,y)),p(B,y)),B,p(p(A,p(B,y)),y))$
    D $DQ(p(p(A,p(B,y)),p(B,y)),B,p(p(A,p(B,y)),y))$

3.4 The resolution proof method

3.4.1 Resolution step

The resolution proof method involves combining unification and elimination in one operation. If U is a set of substitutions, for any clause or literal G let G/U be the version of G where these substitutions have been applied.

Two clauses, A and B, can be resolved if they each have a literal – L_a and L_b – with opposite signs, so that L_a and L_b can be unified. Without loss of generalization, assume that L_a and L_b appear first, and that the other literals are collected in subformulae R_a and R_b so that:

$$A = L_a \lor R_a$$
$$B = {\sim}L_b \lor R_b$$

Let U be the most general substitution that makes L_a and L_b equal, i.e.:

$$L_a/U = L_b/U \qquad\qquad (3.1)$$

Then $A/U = L_a/U \lor R_a/U$
and $B/U = {\sim}L_b/U \lor R_b/U$
$= {\sim}L_a/U \lor R_b/U$ (because of (3.1))

Now, using the elimination rule, it can be concluded:

$$A/U \land B/U \Rightarrow R_a/U \lor R_b/U = (R_a \lor R_b)/U$$

The last clause, $(R_a \lor R_b)/U$ is called a **resolvent** of A and B – there may be several. It is itself in clausal form, and may be written $(A - L_a, B - L_b)/U$, i.e. the union of the literals in A and B except for the literals which were unified.

The resolution can be seen to be correct, because each resolvent of A and B, $\mathrm{Res}(A,B)$, is logically implied by the conjunction of A and B. This follows from the fact that:

$A \Rightarrow A/U$ (because A/U is a special case of A)
$B \Rightarrow B/U$ (because B/U is a special case of B)
$A \land B \Rightarrow (A/U \land B/U)$
$\qquad\qquad \Rightarrow \mathrm{Res}(A,B)$ (by the elimination rule)

3.4.2 Resolution proof

The resolution proof method repeatedly selects pairs of clauses which can be resolved and derives new resolvents by the resolution rule until the empty clause is derived.

There may be several search strategies for the repeated selection of clauses. If the strategy is such that no resolvable clauses are omitted forever, then the resolution proof method is complete. This was proven by Robinson (1965).

The search for a proof is usually full of blind alleys and dead ends. However, when a proof is found, the successful combinations can be reconstructed and presented as the proof. For example:

(1) $P(H)$
(2) $\leftarrow P(v),G(v,H)$
(3) $P(f(x)) \leftarrow P(x)$
(4) $G(f(x),x) \leftarrow P(x)$

The proof of inconsistency is as follows:

(5) $P(x),G(f(x),H)$ % (3,2) $v = f(x)$
(6) $\leftarrow G(f(H),H)$ % (1,5) $x = H$
(7) $\leftarrow P(H)$ % (4,6)
(8) $\leftarrow$ % (1,7)

A proper understanding of resolution is necessary to understand the potential of predicate logic, and to assess current logic programming languages with proposed extensions. It also helps to understand the various logic program transformations and aids deeper understanding, which is a prerequisite for creativity.

Factoring

A complication with the resolution of non-Horn clauses, which were omitted from the first presentation, is that binary resolution alone is not complete, as shown by the following example:

(1) $P(x),P(A) \leftarrow$ % $m = 2$ literals
(2) $\leftarrow P(x),P(A)$ % $n = 2$ literals

This set is obviously inconsistent; however, any resolvent will have two literals, in general, with $m + n - 2 = 2$ literals, where m and n are the number of literals in the parent clauses, but the procedure is not finished until the empty clause has no literals. To achieve this, there is another principle called factoring which merges unifiable literals in the same clause with the same sign.

(1') $P(A)$ % by factoring, i.e. by unifying $P(x)$ and $P(A)$
(2') $\leftarrow P(A)$ % by factoring, i.e. by unifying $P(x)$ and $P(A)$
(3') $\leftarrow$ % (1',2')

Factoring is not necessary for Horn clauses – as an exercise the student may consider why this is so.

3.4.3 Resolution proof search strategies

The proof of a formula depends on finding fortunate clauses to resolve, and many combinations do not contribute to the solution. So, finding search strategies for selecting resolvents so that a proof is achieved in the fewest steps is important.

In general, resolution has no inherent search strategy that can be fixed independently. Searches can be improved by using heuristics (see Chapter 12), or informed guesses at what are the most promising clauses to combine. But without such information, there are still some very general strategies that can be followed.

Unit preference

This is a strategy to select short clauses to resolve, because the ultimate goal is to arrive at the empty clause. A special case is when one of the resolvents is a unit clause, because then that resolvent is one literal shorter than the other.

Input resolution

One of the parent clauses is an original clause, also called an **input clause**.

Linear resolution

An important point about resolution proofs is that the resolution remains complete when the admissible resolvents are chosen. At least one of the literals, therefore, was one of the ancestors on the path of resolvents; the other being either an original clause, or another clause on the same path.

Set of support

This strategy assumes that a problem definition consists of a consistent axiom set and a negated goal, defining clauses that are inconsistent with the former. The negated set is called the **set of support**. Resolvents of clauses only within the consistent axiom set, or new resolvents derived from it alone, will never produce any contradiction or empty clause. It has proven sufficient always to select clauses where at least one stems from the set of support.

Predicate connection graphs

A connection graph is an implementation strategy for resolution, using a network of links between resolvable clauses. This network is maintained during the proof. Links are selected for resolution and deleted afterwards; new clauses are linked into the graph; and clauses with no links are deleted. Connection graphs were invented by Kowalski (1974b) and a complete proof method was provided by researchers from Karlsrühe (Siekmann and Stephan, 1976). Kowalski (1979b) has given an inspiring account of the potentials of multiple search strategies and connection graphs.

Predicate connection graphs allow any search strategy to be implemented and their application in expert systems and parallel inference machines is a promising research topic (Whitney *et al.*, 1985).

Prolog's search strategy

Prolog is a programming language based on resolution of Horn clauses, using a very specialized search strategy. It is a specialized version of linear input resolution, set of support, and a deterministic depth-first search strategy. This search strategy will be explained in Chapter 4.

EXERCISES

3.1   Show the following equivalence:

$$\forall x \ (\text{Grandfather}(x,z) \Leftarrow \exists y \ (\text{Father}(x,y) \wedge \text{Father}(y,z)))$$

is equivalent to:

$$\forall x,y \ (\text{Grandfather}(x,z) \Leftarrow \text{Father}(x,y) \wedge \text{Father}(y,z))$$

3.2   Convert the following sentences to predicate logic:

Tony, Mike and John belong to the Alpine Club.

Every member of the Alpine Club is either a skier or a mountain climber.
Mountain climbers do not like rain, and anyone who does not like snow is not a skier.
Mike dislikes whatever Tony likes and likes whatever Tony dislikes.
Tony likes rain and snow.
Is there a member of the Alpine Club who is a mountain climber, but not a skier?

3.3 Perform the resolution refutation of the following clause set:

$$S \leftarrow C$$
$$S \leftarrow D$$
$$C,D \leftarrow$$
$$\leftarrow S$$

3.4 Prove formally that the following sentences are inconsistent:

John likes everybody who likes logic.
No one likes anyone who likes himself.
John likes logic.

3.5 Translate the following English to clausal logic, add relevant axioms and prove it by resolution:

There are three cakes and two boxes.
Every cake lies in a box.
Show that at least one box contains at least two cakes.

Use the following predicates:

$C(x)$	x is a cake
$B(x)$	x is a box
$L(x,y)$	x lies in y
$E(x,y)$	$x = y$

3.6 Assume the following facts:

$$E(p) \quad G(p)$$
$$E(q) \quad G(q)$$
$$G(r)$$

Now, it is tempting to ask in logic whether it is true that

$$\forall x(E(x) \Rightarrow G(x)) \tag{3.2}$$

However, the implication becomes valid only if it is explicitly stated that p and q are the only x such that $E(x)$:

$$\forall x(E(x) \Rightarrow x = p \lor x = q)$$

With this in mind, prove formula (3.2).

Chapter 4
Predicate Logic as a Programming Language

> Logic is better than programming,
> but I can't prove it.

Prolog is a common name for a family of programming languages which implement the ideas of predicate logic as a programming language. In this text, a particular dialect called Edinburgh-Prolog is considered, specifically the C-Prolog version (Pereira, 1984). However, other dialects are also in use. For certain dialects, there are a number of implemented versions which may vary in detail.

The semantics of Prolog are at the core the same as those described by Horn clause logic. However, the syntax differs and there are features derived from other programming languages which have no root in logic.

4.1 Syntax

4.1.1 Basic syntax

Prolog has a convention that all identifiers beginning with upper-case letters are logical variables, while constant identifiers begin with lower-case letters.

The convention was devised to mark variables as special identifiers, in the same way as proper names, such as Aristotle, are distinguished from ordinary words by capital letters. However, the convention implies that Aristotle becomes a logical variable.

An underscore is allowed as an identifier character, but if it is the first character, then the identifier is regarded as a variable. A single underscore is a special, anonymous variable, different from all other variables in the clause. It has the same effect as a variable with only one occurrence in the clause, though to save time, no substitutions are performed. For example, **socrates**, **blue** and *x* are constant identifiers, while **USA**, **Warren**, **Prolog** and **_blue** are variables.

In addition, there are numeric constants:

| 12 | integer |
| 3.14 | real |

and quoted identifier constants

'Prolog', 'USA', 'Warren'

When the text inside the quote is a legal constant identifier, then the quotes are redundant, i.e.

'blue' = blue

4.1.2 Functions

Functions in Prolog have the same syntax as literals, and start with a lower-case letter. Functions are never evaluated automatically. For example:

tree(Root,X,Y)
max(sin(3.14159265),0)

4.1.3 Clause syntax

In Prolog, the reverse implication is written as :– instead of $<-$. Thus, a goal is initiated by :–.
　　For example:

big('IBM').
blue('IBM').
bigblue(X):–big(X),blue(X).
:–bigblue(X).

4.1.4 Program structure

A Prolog program consists of clauses, which may be of three kinds:

(1) The **facts** are unconditional conclusions

mother(sonja,martha).
mother(sonja,magnus).

father(harald,martha).
father(harald,magnus).

father(olav,harald).

(2) The **rules** are conditional clauses consisting of a conclusion, followed by a ':–', followed by a sequence of conditions, separated by a ','.

parent(X,Y):–mother(X,Y).
parent(X,Y):–father(X,Y).

grandfather(X,Y):–parent(U,Y),father(X,U).

(3) A query logically specifies the conditions to be solved:

:–grandfather(G,magnus).

4.1.5 Describing predicates

For the description of predicates, a meta-variable must often be used to stand for a term which may be either a Prolog variable or a Prolog term. This book uses the very pragmatic convention of using Prolog variables as meta-variables, but will describe what kind of terms they may stand for.

Also, giving examples of items informally requires a notation, so that the English is not disturbed. We will let single quotes, '', surround such items; double quotes have a special meaning in Prolog. In the phrase 'fishandchips', for example, there must be blanks between 'fish' and 'and' and 'chips'.

4.1.6 Input/output and comments

Input/output (I/O) is performed by special predicates. For the time being, the predicate **answer(X)** will print out a term.

A **comment** is everything to the right of a comment sign, which is a % preceded by at least one space. Comments are ignored by the interpreter. Comments in the text after output from Prolog are just supplied by the author for explanation.

p.   % This is a comment
q.   This is not a comment (*sic*)

4.2 The semantics of Prolog

The semantics of Prolog as a programming language are inherited from the semantics of Horn clause logic: it uses both **declarative semantics** and **procedural semantics**. The declarative semantics can be stated as follows:

A condition is provable if it is the conclusion of an instance of some clause, and each of the conditions of that clause is provable.

The procedural semantics of Prolog are defined by a very specific proof search strategy. At any time, Prolog keeps a current sequence of conditions which it tries to solve simultaneously, with the same substitutions for all the shared variables. Such a condition sequence is called a **goal**.

The first condition in the current goal is attempted, unified with a conclusion of a rule or a fact in the program. The conclusions are tried one by one in the same sequence as in the program. If it finds a clause A with a matching conclusion, a new current goal is formed from the previous goal and A, using a single resolution step. If it finds no clause to match, it will forget the current goal, and **backtrack** to the most recent previous goal which still has another untried conclusion.

Prolog's execution strategy can be summarized as:

top-down	only goals are executed
left-to-right	of the conditions
first-to-last	of the conclusions
depth-first	search with backtracking

Indentations in the trace show the depth of the calls. Goals starting in the same column are instances of literals derived from the same predecessor. The goals with no successors are marked with 'FAIL'.

```
mother(sonja,martha).
mother(sonja,magnus).

father(harald,martha).
father(harald,magnus).
father(olav,harald).

parent(X,Y):-mother(X,Y).
parent(X,Y):-father(X,Y).

grandfather(X,Y):-
  parent(U,Y),
  father(X,U).
```

CURRENT GOAL

```
:-grandfather(G,magnus),answer(G).
  :-parent(U,magnus),father(G,U),answer(G).
    :-mother(U,magnus),father(G,U),answer(G).
      :-father(G,sonja),answer(G).  % FAIL
    :-father(U,magnus),father(G,U),answer(G).
      :-father(G,harald),answer(G).
```

:–answer(olav).

==> olav

It is easy to get the false impression that Prolog is grossly inefficient, copying lots of data. However, using an implementation technique called structure sharing (Boyer and Moore, 1972), it is all implemented by means of pointers. It is just the trace printing that gives the copy impression.

There are other ways of describing the behaviour of logic programs. However, the best way to understand Prolog properly is to regard it as a logical deduction process, and explain the execution within a search tree.

4.3   Search tree

The Prolog interpreter searches for a solution. When the set, or space, of all possible solutions is considered, this can be seen as a tree, where each node represents a current goal, and each of the successors of a node is a branch node, representing the successors of the goal.

This search tree is traversed in a strict top-down, depth-first and left-to-right manner. The whole search tree does not exist in memory at any time, only the current goal, and all its parent nodes (the path). Nodes with more branches than the one actually being tried are called **reactivation points**.

Compare the following example with Figure 4.1.

(1) $p(X):-g(X),r(X)$.
(2) $p(scrmph)$.
(3) $q(a)$.
(4) $q(b)$.
(5) $q(c)$.
(6) $r(b)$.
(7) $r(c)$.
(8) $s(b)$.
(9) $s(c)$.
(10) $w(U):-s(U)$.
(11) goal:–$p(U),w(U)$.
(12) goal:–alter(ego).

4.4   Recursion

Prolog definitions may be recursive; this is in fact a natural and necessary part of the language. For example, to define an ancestor relation requires

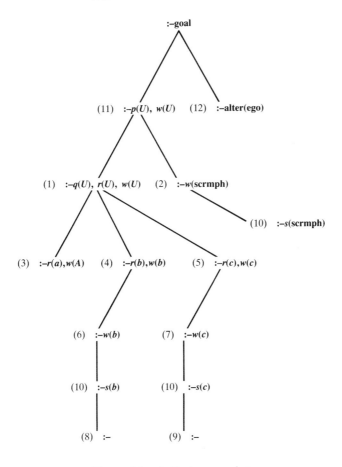

Figure 4.1   A Prolog search tree.

a transitive extension of the parent relation defined in Section 4.2.

ancestor(X,Y):–parent(X,Y).
ancestor(X,Z):–parent(X,Y),ancestor(Y,Z).
:–ancestor(X,adam).

The search tree of this definition is infinite. Great care must be taken in order not to fall into a **recursive trap**, also known as a shaft, well, hell or catch, amongst other things. Here a problem's solution is attempted by means of a more general version of itself. The above example is **right-recursive**, because the recursive call appears to the right of the other condition parent. However, if the definition is **left-recursive**, there is a danger: conditions after the recursive call will never be reached, even if they are unsolvable and could stop the whole evaluation. Also, potentially successful rules defined after a left-recursive rule are actually never tried. As the following example shows, Adam has no parents, so the problem is unsolvable, but this is never discovered:

> parent(adam,cain).
> parent(adam,abel).
>
> ancestor(X,Y):–parent(X,Y).
> ancestor(X,Z):–ancestor(X,Y),parent(Y,Z).
>
> CURRENT GOAL
>
> :–ancestor(W,adam)
>   :–parent(W,adam)   % FAIL
>   :–ancester(W,Y),parent(Y,adam)
>   :–parent(W,Y),parent(Y,adam)
>   :–parent(cain,adam)   % FAIL
>   :–parent(abel,adam)   % FAIL
>   :–ancestor(W,Y'),parent(Y',Y),parent(Y,adam)
>   .
>   .
>   .

and so on.

There will be many more examples of recursion in the later chapters, but the concepts of left-recursion and right-recursion must be kept in mind.

4.5   On variable bindings

Different variables do not necessarily denote different values. This is demonstrated by the following example:

> X and Y are brothers if they have the same father.
>   brother(X,Y):–father (F,X),father (F,Y).
>   father(adam,cain).
>   father(adam,abel).
>   :–brother(cain,Y).

This gives both Cain and Abel as answers, that is, Cain is postulated to be his own brother. To avoid this, inequality must be tested for explicitly (see Section 4.8.5).

4.5.1 Anonymous variables

As mentioned in the syntax section, a single underscore denotes a dummy variable. The following example demonstrates how these are used.

> $p(a,b)$.
> :–$p(\_X,\_X)$.   % will not succeed
> :–$p(\_,\_)$.   % will succeed

4.5.2 Renaming variables

It is important at some point to understand the details of Prolog execution. They are an adaptation of the unification mechanism in resolution, applied to Prolog. When the first condition in the current goal is to be unified with the conclusion of a clause, it must be considered as if a copy were made of the clause, where all the free variables in the clause are renamed before unification starts. This is called the **renaming principle**. Consider the example:

> $p(X)$.
> :–$p(a),p(b)$.

In the unification, a copy of the clause $p(X)$ is made, the X is replaced by a new variable (X_0), and the resolvent is found after setting X_0 to a. The point is that the variable X itself is not bound to a when the next condition is tried:

> :–$p(b)$

Now, a new copy of the clause $p(X)$ is made and a new variable, X_1, replaces X, and X_1 is then bound to b.

> :–

Another effect of the renaming principle is that variable names in the goal, and in the clause with the matching conclusion, are initially different before unification starts, even though they superficially have the same name. Consider the example:

> **granny**(X,Z):–
>   **mother**(X,Y),**mother**(Y,Z).
>
> :–**granny**(maud,Y).

If the resolution were naively performed without the renaming, it would give:

> :–mother(maud,Y),mother(Y,Y).

Here Y is asked to be the mother of herself. What is actually happening is that when the conclusive clause is renamed, a new set of different variables is developed.

> granny(X_10,Z_11):–
>   mother(X_10,Y_12),mother(Y_12,Z_11).
> :–mother(maud,Y_12),mother(Y_12,Y).

The renaming principle should be kept in mind when studying Prolog examples, because the explanations sometimes conceal it for reasons of simplicity.

4.5.3 Occur check

If the following condition must be unified:

> :–eq(Y,$f(Y)$).

with this fact:

> eq(X,X).

unification will be attempted in two steps, bearing in mind that the renaming of eq(X,X) is initially done once.

(1) The first argument is unified by letting a copy of X be substituted by Y:
    eq(Y,Y).
    Now the same variable Y occurs in both literals.
(2) An attempt to unify the second argument will lead to the substitution $Y -> f(Y)$.

However, if an attempt is made to find the value of Y, it will be caught in an infinite self-referencing loop:

$$Y = f(f(f(f(f(\ldots$$

Actually Prolog systems usually do not check this at the time of unification, for efficiency reasons, so it comes as a nasty surprise in the shape of a stack overflow when access of the mal-substituted variable is attempted.

eq(X,X).
   :–eq(Y,$f(Y)$).   % Nothing happens. Y is actually bound to
                       % $f(Y)$, but this is not checked.

   :–eq(Y,$f(Y)$),answer(Y).
$f(f(f(f(f(...–$ % % % Stack overflow

The reason for not checking the occurrence of a variable when this variable is substituted is that this check would take a time proportional to the size of the term. (The unification procedure would have to scan the whole term.) On average, the unification will take a time proportional to the size of the goal condition, which is typically large. Without an **occur check**, the unification will take a time proportional to the size of the conclusion, which is usually smaller.

An empirical result is that the occur check has hardly any practical purpose – in almost all cases, a variable bound in this way is a sign of a programming error. An interesting variant of Prolog, Prolog II (Giannesini *et al.*, 1986) actually allows infinite self-referencing of terms.

4.6   Symmetry properties

Prolog exhibits some good symmetry properties inherited from logic. 'Truth is independent of sequence', for example.

4.6.1   Symmetry of sequence of conclusions

From the earlier example:

     father(harald,magnus).
     father(harald,martha).
     father(olav,harald).

But, the sequence of these clauses could equally well be permuted as follows:

     father(harald,magnus).
     father(olav,harald).
     father(harald,martha).

4.6.2   Symmetry of sequence of conditions

From an earlier example:

     grandfather(X,Z):–parent(U,Z),father(X,U).

However, the program would work as well with the definition:

grandfather(X,Z):–father(X,U),parent(U,Z).

Sometimes, however, the sequence of conditions is important for reasons of efficiency, and if the search tree is infinite, as in recursive examples, an awkward sequence will cause an endless recursion in an infinite part of the search tree.

4.6.3   Test-or-generate symmetry

In the grandfather example, the definitions of grandfather were used to generate (i.e. find and instantiate) a grandfather of Magnus, G = **olav**.

    :–grandfather(G,magnus).

However, if the definition had let G = **olav**, the condition:

    :–grandfather(olav,magnus).

would succeed as a test that Olav is the grandfather of Magnus.

4.6.4   Input/output parameter symmetry

This is a special case of the test-or-generate symmetry. For instance, the program above can be used either to find the grandfather of Magnus, or find the grandchild of Olav. This principle is sometimes called input/output symmetry, although it has nothing to do with ordinary I/O.

4.7   Cutting the search tree

Prolog searches through the search tree in a strict top-down, left-to-right, depth-first order. Because of this, it is possible to cut the remaining alternative branches of a goal by use of the special predicate !, called the **cut**. The cut is a solvable condition itself, but has the effect of cutting away unexplored branches of the search tree. In the following example, the search tree developed in Section 4.3 will be used, but adding the cut ! at the end of the first clause (see Figure 4.2).

    (1) $p(X)$:–$q(X)$,$r(X)$,!.
    (2) p(scrmph).
    (3) $q(a)$.
    (4) $q(b)$.

(5) *q(c).*

(6) *r(b).*

(7) *r(c).*

(8) *s(b).*

(9) *s(c).*

(10) *w(U):–s(U).*

(11) **goal**:–*p(U),w(U).*

(12) **goal**:–**alter(ego).**

The effect of the cut ! is to cut away from the search tree all alternatives that have been created since the call of the condition that called the clause with the !, *p(U)* in the figure. The branches cut away in

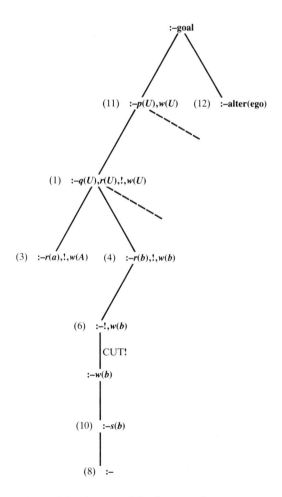

Figure 4.2 A pruned Prolog search tree.

this example are indicated by dashes (---). In other words, as soon as a '!'
is executed, the conclusion of the rule where this ! occurred (clause 1) is
accepted as the only possible solution to the calling condition. Note that
the alternative to the goal (clause 12) is not cut from the search.

4.8   Using the cut operator, !

The cut has several purposes:

- to implement pattern matching, so that when a pattern is found,
  the other patterns are discarded;
- to implement negation as failure;
- to cut the search for alternative solutions when one suffices;
- to cut the search when continuing would lead to an infinite search;
- to save storage space because the interpreter can forget the
  reactivation points.

Some of these applications will be illustrated using the following
definitions:

father(hans,gerhard).	% Hans is the father of Gerhard
mother(lise,gerhard).	% Lise is the mother of Gerhard
father(ivan,heinz).	
parent(X,Y):–father(X,Y).	
parent(X,Y):–mother(X,Y).	
hasparent(Y):–parent(X,Y).	% Y has a parent if there is an X
	% who is parent of Y
child(gerhard).	
child(heinz).	
child(beate).	
status(gerhard,healthy).	
status(heinz,sick).	

4.8.1   Negation as failure

A peculiarity of clausal logic is that it is not straightforward to prove the
negation of a formula.

   In the example, Beate is a child with no parents (she is an orphan), but that is not derived as a conclusion of an inference, but only by the fact that it is impossible to prove that she has a parent. In Prolog, this is implemented by combining cut with a special predicate called **fail**, which deliberately cannot be solved – it is insoluble.

  (1) **orphan(X):–child(X),noparent(X).**
  (2) **noparent(X):–parent(Y,X),!,fail.**
  (3) **noparent(X).**   % always succeeds if control
                                    % reaches here

Study the effect of the goal **noparent(beate)**:

    :–noparent(beate).   % has two alternatives 2,3

    (2)   **:–parent(Y,beate),!,fail.**
             :–father(Y,beate),!,fail.
             :–mother(Y,beate),!,fail.
    (3)   **:–**

noparent(beate) succeeds by the default clause 3, saying that everything else satisfies **noparent**. However, this fails if a person who is not an orphan is considered:

    :–noparent(gerhard).   % two alternatives 2,3

    (2)   **:–parent(Y,gerhard),!,fail.**   % cut is introduced here
             :–father(Y,gerhard),!,fail.
                :–!,fail.

The cut operator comes into effect here, and cuts alternative solutions for the goal **noparent(gerhard)**. Thus, clause 3 is cut off from trial.

        :–fail.

This goal is insoluble and causes backtracking. However, since the cut has removed the other alternatives, there are no other solutions, and the whole goal fails.

    The underlying assumption that negation may be deduced as failure is called the **closed world assumption** (CWA) (Reiter, 1978). The meaning of the world being closed is that all information about the world is available, and that everything that is not a logical consequence of this information is false. Negation as failure, on the other hand, is based on this assumption; a goal is false if all attempts to prove it terminate unsuccessfully.

4.8.2 Cut unnecessary search

Let us suppose we want to find if Gerhard is a child who has a parent, and is sick.

:–hasparent(gerhard),status(gerhard,sick).	
:–parent(Y,gerhard),status(gerhard,sick).	
:–father(Y,gerhard),status(gerhard,sick).	%% Y=hans
:–status(gerhard,sick).	%% no, backtrack
:–mother(Y,hans),status(gerhard,sick)	%% redundant,
:–status(gerhard,sick).	%% no, backtrack

Gerhard is not a solution, because Gerhard is not sick. We see that even though one parent of Gerhard would suffice, the automatic search regime of Prolog tries all possibilities when backtracking, so both the father and mother of Gerhard are tried in vain.

To avoid this kind of redundancy, the **hasparent** predicate could be defined as follows:

hasparent(X):–parent($\_$,X),!.

Now, as soon as one parent is found, all searches for other parents are stopped.

Note that the cut only has effect on the conditions to the left of the cut:

$p(X,Y)$:–$q(X)$,!,$r(Y)$.
$q(a)$.
$q(b)$.
$r(c)$.
$r(d)$.
$r(e)$.
:–$p(X,Y)$,answer(solution(X,Y)),fail.

solution(a,c)
solution(a,d)
solution(a,e)

Note, also, that the alternatives of q are cut from the solution space, but not the alternatives of r.

4.8.3 Cut destroys symmetry

The introduction of the cut may have some ill effects on the program. Generally speaking, the cut destroys symmetry properties, and therefore destroys the declarative reading of a program. More is said about the use and misuse of the cut in Chapter 7.

4.8.4 Variable conditions

In Prolog, there is the same syntax for terms and facts. It is also possible to call a term as a condition. A particularly good example is the **not** predicate defined by

```
not(X):-X,!,fail.          % i.e. not possible
not(X).                    % otherwise
```

Thus, the orphan example can be rephrased as:

```
orphan(X):-not(parent(Y,X)).
:-orphan(gerhard).
  :-not(parent(Y,gerhard)).
    :-parent(Y,gerhard),!,fail.
      :-father(Y,gerhard),!,fail.
        :-!,fail.
          :-fail.
```

Thus, **orphan(gerhard)** fails.

There are a number of other uses of condition variables:

```
and(X,Y):-X,Y.             % succeeds if both X and Y succeed
or(X,Y):-X.                % succeeds if X or Y succeeds
or(X,Y):-Y.
```

The parent predicate could be rephrased as:

```
parent(X,Y):-or(father(X,Y),mother(X,Y)).
```

An **exist** predicate finds only the first solution, if any:

```
exist(X,Y):-Y,!.
```

The **hasparent** example could be stated as:

```
hasparent(X):-exist(Y,parent(Y,X)).
```

An important property of **not(X)** is that if **not(X)** succeeds, by failing X, then no instantiation will be done for X.

test(X):–not(not(X)).

test(X) succeeds if and only if X succeeds at least once, but exploits the effect of the **not** predicate that all substitutions are undone. For example:

hasparents(X):–test(parent(Y,X)),answer(Y).
:–hasparent(gerhard).
Y_0

The variable Y, once bound to **hans**, is unbound.

4.8.5 Equality and inequality

Prolog is one of the very few programming languages where equality is not necessarily a primitive operation. For example, it is easy to define an equality predicate which matches any two arguments that are possibly equal or unifiable:

eq(X,X).

The effect is as follows:

:–eq(a,a)   success
:–eq(X,X)   success
:–eq(a,b)   failure
:–eq(X,a)   success by substitution ($X = a$)
:–eq(tree(L,node,b),tree(a,node,R)) ($L = a,R = b$)

However, inequality is not definable by unification alone.
    Inequality can be defined in many equivalent ways, but, strangely enough, not without using the cut in some way or other.

(1) ne(X,Y):–not(eq(X,Y)).
(2) ne(X,Y):–eq(X,Y),!,fail.
     ne(X,Y).
(3) ne(X,X):–!,fail.
     ne(X,Y).

The opposite effect is achieved:

:–ne(a,a)	% failure
:–ne(X,X)	% failure
:–ne(a,b)	% success
:–ne(X,a)	% failure
:–ne(tree(L,node,b),tree(a,node,R))	% failure

EXERCISES

4.1 Write the animal example in Prolog, and extend it with other kinds of animals, such as birds and fishes of various kinds.

4.2 Extend the rules for families (father, mother, grandmother) to concepts such as sibling, uncle, aunt and cousin, and use your own family as an example.

4.3 Define a recursive predicate **partof** in Prolog considering parts of a bicycle, e.g.

wheel, frame, pedal, saddle, handlebars, lighting-system, brake-system, hub, spokes, gear-cogs, brake-cable, brake-block, dynamo, lights, electric-flex, etc.

Use it to answer questions such as:

What is a hub part of?

What are the parts of the lighting system?

4.4 Show that it is not possible to define inequality in Prolog without the cut being used, directly or indirectly.

4.5 Define by using variable conditions a predicate implies(X,Y) which is true if, for all satisfiable instances of X, the Y is simultaneously true.

4.6 Look at the following definition:

```
cut:-!.
notatall(X):-X,cut,fail.
notatall(X).
```

Explain why **notatall** does not implement negation as failure.

Chapter 5
Programming in Prolog

Logic Programming:– % is
 Logic, % as long as we don't use the
 !, % which brings us irrevocably into
 Programming. % with no way of backtracking.

5.1   Predicate library

Software engineering is a collective endeavour, and the use of program libraries facilitates co-operation. In Prolog, programs are defined by various hierarchical levels of predicates:

- **built-in** or **predefined predicates**, which are considered essential by the creators of the Prolog system, but which cannot efficiently be implemented by more primitive predicates;
- **general predicate library**, containing very useful and general predicates and referred to for ease of explanation and exchange of programs. This book uses the general predicate library summarized in the Appendix;
- **application predicate library** which may be chosen as standard within a programming project, or an application;
- **user program**.

Some principles and techniques for programming in Prolog follow, and the essence of the technique will usually materialize in a set of useful predicates which may generally be applied. This section describes some predicates of a very general kind, while others will appear in other contexts. Some of the predicates will be used throughout the book without being redefined, so if a predicate is not defined where used, it may be found in the Appendix. This book is not systematic about application predicate libraries, but the principle should be noticed in practical work.

Using predicate libraries has its own merits: it shortens program development, and makes exchange of programs much easier although it does make such exchange difficult if the libraries are not identical.

5.2 Interactive Prolog

Most Prolog implementations are interactive. The following description is typical, and corresponds to our chosen reference language, the C-Prolog.

The initial use of Prolog is via a terminal, where the user is in a query mode, prompted by:

    | ?–

Here, the user may input any goal (sequence of conditions) separated by ',', and ending with a '.'.

When a goal is entered, the Prolog system finds one solution, prints the values of the variables occurring in the goal, and returns control to the user. The user may type a carriage return (CR) to end the query, or type a ';', in which case Prolog continues to try to query, their instantiations will be printed. Prolog will respond with a **yes** when a query without variables succeeds, or after a CR. If the query fails, or if there are no more answers, Prolog replies **no**. This interaction is called the **Prolog standard response**. It is only relevant for queries interactively typed in at the keyboard.

The user may switch to programming mode by typing:

    | ?–consult(user).

whereby the following lines of programming code will be read and analysed, and the goals executed. The programming mode is terminated by:

    end_of_file.

or a special control character, such as:

    ctrl-Z for VAX/VMS,
    ctrl-D for VAX/UNIX,

leading back to the query mode.

A sample Prolog dialogue runs as follows:

    | ?–consult(user).
    | father(ole,tore).
    | (ctrl-Z)
    yes   (exit consult)
    | ?–father(ole,tore).
    yes

```
| ?–father(X,tore).
X = ole   (CR)
yes
| ?–father(ole,brit).
no
| ?–consult(user).
| father(ole,brit).
| (ctrl-Z)
yes     (exit consult)
| ?–father(ole,brit).
yes
| ?–father(ole,Y).
Y = tore;          (; is typed)
Y = brit;          (; is typed)
no                 (no more answers)
| ?–father(X,Y).
X = ole
Y = tore;
X = ole
Y = brit;
no
| ?–father(X,Y).
X = ole
Y = tore   (CR)
yes        (although there are more answers)
| ?–halt.
[Prolog execution halted]
```

In this book Prolog examples typically occur in Prolog programs, and are not typed in directly from the terminal. The **consult(user)** and the return character, ctrl-Z, are usually dropped, therefore, and the program followed by examples of goals to illustrate the working of the programs.

Programs can be edited on file, and read and analysed by the **consult** predicate. An alternative form of consult might be:

$$?–[f_1,f_2,...,f_n].$$

This can be used to consult the files $f_1,...,f_n$ in sequence.

5.3   Basic input and output

A complete definition of input/output in Prolog is found in your reference manual. For the purposes of this book, the following predicates will suffice:

print(X)	print the term X	will print the current value of the term X on the terminal, as it is instantiated at the moment of printing, without any trailing blanks;
nl	print a new line	
read(X)	read a term X	will input a term from the terminal, and assign it to X The input must be terminated by a '.';
tab(N)	print N blanks	N must be a number.

In the following example:

```
colour(blue).
?–print(X),
   nl,
   colour(X),
   print(the),
   print(sky),nl,
   print(is(X)).
```

will print:

X_0	% internal variable name for the free variable X.
thesky	% note no automatic spacing.
is(blue)	% X is now bound to blue.

Actually, C-Prolog only outputs _0 for the variable X. This book occasionally uses the source listing variable name as a prefix for all output variables, to explain the ideas, because the C-Prolog format is not pertinent to Prolog, unless someone standardizes it.

```
?–read(X),print(X).
```

|hansen.	% | is a so-called 'prompt'
hansen	% output

The following text frequently uses the more convenient predicates, defined by:

output(X):–print(X),nl.   % print X with new line

out(X):–print(X),print(' ').   % print X with a space

input(X):–print('>'),read(X).   % conventional prompt for input

Some rudimentary predicates are sketched here for input/output, just to demonstrate Prolog. However, there are more advanced features for file handling.

First, the user may switch input/output files, so that input is taken from some files, and output is sent to others:

see(File)   % file becomes the new input

seen   % returns input file to terminal

tell(File)   % directs output to file

told   % redirects output back to terminal

Unfortunately, it is not possible to have output directed to the terminal, and at the same time to have a copy of everything that appears on the screen on a separate file for later inspection and documentation.

5.4   Built-in operators in Prolog

So far, this book has covered functional terms and predicates to explain the language concepts. Prolog is an interactive language, and operators can be used to implement a user language of almost any kind. A useful property of operator expression is economy of expression, i.e. few parentheses. Also, infix notation is often more natural than prefix notation. It is possible to have an operator syntax for the terms. Some of these are built-in, but it is also possible to define your own operators.

Here is a list of the built-in operators that will be used in this book. Their use will be described later. Other operators may be found in your reference manual.

?–	query operator
:–	command or conditional operator
$X = Y$	equality by unification (eq(X,Y));
	inequality is expressed by not $X = Y$
$X < Y$	X is less than Y, for numbers
$X > Y$	X greater than Y
$X =< Y$	X less or equal Y
$X >= Y$	X greater or equal Y

$X == Y$ X identical to Y without unification
$X =/= Y$ X not identical to Y
X,Y same as and(X,Y)
$X;Y$ same as or(X,Y)
not X same as not(X)
X **is** Y evaluate the expression Y and let X be the result
$X + Y$ addition, or just prefix
$X - Y$ subtraction, or negative prefix
$X * Y$ multiplication
X / Y division
$X \char94 Y$ power raising
$X =.. Y$ splitting a functional term X into its components

5.5   Evaluation of expressions

In algorithmic languages such as FORTRAN and Pascal, formulae are used to evaluate numerical results. In Prolog, expressions are not evaluated automatically, as the following example demonstrates very clearly:

> ?-X = 1 + 2 * 3.   % the query, X is unified with $1 + 2 * 3$
> X = 1 + 2 * 3   % the answer, which is the expression itself

The **is** operator allows an expression consisting of arithmetic operators and numbers to be calculated automatically. As programmers know, expressions such as:

> 1 + 2 * 3

are ambiguous unless the operators are given priorities. Therefore, the above expression is calculated as:

> 1 + (2 * 3)

To make this fully clear, study the following examples:

> ?-X is 1 + 2 * 3.
> X = 7
> ?-X is 3.1415 * 30^2.
> X = 2827.35
> ?-X = 3.1415 * 30^2.
> ?-X is 3.1415 * R^2, R = 30.
> **∗∗Error. Uninstantiated variable in arithmetic expression.**

?–R = 30, X is 3.1415 ∗ R^2.
X = 2827.35.

In this way, a Prolog system also acts as a superior programmable calculator.

5.6 Query processing

Sometimes, the standard response gives much irrelevant information, and it is also cumbersome to have to sign for each new solution using a ';' character. Instead, a predicate **all**(X) is used to print out X for each solution of the query.

all(X):–print(X),nl,fail.

all(X) is an insoluble predicate that outputs the solution before it fails, in effect forcing all the solutions to be output. For example:

$p(a)$.
$p(b)$.
$p(a)$.
?–$p(X)$,all(X).
    a
    b
    a
    no   % no more answers
                   % we omit this **no** from now on

Note that solutions are printed out even if they are not unique. The **all** predicate may be used with an arbitrary term as argument, as in the following examples:

$p(a)$.
$p(b)$.
  ?–$p(X)$,all(point(X)).
point(a)
point(b)
  ?–$p(X)$,all(X + 1).
a + 1
b + 1

The **all** predicate is intended for interactive use, and should not be used inside programs where the predicate is supposed to succeed after the last output. Even when only one solution is expected, it may be revealing to use the **all** predicate. Otherwise, when one specific answer is required to be printed out, the following predicate is used:

output(*X*)

All the other variable instantiations caused by the standard response as follows are not shown:

?–*p*(*X*),output(*X*).

a

5.7 Manipulating the database

The Prolog program consists of a set of facts, called the **database**, a set of rules, and queries. In pure Prolog, the facts are supposed to be given, and be invariant during the execution, while all the answers to the queries are deduced from the facts and the rules. Sometimes, this simple philosophy is not adequate because it may be desirable, or even necessary to change the database dynamically during the execution; to add or delete facts.

To this end, two predicates are built-in: **assert** and **retract**.

5.7.1 Assert

assert(*X*) will assert the term *X* as a fact in the database, even if the same fact appears before. **assert**(*X*) will always succeed.

For example:

?–assert(*q*(1)),
   assert(*q*(2)),
   assert(*q*(1)).

will cause the facts *q*(1), *q*(2) and *q*(1) to be true, as demonstrated by the query:

?–*q*(*X*),all(*X*).
1
2
1

Programmers need the facility of inserting only unique facts; that is the ability to check before inserting a new fact, if it is already known to be true. This is done using the predicate:

    remember(*X*).

defined by:

    remember(*X*):–*X*,!.
    remember(*X*):–assert(*X*).

As an example, starting with the predicate:

    likes(god,*X*).

a call for:

    ?–remember(likes(god,me)).

will find out that

    likes(god,me)

is true, as a special case, so **likes(god,me)** will not be added to the database. Its straightforward use is to test if a fact is already in the database to avoid duplication. For example:

    ?–remember(*r*(1)),
       remember(*r*(2)),
       remember(*r*(1)).
    ?–*r*(*X*),all(*X*).
  1
  2

5.7.2 Retract

The reverse of the assert function is to remove facts from the database by the built-in predicate:

    retract(*X*)

which removes the fact unifiable with *X*. **retract(*X*)** only removes one fact at a time, and fails if there are no facts matching *X*. What is often needed is a predicate that removes all facts supporting a condition, e.g.:

    ?–forget(*p*(*a*)).

should delete the fact *p*(*a*), while

    ?–**forget**(*p*(*X*)).

should delete the facts *p*(*a*), *p*(*b*) and so on, if present.
forget is easily implemented as a library predicate:

    forget(*X*):–*X*,**retract**(*X*),**fail**.
    forget(*X*).

Note that the terms inside a retracted fact are not removed by the retract
function:

    p(abra).
    ?–*p*(*X*),
        retract(*p*(*X*)),
        output(*X*).

should produce

    abra

which means that the term **abra** exists somewhere, even if the only fact
containing it is retracted.
    It is also possible to add and delete conditional clauses, but this
activity is very much the same as writing a self-modifying code, which
should be avoided according to fundamental software engineering
principles. No use of dynamic rule modifications will be shown, because,
except for pathological examples, it can easily be simulated by database
modification.

5.8 Operator declarations

The operators defined earlier are built-in, but it is possible to declare
your own operators.
    An expression containing operators is represented as a tree, with
the main functor at the root, and subtrees at the branches. The operator
priorities tell which of the adjacent operators are root operations,
relatively speaking.
    The priorities are indicated by integers from 1 at the leaf side to
1200 at the root side. For example:

    '+' **has priority 500**
    '*' **has priority 400**

Therefore, *a* + 4 * *b* can be represented internally as:

'+' (*a*, '*' (4,*b*))

and can be depicted as a tree (see Figure 5.1).

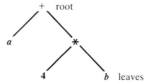

Figure 5.1 An operator expression tree.

All operator expressions can be put into round parentheses. Then the whole bracket acts as an operand. This then has a priority of 0. The operators are declared by a command as follows:

:–op(priority,type,name).

The type is a code with 3 main categories:

prefix: *fx,fy*
infix: *xfx,xfy,yfx,yfy*
postfix: *xf,yf*

Below is a list of the built-in operators in C-Prolog that are used in this book, although there are more than these.

:–op(1200,*xfx*, [:–]).
:–op(1200,*fx*, [:–,?–]).
:–op(1100,*xfy*, [;]).
:–op(1000,*xfy*, [',']).
:–op(900, *fy*, [not]).
:–op(700,*xfx*, [=,is,=..,==,=/=,<,>,=<,>=]).
:–op(500,*yfx*, [+,–]).
:–op(500, *fx*,[+,–]).
:–op(400,*yfx*, [*,/]).
:–op(200,*xfy*, [ˆ]).

This priority list defines how an expression is represented, but the semantics of each is defined by built-in Prolog predicates.
    The priorities unambiguously define the tree structure of an operator expression, except when two operators with the same priority, for example, the same operator, are adjacent. Therefore, main types of operator are subdivided according to whether they are inclined to the left or to the right.

fx   prefix, operand of lower priority
fy   prefix
xfx   infix, operands must be of lower priority
xfy   infix, right-associative. Left operand must be lower
yfx   infix, left-associative. Right operand must be lower
yfy   (not used)
xf   postfix, left operand lower
yf   postfix

For example,

$$X - Y - Z$$

means

$$(X - Y) - Z$$

and not

$$X - (Y - Z)$$

because $-$ is of type *yfx*, and therefore 'left associative'. Similarly, an expression with $+$, such as:

$$a + b + c + d$$

which is an infix operator of subtype *yfx*, is internally represented the same way as:

$$(((a + b) + c) + d)$$

The comma ',' is both a separator and an infix operator (see Figure 5.2).

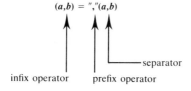

Figure 5.2 The anatomy of the comma.

It has a subtype *xfy* and a priority of 1000. This means that the comma is 'right-associative', in contrast to '+'. Thus:

$$a,b,c,d$$

is internally represented in the same way as:

$(a,(b,(c,d)))$.

which is the reverse grouping to that of the + expression. The parentheses are included to clarify the order of the operations.

Here is an illustration of user-defined operators, prefaced with some operator definitions from the predicate library.

```
:–op(1100,  fx, [list,listall]).
:–op( 980,  fx, if ).
:–op( 979,xfy, else).
:–op( 978,xfx, then).
:–op( 960,xfx, impl).
:–op( 950,  fx, table).
:–op( 950,xfy, or).
:–op( 940,xfy, and).
:–op( 900,xfx, has).
:–op(   1,xfx, ':').
```

The examples are as follows:

> *X* impl *Y* is represented as impl(*X*,*Y*)
> *X* or *Y* as or(*X*,*Y*)
> *X* and *Y* as and(*X*,*Y*).
>
> not *X* is built-in as equal to not(*X*)

The operator notation and the functional notation become identical, except that Prolog stores the expressions as terms, but presents them as expressions. The following examples illustrate these points:

> ?–(*a* and *b*) = and(*a*,*b*).
>   yes.
> ?–*X* = and(*a*,*b*).
>   *X* = *a* and *b*.

Literals and terms have the same syntax. This also applies to literals defined by operators. For example, if the operators **and** and **or** are declared as above:

> *X* and *Y* :−*X*,*Y*.
> *X* or *Y* :−*X*.
> *X* or *Y* :−*Y*.

define predicates with operator syntax. For another demonstration, some operator predicates are defined for listing answers to a goal:

list *X,Y:–Y*,all(*X*).

This operator is used to list all solutions *X* to the query *Y*, as in the example:

p(a). p(b). p(c). p(d).
?–list*X,p(X)*.

a
b
c
d

Note that the condition sequence is stored as an operator expression with the comma as an infix operator having a priority of 1000. This must be taken into account where other operators are to be mixed with comma operations, unless they are shielded by parentheses.

However, prefix operators can also be used as if they were predicates or functors, as before.

?–list(*X,Y*)   is interpreted as list (*X,Y*).
which is the same as list *X,Y*
because list has priority > 1000

Another operator is **listall**

listall *X:*–list*X,X*.
?–**listall** *p(X)*.

p(a).
p(b).
p(c).
p(d).

5.8.1 Extralogical features

Prolog is based on predicate logic, and inherits its main characteristics from that. However, there are specific programming features that break with the principles of logic. These are called **extralogical features**. The following summary puts them into perspective.

- Input/output makes irrevocable changes on the environment.
- Cut manipulates the search space, and is only meaningful for a special predictable search strategy.

- Assert and retract can manipulate truth without any logical justification.

In addition there are built-in predicates that check the current status of a term.

var(X)	X is currently a variable
atom(X)	X is a constant identifier
number(X)	X is a number
$X == Y$	X is identical to Y without unification

EXERCISES

5.1 Make a table of Presidents or Prime Ministers of your country, with information about:

name, date of assignment, date of retirement

Write Prolog programs to answer queries such as

- which Presidents or Prime Ministers were appointed from 8 May 1945 to the present time;
- which Presidents or Prime Ministers retired between 8 May 1945 and the present.

5.2 Let father and mother be two predicates and let there be a number of facts about these. Write Prolog programs and queries for finding persons who have

- no parents,
- one parent,
- two parents,
- no children,
- one child,
- several children,

in addition to finding errors such as:

- more than one mother or father,
- a person is his own ancestor.

5.3 Write a Prolog program to evaluate the logical value of an expression containing:

truth values   **true,false**
operators   **and or not impl**

For example:

(true or false) and (true impl false)
==> false

5.4 Show how you can exploit Prolog's capabilities as a programmable desk calculator.

5.5 Define a predicate similar to **all**, except that only unique answers are printed out.

5.6 Write a Prolog program to compute Ackermann's function:

$ack(0,N) = N + 1$
$ack(M,0) = ack(M - 1,1)$ if $M > 0$
$ack(M,N) = ack(M - 1,ack(M,N - 1))$ if $M > 0$, $N > 0$

5.7 The Tower of Hanoi problem is as follows:

There are three pegs, X, Y and Z.
On peg X, there are N discs of decreasing size.
The discs shall be moved one by one so that finally
all the discs are on peg Z in order of decreasing size.
All the pegs may be used for temporary storage, but
a larger disc may not be put upon a smaller one.

Define a recursive predicate as follows:
$move(N,X,Y,Z)$

that moves N discs from peg X via peg Y to peg Z.

Chapter 6
List Processing

(THE SENTENCE
  (THE SENTENCE
    (TRUTH IS BEAUTY AND BEAUTY IS TRUTH)
    IS BEAUTIFUL BUT NOT TRUE)
  IS TRUE BUT NOT BEAUTIFUL)

Freely from Keats

6.1 List processing

An important class of Prolog data structures is composed of symbolic expressions usually referred to as **S-expressions**. **List-structures** of indefinite length are kinds of trees where the branches – also called subtrees – are put together with parentheses and other delimiters to form larger branches. The tree itself is a special kind of branch, and the leaves of a tree consist of atoms or terms.

The analogy between nested list-structures and trees is fundamental for understanding the explanation of list operations. The syntax of list-structures in Prolog is a variant of the syntax of LISP (Winston and Horn, 1981), which is the traditional language for symbolic computation.

All list structures are of one of two kinds, **S-expressions** or **lists**, where S-expression is the basic notation mechanism, while lists are a more user-friendly, short-hand notation for certain types of list-structures.

6.2 S-expressions

S-expressions are written in what is called **dot notation**. They are composed of:

- atoms (variables, constants or numbers);
- functional terms;
- dotted pairs using the punctuation marks [|], that is [a|b] is a dotted pair of a and b. [a|b] is represented internally as a functional term '.'(a,b).

These symbolic data structures were originally defined in a symbolic programming language called LISP. This used a slightly different syntax from Prolog, with round parentheses and a dot – (*a.b*) – it is for this reason that such a pair is called a dotted pair.

An S-expression may be an atom or a pair of S-expressions (thus, the definition of S-expressions is recursive). This is illustrated in the following examples.

S-expressions represent strict binary trees, with subtrees called LEFT and RIGHT (in LISP these are called CAR and CDR) which are themselves S-expressions. Figure 6.1 shows a simple S-expression with two subtrees. The left subtree consists of the atom *a*, while the right subtree consists of the atom *b*; the S-expression is therefore the dotted pair [*a*|*b*].

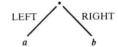

Figure 6.1   A dotted pair.

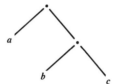

Figure 6.2   The S-expression [*a*|[*b*|*c*]].

The S-expression in Figure 6.2 consists of the atom *a* and another S-expression [*b*|*c*], of two atoms.

Note that when describing S-expressions the order of the subtrees is significant, that is [*a*|*b*] is different from [*b*|*a*].

6.3   The empty node

At the leaf nodes of an S-expression there are only atoms. However, in Prolog, there is a special symbol [] to denote an empty place with no proper atom. This symbol has a similar role in list processing as 0 in the arithmetic of addition. In LISP it is called NIL. Figure 6.3 shows Prolog's use of the empty subtree symbol [].

[a|[]]

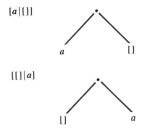

[[]|a]

Figure 6.3   Two different S-expressions.

In Figure 6.3 the two S-expressions each have only one proper atom, *a*. However, the subtree in which the atom occurs is significant. Thus, as with the previous example, the two S-expressions above are different.

The [] symbol also plays an important role in list notation.

6.4   List notation

Dot notation is necessary and sufficient to represent all list structures in Prolog. However, it leaves much to be desired as a convenient programming notation. In practice, list structures are often used to represent a sequence of symbols – *a,b,c,d* say. With S-expressions, the way to represent this is as follows:

[a|[b|[c|[d|[]]]]]

or graphically as in Figure 6.4.

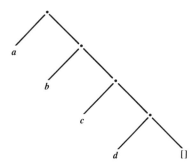

Figure 6.4   A list structure.

As lists are frequently used, the following **list notation** is introduced:

[a,b,c,d]

(This list would be represented in LISP as (*a b c d*).)

A list consists of **elements**, which may themselves be sublists, and these sublists may also have sublists, and so on. For example, the list:

[a,[b,c],[d]]

is a list of three elements

a
[b,c]
[d]

as illustrated in Figure 6.5.

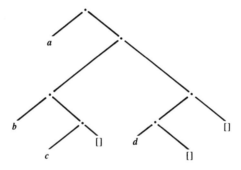

Figure 6.5   A nested list structure.

List notation may be freely intermixed with dot notation, and vice versa. In Figure 6.5, the list [b,c] may be represented by the S-expression [b|[c|[]]], while [d] is represented as [d|[]]. It is important to acknowledge the difference between the dotted pair [a|b] and the list with two elements [a,b]. As explained:

[a,b] = [a|[b|[]]]

[w,x,y|z] is a legal shorthand notation for the S-expression [w|[x|[y|z]]].

Note also in the above example that the list [d] is a list with one element *d*. This list is different from the atom *d* without parentheses. We repeat that the empty list in list notation is denoted by a list with no elements:

[]

Drawing a parallel between the list and S-expression structure, it was noted earlier that the S-expression has two components, LEFT and RIGHT. When considering lists, it is more natural to talk about FIRST and REST. The FIRST of [*a,b,c*] is the element *a*, while the REST is [*b,c*], i.e. the list of the remaining elements. Thus, the FIRST part of a list is exactly the same as the LEFT part in dot notation. This is similar for the REST part of a list, and the RIGHT part of an S-expression.

It can then be seen that there is a perfect symmetry in the two interpretations of the [] symbol as an empty list or empty node, as follows:

List	S-expression
[*a,b,c*]	[*a*|[*b*|[*c*|[]]]]

Remove FIRST successively in the list, and remove LEFT successively for the S-expression on the right:

[*b,c*]	[*b*|[*c*|[]]]
[*c*]	[*c*|[]]
[]	[]

6.4.1 Transforming list notation to dot notation

All lists in list notation can be transformed to an equivalent dot representation, but not vice versa. S-expressions exist that cannot be represented as lists and these are described in Section 6.4.2.

There are two simple rules for a stepwise transformation of a list into an S-expression. The rules are applied recursively, as long as there are components of the structure not in dot notation.

(1) [*x*] is converted to [*x*|[]]
(2) [*x,y,...,z*] is converted to [*x*|[*y,...,z*]]

For example, the compound list [*a*,[*b,c*],[*d*]] is transformed into mixed notation as follows:

[*a*|[*b*|[*c*|[]]],[*d*|[]]]

and then into pure dot notation:

[*a*|[[*b*|[*c*|[]]]|[[*d*|[]]|[]]]]

6.4.2 Transforming dot notation to list notation

As was mentioned in the previous section, it is not always possible to transform a dotted pair – e.g. [a|b] – into a list. However, even if we cannot transform the whole expression, there is an algorithm that will eliminate as many | signs as possible, leaving a pure list notation, if that is possible. The process is called **linearization**, and an algorithm is formulated as a set of recursively-defined rules that are to be applied whenever possible to transform the S-expression by steps.

(1) [x|[]] is converted to [x]
(2) [x|[y,...,z]] is converted to the list [x,y,...,z]

Note that y,...,z means a sequence of one or more elements, while x may represent a sequence, e.g. x_1,x_2.

In this example, the transformation proceeds from inside out:

[a|[[b|c]|[d|[]]]]

apply rule (1):

[a|[[b|c]|[d]]]

apply rule (2):

[a|[[b|c],d]]

apply rule (2) again:

[a,[b|c],d]

This list can be reduced no further, as the second element [b|c] cannot be represented as a list. However, the expression is now simpler and perfectly valid, even if it is in a mixed notation. When Prolog outputs an S-expression, it will always be linearized as much as possible.

6.4.3 Extension to Prolog S-expression

In Prolog, there are a few extensions to classical S-expressions. The first extension is a **logical variable**, which is treated as an atom when not instantiated. On the other hand, if instantiated to a list, say, it will change the list structure from mixed mode to a list. The other extension is **functional terms**, which are not atomic, but since they are not lists either, they are treated as atoms in list processing.

6.5 Elementary list predicates

When unifying a dotted pair [X|Y] with a list, the FIRST and REST parts of the list are selected by assigning X to the first part and Y to the REST part.

   ?-[X|Y] = [a,b,c].

will produce:

   X = a
   Y = [b,c]

To illustrate the use of list structures, some useful predicates are defined here. (Some of these are collected in the predicate library.)

6.5.1 The cons predicate

List structures may be defined and transformed in Prolog using predicates in many ways. The first necessity is to be able to construct an S-expression from its LEFT and RIGHT subparts. The predicate **cons** may be completely defined by the definition:

   cons(X,Y,[X|Y]).

For example:

   ?-cons(a,b,Z).
   Z = [a|b]

During unification, X is bound to a, Y is bound to b, and Z is bound to [X|Y], which is equal to [a|b] due to the values of X and Y.
   If X is an element, and Y is a list, then [X|Y] is a new list with X as the first element, as in the example:

   ?-cons(a,[b,c],Z).
   Z = [a,b,c]
   ?-cons(a,[],Z).
   Z = [a]

Also, the generality of the unification allows a result to be defined implicitly:

?–cons(*a*,*X*,[*a*,*b*,*c*]).
X = [*b*,*c*]

In the last example the input/output symmetry is applied to a kind of equation solving; an *X* is found so that [*a*|*X*] = [*a*,*b*,*c*]. If the second argument is not a list, then neither is the third argument. For example:

?–cons([*a*,*b*],*c*,*X*).
X = [[*a*,*b*]|*c*]   (in mixed notation)

Also, if the first argument is a list with say three elements, and the second argument has two elements, then the third argument will not be a list with five elements. On the contrary, the first element in the new list will be the entire list of the first argument.
    Try to draw a tree of this list:

?–cons([*a*,*b*,*c*],[*d*,*e*,*f*],*Z*).
Z = [[*a*,*b*,*c*],*d*,*e*,*f*]

    Later an **append** predicate will be defined, which makes a list from the elements of two lists.

6.5.2   The member predicate

Another basic question encountered is whether a term is a member of a list. Consider the predicate:

member(*X*,List)

which is true if *X* is a member of the list **List**. This predicate is typical of recursive list processing in logic programming generally.
    The following examples, with instantiations of *X* and **List**, are required to be true.

?–**member(*a*,[*a*,*b*,*c*]).**
    yes
?–**member(*a*,[*b*,*c*,*a*]).**
    yes
?–**member(*a*,[*a*]).**
    yes
?–**member([*a*,*b*],[*c*,[*a*,*b*],[]]).**
    yes

In the last example, the first argument, list [*a*,*b*], is a member of the other list.

However, the following examples should *not* be true:

?–member(*a*,*a*).
    no
?–member(*a*,[*b*,*c*,*d*]).
    no
?–member(*a*,[]).
    no
?–member(*a*,[*b*,[*a*],*c*]).
    no

With a clear picture of what is needed, the predicate is defined as follows:

(1)	**member(*X*,[*X*|*Y*]).**	% *X* is a member	
		% if *X* is the first element	
(2)	**member(*X*,[*U*|*V*]):–**	% *X* is a member of the list	
	member(*X*,*V*)–	% if *X* is a member of the rest	
		% of the list	

This example is a good illustration of the dual reading of a Prolog predicate. It is a definition of membership, but it is also a program to test membership. The execution of this program is traced here:

?–**member(*c*,[*a*,*b*,*c*,*d*]).**
    :–**member(*c*,[*b*,*c*,*d*]).**   % <= 2 by $X = c$, $U = a$, $V = [b,c,d]$
        :–**member(*c*,[*c*,*d*]).**   % <= 2 by $X = c$, $U = b$, $V = [c,d]$
            :–   % <= 1 by $X = c$, $Y = [d]$

and it has proven that *c* is a member of [*a*,*b*,*c*,*d*]. A final example shows the versatility of the member definition: output all members of a list:

?–**member(*X*,[*a*,*b*,*c*,*d*]),all(*X*).**
    a
    b
    c
    d

6.5.3 The append predicate

Prolog is a language which does not change existing structures other than by instantiating logical variables. So when Prolog is used for list processing, it defines the relations between input and output list structures. The next problem illustrates this kind of difficulty, which often occurs in list processing. The problem is to add the elements of two lists and make a new list using those elements.

?–append([a,b],[c,d,e],X).
X = [a,b,c,d,e]

Let the **append** predicate be defined as follows:

append([ ],List,List).
append([First|Rest],List,[First|Templist]):–
   append(Rest,List,Templist).

The important point to notice is the stepwise building of the result in the
third argument.

?–append([a,b],[c,d,e],Res),output(Res).
   :–append([b],[c,d,e],Templist),output([a|Templist]).
      :–append([ ],[c,d,e],Templist'),output([a|[b|Templist']]).
         :–output([a|[b|[c,d,e]]]).
   ==>[a,b,c,d,e]

The result is output in list form. (**Templist'** is just a renamed version of
Templist.)

6.5.4   The delete predicate

A predicate that removes one element from a list is a useful predicate.
The problem is nondeterministic in the sense that any of the elements can
be removed, and thus represents a solution of the problem.

delete(X,[X|Y],Y).
delete(X,[U|V],[U|W]):–
   delete(X,V,W).

For example:

?–delete(X,[a,b,c],Y),all(X + Y).
a + [b,c]
b + [a,c]
c + [a,b]

In this example, each common element is removed:

?–delete(X,[a,b,c],Y),
delete(X,[d,c,b],Z),
all(Y + Z).
[a,c] + [d,c]
[a,b] + [d,b]

6.5.5 Naive reverse

The facility of reversing a list, i.e. to put it in reverse order, is useful for many purposes. It can be done in a number of ways:

    reverse([a,b,c],[c,b,a]).
    reverse([],[]).
    reverse([a,[b,c],c],[c,[b,c],a]).

There is one approach which is very straightforward, although the execution time is actually a quadratic function of the length of the list:

(1) Take out the first element;
(2) Reverse the rest;
(3) Append the list of the first element to the reversed rest.

In Prolog, this is written:

    reverse([],[]).
    reverse([X|Y],Z):–
       reverse(Y,Y1),
       append(Y1,[X],Z).   % note: not 'append(Y1,X,Z)'

This program (together with **append**) has gained status as a benchmark test for Prolog systems. It is called a **naive reverse**, and when the number of logic inferences or Prolog calls is divided by the number of seconds used, the number measures the speed of the Prolog system in LIPS, logic inferences per second.

C-Prolog, which is an interpreter, has a speed of approximately 1500 LIPS (1.5 kiloLIPS) on a VAX11/780, but will vary with the computer power. Prolog compilers, which are more expensive, are in general 10–20 times faster than interpreters. The fastest Prolog implementation the author is aware of runs on an IBM 3090 with 750 kiloLIPS.

6.5.6 Smart reverse

This version of the reverse is faster but less easy to understand. The time is proportional to the length. An extra argument, first, builds the results up and outwards from the empty list, using the recursive predicate **outwards**.

    reverse(X,Y):–
       outwards([],X,Y).
    outwards(L,[],L).

```
outwards(L,[X|Y],Z):-
    outwards([X|L],Y,Z).
```

6.6   Lists and sets

The fundamental mathematical concept of a set is easily represented in Prolog. A **set** is a list with no duplicate elements, and with an arbitrary order of elements. Examples of lists which are sets include:

$[a,b,c]$	% straightforward
$[[a,b],a]$	% $[a,b] \neq a$
$[a,b,[a,a]]$	% $[a,a]$ is not a set, but the whole list is
$[]$	% the empty set
$[[a,b],[b,a]]$	% yes, but problematical

Examples of lists which are not sets include:

$[a,a]$

$[a,[b,c],d,e,[b,c]]$

There is no automatic mechanism in Prolog to support the uniqueness of elements in a set, but this is readily done in Prolog itself by a number of set-predicates. Consider the following set operations from set theory:

•	intersection	$A \cap B$	X is a member of $A \cap B$ *iff* (if and only if) X is a member of A and X is a member of B
•	union	$A \cup B$	X is a member of $A \cup B$ iff X is a member of A or X is a member of B
•	difference	$A \setminus B$	X is a member of $A \setminus B$ iff X is a member of A and X is not a member of B

Compare them with these set test predicates:

•	**empty**(S)		S is empty if it contains no elements
•	**set inclusion**	$A \subset B$	All elements in A are also in B
•	**set equality**	$A = B$	Two sets are equal if they contain the same elements

The Prolog predicates for these set operations follow a typical pattern of recursive definition:

```
intersection([],Set,[]).
intersection([X|Y],Set,Z):-
   not(member(X,Set)),
   !,                             % eliminate the alternative below
   intersection(Y,Set,Z).        % X is not a member of the result
                                  % Because of the ! above,
intersection([X|Y],Set,[X|Z]):-  % we know that X is in Set so
   intersection(Y,Set,Z).        % X is a member of the result

union([],Set,Set).
union([X|Y],Set,[X|Z]):-
   not(member(X,Set)),
   !,
   union(Y,Set,Z).
union([X|Y],Set,Z):-             % here we know X is in Set
   union(Y,Set,Z).

difference([],Z,[]).
difference([X|Y],Set,[X|Z]):-
   not(member(X,Set)),
   !,
   difference(Y,Set,Z).
difference([X|Y],Set,Z):-        % we know X is in Set
   difference(Y,Set,Z).

emptyset([]).
inclusion(A,B):-implies(member(X,A),member(X,B)).
implies(X,Y):-not(and(X,not(Y)))%%% see predicate library
equalset(A,B):-inclusion(A,B),inclusion(B,A).
```

Consider the following examples of standard set operations.

```
?-intersection([a,b,c],[d,c,b],X).
X = [b,c]
?-intersection([a,[b,c]],[b,c],X).
X = []
?-intersection([a,[b,c]],[[b,c]],X).
X = [[b,c]]
?-union([a,b,c],[b,c,d],X).
X = [a,b,c,d]
?-difference([a,b,c],[a],X).
X = [b,c]
```

```
?–inclusion([a],[b]).
no
?–inclusion([a],[a]).
yes
```

6.6.1   Representing information as lists or as facts

In Prolog, there are two different ways of explicitly representing information, either by facts in the database, or as a list. An example of database representation is as follows:

```
king(haakon).
king(olav).
king(harald).
king(magnus).
?–king(X),all(X).

haakon
olav
harald
magnus
```

An example of list representation:

```
kings([haakon,olav,harald,magnus]).
```

It is possible to switch from the list representation to the database representation:

```
king(X):–kings(Z),member(X,Z).
```

This definition of 'king' gives exactly the same solutions as the database representation above, by the query:

```
?–king(X),all(X).
```

It also has the same external behaviour, although the recursion in **member** makes them different internally. It is more difficult, however, to move from the database representation to the list representation. What is needed is a general predicate:

```
setof(X,Y,Z)
```

where Z is the set of unique X such that Y is represented as a sorted list.

Such a predicate is actually built-in, but a simpler version will be considered here to demonstrate programming techniques. Also, there are some drawbacks to the built-in version, which makes it worthwhile to develop our own definition.

The problem is that database retrieval is based on backtracking, which has the consequence of undoing all the substitutions carried out since the last retrieval. The program must construct a list of solutions, but the backtracking will also undo the substitutions that comprise the list structure. To overcome this, the intermediate solutions must be stored by using **remember**. When all solutions are stored, the **reap** predicate collects them into a list.

findall(X,Y,Z):–
  Y,   % whenever Y is true,
  remember(new(X)),   % remember a new fact;
  fail.   % new must be a unique predicate name

findall(X,Y,Z):–
  reap(Z).   % collect the facts into a list Z

reap([$X|Y$]):–
  retract(new(X)),   % new as above
  !,
  reap(Y).
reap([ ]).

remember(X):–X,!.   % check if X is already true;
remember(X):–assert(X).   % assert if not

These can be used in the following example:

?–findall(X,king(X),Ks),output(Ks).
[haakon,olav,harald,magnus]

The definition of **findall** does not take nested sets. For instance, if a program requires a set of all fathers, together with the set of their children, as follows:

[[haakon,[olav]],[olav,[ragnhild,astrid,harald]]]

programmers have to be slightly more general. This is, however, left as an exercise.

6.6.2   The unexpected nature of the built-in setof

The built-in predicate **setof** works in an unexpected way. For example, let a father relation be as follows:

father(haakon,olav).
father(olav,ragnhild).
father(olav,astrid).
father(olav,harald).

Then the question:

'Who are the fathers?'

could be solved by:

?–setof(X,father(X,Y),Z).

But instead of the list **[haakon,olav]** only one answer is given:

Y = astrid
Z = [olav]

By successive backtracking, the other answers are given:

Y = harald
Z = [olav]
Y = olav
Z = [haakon]
Y = ragnhild
Z = [olav]

The key to this behaviour lies in the handling of free variables, such as Y in the example. To preserve the symmetry of the declarative semantics, it should be irrelevant whether this variable is instantiated before or after the **setof** call.
    Consider this example:

female(ragnhild).
female(astrid).

Now the query 'Who are fathers of females?', can be posed in two equivalent ways with the same answers.

?–female(Y),setof(X,father(X,Y),Z).

?–setof(X,father(X,Y),Z),female(Y).

The **setof** construction becomes more predictable when an ^ operator is used:

```
?–setof(X,Y^father(X,Y),Z).
Z = [haakon,olav]
```

The ^ operator is interpreted as an existential quantifier, and the expression could be read 'Z is the set of X such that there exists a Y so that father(X,Y) . . .'.

In addition to these surprises, there is a requirement that the result set is not empty. Otherwise backtracking is caused as if there were something wrong with empty sets.

6.6.3 Set construction without databases

It is possible to construct sets without having side-effects on the database in the form of assertions. It is not recommended, however, because it is inherently inefficient, but it is instructive when learning Prolog.

```
oddsetof(Predname,Z):–
  accset(Predname,[],Z).
accset(Predname,Found,Z):–
  callpred(Predname,X),
  not(member(X,Found)),
  !,
  accset(Predname,[X|Found],Z).
accset(Predname,Found,Found).
```

An example of the use of this procedure is as follows:

```
callpred(p,X):–p(X).      % p is a constant
p(a).
p(b).
p(a).
p(c).
?–oddsetof(p,Z).
Z = [c,b,a]
```

The trick is to add an argument, **Found**, containing the elements found so far, and to make the predicate **accset** recursive, and check that the new element is not already found. The **callpred** predicate must have one tailor-made clause for each new predicate, e.g. *p*. The standard operator =.. explained later, makes it more general:

callpred(*P,X*):–*Z* =..[*P,X*],*Z*.   % *P* is a variable

The inefficiency of **oddsetof** lies in the fact that Prolog starts from the beginning for each new element, so the elements in the **found** list will be rediscovered in vain until new elements are found.

6.7   D-lists

The **append** example highlights a problem when an element must be placed at the rear of a list. This is actually done by going recursively through the whole list, to find the end of it, while simultaneously building up a whole new list. This operation requires as many Prolog calls as the number of elements in the first list. A technique known as D-list (Clark, 1978) solves this problem and appends lists with one unification.

An ordinary list has a [] as its last, and hidden, element:

[*a,b,c*] = [*a*|[*b*|[*c*|[]]]]

If a new element, say *d*, must be added, then [] should be replaced with [*d*|[]]:

[*a,b,c,d*] = [*a*|[*b*|[*c*|[*d*|[]]]]]

The trick is to let a so-called tail-variable be the last element in a term, e.g.

t(Dlist,Tailvar)

It is, however, more meaningful and more readable to use the infix operator –, so that:

Dlist – Tailvar

holds both the Dlist and the tail variable itself. However, the – operator will not have any arithmetic significance, in subtraction, for example.

To put an element *d* at the rear of this line:

[*a*|[*b*|[*c*|*X*]]] – *X*

it suffices to replace *X* with [*d*|*Y*] and let *Y* be the new tail variable in the new D-list, as follows:

[*a*|[*b*|[*c*|[*d*|*Y*]]]] – *Y*

Ordinary lists may be called S-lists as distinct from D-lists. The D-list data structure allows any of the following operations in one unification:

- add an element to the front (also possible for S-lists);
- remove an element in the front (also possible for S-lists);
- add an element at the rear;
- append two lists.

6.7.1 D-list manipulation

The **d_queue** predicate is used to add an element to the rear of a D-list:

> **d_queue(ListX − [Element|Y],Element,ListX − Y).**

In this example:

> **?−d_queue([a|[b|X]] − X,c,Dz),output(Dz).**
> **[a,b,c|Y] − Y**

The **d_stack** predicate puts an element in front of a D-list (or takes one out according to how it is used).

> **d_stack(Element,List − Tail,[Element|List] − Tail).**

An empty D-list is created by the predicate

> **d_empty(X − X).**

By setting the tail variable to [], the D-list is converted to an ordinary list:

> **d_convert(List − [],List).**

Conversion the other way, from an S-list to a D-list, however, has to be carried out by a recursive program, which is left as an exercise.

D-list is a short-name for Difference list, because the list is logically viewed as the difference between the elements in two lists. This is demonstrated by the predicate **d_append**, which appends two D-lists into a third D-list:

> **d_append(A − B, B − C, A − C).**

This adds $A − B$ to $B − C$ giving $A − C$.

6.7.2 Limitations of Prolog list structures

In ordinary programming languages such as Pascal, it is possible to create data structures, such as doubly-linked lists, that allow any element to be inserted or deleted anywhere in a list. In Prolog, the data structures are essentially tree structures, so it is not possible with one unification to remove any other element than the first, or to add elements in the middle. This would demand circular data structures, where elements are pointing to each other. When such a structure is interpreted as a tree, it becomes infinite.

6.8 An application: sorting

Sorting sequences of numbers is an important application in any programming language. In Prolog, programmers often need to sort lists of numbers. There are two general sorting methods presented here: **mergesort** and **quicksort**. Mergesort uses ordinary lists, while quicksort uses D-lists, and both are good examples of nontrivial applications of list processing.

6.8.1 Mergesort

There is a sorting predicate **mergesort**, which works on the following principles:

(1) Make a predicate **split(List,Lista,Listb)**, where **List** is split into two sublists, **Lista** and **Listb**, so that every second element is put into **Lista**, and the others into **Listb**. For example:

   split([7,1,3,5],[7,3],[1,5])

(2) Make a predicate **merge(Lista,Listb,List)**, which creates a sorted list from two sorted lists, **Lista** and **Listb**. For example:

   merge([1,13,15],[2,4,6],[1,2,4,6,13,15]])

(3) Finally, create a predicate **mergesort**, which works as follows:

   split the list into two sublists,
   mergesort each list separately
   merge the two sorted lists.

The actual predicates are as follows:

```
split([],[],[]).
split([X|Z],[X|U],V):-split(Z,V,U).
merge([Xa|Ya],[Xb|Yb],[Xa|Z]):-
  before(Xa,Xb),
  !,
  merge(Ya,[Xb|Yb],Z).
merge([Xa|Ya],[Xb|Yb],[Xb|Z]):-
  merge([Xa|Ya],Yb,Z).
merge(X,[],X).
merge([],X,X).
mergesort([],[]):-!.
mergesort([X],[X]):-!.

mergesort(List,Sorted):-
  split(List,Left,Right),
  mergesort(Left,Sleft),
  mergesort(Right,Sright),
  merge(Sleft,Sright,Sorted).
before(X,Y):-X < Y.
```

Actually, the **before** predicate is to be adapted to the application. For instance, if the elements of the list are terms p(**Node**,**Value**), then **before** could be defined as

```
before(p(N1,V1),p(N2,V2)):-V1 < V2.
```

The idea of **mergesort** in Prolog is further elaborated in O'Keefe (1982).

6.8.2 Quicksort

The quicksort method (Hoare, 1962) uses a slightly different approach:

(1) Take the first element E in **List**.
(2) **Partition List** into two, so that:

    all the elements $<E$ are put into **Lower**;
    all the elements $>E$ are put into **Higher**.
(3) **quicksort Lower** and **Higher** recursively.
(4) Finally, **append Lower**, E, and **Higher**.

The last **append** operation suggests that if D-lists are not used, the **append** operation will be a relatively costly operation. Using D-lists makes it more complicated, but faster. The predicates are as follows:

- quicksort(List,Sortlist):–
      qdsort(List,Dlist),   % produce a sorted D-list
      d_convert(Dlist,Sortlist).   % and convert to S-list

- qdsort([],$X - X$).

- qdsort([E|Rest],Dsort):–
      partition(E,Rest,Lower,Higher),
      qdsort(Lower,Dsortlow),   % sort lower part
      qdsort(Higher,Dsorthigh),   % sort higher part
      d_queue(Dsortlow,E,DE),   % put E behind lower part
      d_append(DE,Dsorthigh,Dsort).   % put together

- partition(E,[],[],[]).
  partition(E,[First|Rest],[First|Left],Right):–
      before(First,E),   % see definition and comment
      !,   % on before in Section 6.8.1.
      partition(E,Rest,Left,Right).

- partition(E,[First|Rest],Left,[First|Right]):–
      partition(E,Rest,Left,Right).

6.9   Alternative list syntax

6.9.1   Strings

A string in Prolog is a sequence of ASCII characters, stored as a list of numerical ASCII values. The list structures above only apply to square brackets. However, a **string constant** is a sequence of characters, enclosed in double quotes; for example:

"AZaz09. "

which is stored as

[65,90,97,122,48,57,46,32]

The strings must not be confused with text constants, which use single quote marks, as in

'Azaz09. '

which is a unique atomic item. It is possible to convert between the two types of constants by the built-in predicate:

name(Constant,String).

This works either way:

>   :–name('ABC',X).
> X = [65,66,67]
>   :–name(X,[48,46,57]).
> X = 0.9

As Prolog does not know if a list of numbers is meant to be a string or not, the programmer uses a predicate to print out strings.

printstring(Xs):–name(Xc,Xs),print(Xc).

6.9.2   Round lists

The list structures described earlier apply square brackets as the standard list notations in Prolog. However, there are two other kinds of list structures that should be mentioned:

(1) **'round' lists**, which are standard Prolog notation with round parentheses, ();
(2) **LISP lists**, which use round parentheses with the same semantics as Prolog square brackets, but are incompatible with Prolog syntax.

A round list is, in fact, an operator expression, using the comma as the operator (see Chapter 5). The rules for parentheses apply to ordinary operator expressions as well, making these two round lists identical:

> (a,b,c)
> $(a,(b,c))$

They have a well defined meaning in Prolog as a combined term

> ',' $(a,','(b,c))$

where ',' is an internal functor representing ',' as an operator; the comma in (b,c) is a separator.

Round lists are very important, because in Prolog round lists represent conjunctive goals:

> p :–q,r,s

is represented as the term:

> $(p:–(q,(r,s)))$

where the parentheses have been added for emphasis. By using the round list concept, Prolog is capable of manipulating its own programs, an idea which is pursued under the concept of **meta-programming**. Although parentheses and commas have wider areas of application in Prolog, compare their use with that in standard lists.

There are three important differences between round lists and square lists.

(1) *[a]* is different from *a*, but *(a)* is identical to *a*;
(2) [] is an empty square list, while () is illegal;
(3) Square lists always have an empty element [] as a hidden last element, while round lists have none. Therefore:

[a,b,c] is represented as '.'(*a*,'.'(*b*,'.'(*c*,[])))

while

(a,b,c) is represented as ','(*a*,','(*b*,*c*)).

6.9.3   List processing with round lists

The syntax of round lists allows the construction of data structures which are usually called **elementary lists**. An elementary list is uniquely defined by the sequence of innermost elements that are not elementary lists themselves.

The principle can be implemented by square or round lists, but it is shown here for the latter. Since there is no standard empty list concept, such as [] for square lists, nil must be used. A predicate to find the innermost elements may be given:

```
element(X,Y):-
    var(Y),            % If Y is a variable
    !,                 % avoid trap
    X = Y
element(X,(U,V)):-!,
    (element(X,U);
    element(X,V)).
element(X,X):-not X = nil.
?-element(X,(a,(b,c))),all(X).
a
b
c
```

By disregarding the parenthetical structure, the ',' is regarded as an associative operation, but it is not commutative. For example:

(*a*,(*b*,*c*)) is equivalent to ((*a*,*b*),*c*)
(*a*,(*b*,*c*)) is not equivalent to ((*b*,*c*),*a*)

This means that concatenation of elementary lists can be performed in one operation.

e_append(*X*,*Y*,(*X*,*Y*)).

EXERCISES

6.1   Write a predicate, **score(*X*,*Y*,*B*,*W*)**, so that *X* and *Y* are lists of equal length of integers, and *B* is the number of places where the lists have identical elements, while *W* is the number of digits that occur in both lists, but at different places. For example:

score([7,2,3,4],[2,3,4,4],1,2).

6.2   Write a program that outputs all lists of length *n* where *b* is an element.

6.3   Write a program that reverses a list of elements, but also recursively reverses the elements when they are sublists.

6.4   Write a predicate that converts an S-list to a D-list.

6.5   Write a program in Prolog that finds all the permutations of a list, according to the following algorithm:

>   Take out the first element of the list;
>   Make all the permutations of the rest of the list;
>   Put the element back at an arbitrary place.

For example:

[*a*,*b*,*c*] ==> *a* + [*b*,*c*] ==> [*a*,*b*,*c*]
                                    [*b*,*a*,*c*]
                                    [*b*,*c*,*a*]
                  a + [*c*,*b*] ==> [*a*,*c*,*b*]
                                    [*c*,*a*,*b*]
                                    [*c*,*b*,*a*]

6.6   Write a predicate that uses the **append** predicate to remove the last element from a list.

6.7   Define the set operations **intersection**, **union** and **difference** by using the defined predicate **findall**.

6.8   Find the number of inferences needed to compute the reverse of a list by the naive reverse method. Measure the speed of your own Prolog implementation.

6.9   Concatenation of elementary lists, using round or square lists, is done in one operation. Utilize this to implement **quicksort**.

6.10 Extend the **findall** predicate to handle nested lists. (Hint: Use a two-argument predicate, **new(NestingLevel,Fact)**, to store elements, and let **reap** collect elements at the right level.)

Chapter 7
Logic Programming Techniques

:–op(1199,*xfx*,'<–').
prove(true).
prove((*X*,*Y*)):–prove(*X*),prove(*Y*).
prove(*H*):–(*H* <– *B*),prove(*B*).

Prolog interpreter written in Prolog

Logic programming seems to be a very promising technique. It is true that the declarative style solves many information retrieval problems automatically, but many problems logic programming meets are algorithmic in nature. This means that programmers must learn to solve algorithmic problems in Prolog. It is also necessary, therefore, to learn how to express algorithms in Prolog.

There is a saying that no matter how high-level the language is, programming is still programming. This is not true for logic itself, but is to a high degree true for present-day Prolog. Also, a small Prolog program may be a sublime creation, but Prolog programs are software, subject to the disciplines of software engineering, where structure and discipline are necessary to avoid chaos.

The Prolog systems available today are not intelligent. This means that no matter how fast the Prolog system executes, it is *easy* to make a program that will soon run out of time and space, even though the program is correct in theory. However, it is the domain of the Prolog expert to discover the range of things that slow down Prolog programs and to improve them. In the era of knowledge engineering, this task will be put into an intelligent Prolog programming environment, where the system itself writes the programs. But for the time being, we must learn to write constructive Prolog programs ourselves.

7.1   Constructing recursive programs

When faced with the problem of defining predicates for recursive list processing problems, it is good heuristics to apply inductive thinking, and solve the following two cases separately:

(1) One of the arguments is [];
(2) The same argument is a dotted pair, say **[First|Rest]**, but the problem is assumed to be solved for **Rest**.

Which argument to make induction on depends on the problem at hand, e.g. **append**. However, the **cons** predicate will make a list from an element and a list, so it is easy to put elements in front of a list and still obtain a new list.

> ?–cons(c,[d,e,f],X).
> X = [c,d,e,f]

This is a hint that induction should be used in the first argument of **append**:

> append([],List,List).   % [] appended to a list gives
>   % the same list as a result;
> append([First|Rest],List,Newlist):–% First is the first element
>   append(Rest,List,Templist),   % this problem is simpler, because
>   % Rest is smaller than [First|Rest]
>   cons(First,Templist,Newlist).

7.1.1   A closer look at recursion

Confronted with the problem of transforming the elements in a list to build another list structure, backtracking cannot be used. Study the following recursive definitions. A list can be copied in one operation:

> copylist(X,X).

but assume that it is done element by element, and the element-wise transformation is just a copy. Then the pattern is:

> copylist([],[]).
> copylist([X|Y],[X|Z]):–
>   copylist(Y,Z).
> :–copylist([1,2,3],V),output(V).

:–copylist([2,3],Z),output([1|Z]).
  :–copylist([3],Z),output([1|[2|Z]]).
    :–copylist([],Z),output([1|[2|[3|Z]]])
     :–output([1|[2|[3|[]]]])

[1,2,3]   % list is printed in linear form

The result in the output condition is built up stepwise, outside inwards, i.e. starting with the outermost brackets. It is therefore called **outside inwards accumulation**.

Another way is called **inside outwards accumulation** where the recursion starts with [], and builds itself up around it. A particularly good example is the smart-reverse list operation (see Section 6.5.6):

reverse(X,Y):–outwards([],X,Y).

outwards(L,[],L).
outwards(L,[X|Y],Z):–
  outwards([X|L],Y,Z).

7.1.2 Path problems

A number of problems concern finding a path through a network. Assume there are five cities, a, b, c, d and e, and assume there are railway connections between some of them as shown in Figure 7.1.

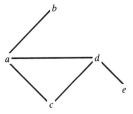

Figure 7.1 Diagram showing the railway connections between cities a, b, c, d and e.

In Prolog, the minimally meaningful elementary facts are represented, the rules defined, and the rest left to Prolog's automatic search.

leg(a,d).
leg(a,c).
leg(a,d).
leg(c,d).
leg(d,e).

A new binary relation **connection** is defined by one or more applications of **leg**. **connection** is said to be the **transitive closure** of **leg**. Two nodes A,B are connected if there is a sequence of nodes $X_0,...,X_n$ such that:

$$A = X_0, \ X_n = B \text{ and } \textbf{leg}(X_{i-1},X_i) \text{ for } I = 1 \ ... \ n.$$

However, Prolog handles such iterative definitions by recursion, so when the following is defined:

```
connection(X,Y):-
    leg(X,Y).
connection(X,Z):-
    leg(X,Y),
    connection(Y,Z).
?-connection(a,e).

yes
?-connection(a,Z),all(Z).

b
c
d
d
e
e
```

Duplicate answers are obtained, one for each path.

7.1.3 Finding the path

The next problem is to find a path between nodes, and to represent this as a list. The method is to create the path by outside inwards accumulation:

```
% connection (Fromnode,Tonode,Path).
connection(X,X,[X]).
connection(X,Z,[X|P]):-
    leg(X,Y),
    connection(Y,Z,P).
?-connection(a,e,P),
    all(P).
[a,c,d,e]
[a,d,e]
```

Assume that the connections between the cities are symmetrical and go both ways; this symmetry is best represented as a rule above the fact level, because

    leg(X,Y):–leg(Y,X).

is a malicious special case of a left-recursive definition which must be avoided.

    It is generally advisable to have a separate data level, containing no rules.

    way(X,Y):–leg(X,Y);leg(Y,X).

But beware; if you define this connection:

    connection(X,X,[X]).
    connection(X,Z,[$X|P$]):–
      way(X,Y),
      connection(Y,Z,P).

you will end up in an infinite loop.

    The deadly logic behind this anomaly is that there is an infinite number of paths when a city can be visited more than once. A path must not therefore revisit any node. To avoid this, reformulate the strategy.

    In addition to the result which is built up outside-inwards, there is now a list of visited nodes, built inside-outwards, starting with the start node. If the goal node is reached, the visited list is the solution.

    connection(A,Z,P):–
      conn(A,Z,[A],P).   % Connection from A to Z, not revisiting A
    conn(X,X,Visited,[X]).   % Invariant:
                               % X is member of Visited
    conn(X,Z,Visited,[$X|P$]):– % X is member of Visited
      way(X,Y),
      not(member(Y,Visited)),
      conn(Y,Z,[$Y|$Visited],P).
    way(X,Y):–leg(X,Y);leg(Y,X).

The visited list is built up in reverse order.

7.2 Constructing iterative programs

Prolog is a recursive language, requiring a maturity in recursive thinking. Also, backtracking is a powerful technique for many purposes. However, recursion and backtracking are difficult to combine, because recursion builds up structures during succeeding calls, while backtracking forgets them, unless assertions are made. But then a very intricate program and data structure is combined.

The situation is improved if some structured programming techniques are used. Not all recursive problems are recursive in a deep sense, they are just iterative, and should be recognized as such.

The most primitive predicate used to perform iteration is the repeat predicate. It is actually built-in as defined by:

```
repeat.
repeat:-repeat.
```

For instance, a loop to perform input/output processing would be

```
loop:-
  repeat,
    input(X),
    process(X,Y),
    output(Y),
% until
  X = stop,!.
?-loop.
```

This would input terms, process, output terms and backtrack until the term typed in was **stop**.

If a program was required to write out all members of the list L, a recursive solution could be:

```
listmembers([]).
listmembers([X|Y]):-
  output(X),
  listmembers(Y).
```

This pattern of recursion is common in Prolog programming, but can be generalized, defining a predicate:

```
for(X,Y):-X,Y,fail.
for(X,Y).
```

so that for all solutions of X, Y will be called. The for loop ends when there are no more solutions to X. This definition leaves:

```
listmembers(L):-
  for(member(X,L),output(X)).
```

Another example problem is to list all numbers from one to ten. A recursive solution might be:

```
listnumbers(N):-N > 10,!.
listnumbers(N):-output(N),
    N1 is N + 1,
    listnumbers(N1).
?-listnumbers(1).
1
2
3
4
5
6
7
8
9
10
```

Instead, a general recursive predicate **in** is defined, which, by backtracking, returns the values from 1 to N:

```
in(I,I,H):-H >= I.
in(I,L,H):-L < H,
    N is L + 1,
    in(I,N,H).
```

So, the new solution is

```
?-for(in(I,1,10),output(I)).
```

The **for** predicate can easily be combined, in various ways, to print out multiplication tables, for example:

```
multtable:-
    for(in(I,1,10),
        (for(in(J,1,10),
            (K is I * J,out(K))),
        nl)
    ).
?-multtable.
```

As an application of the above concept, and at the same time as an exercise in applying operators, some operators are defined to make iterative programs look similar to Pascal programs.

```
:-op(1110,xfy,do).
:-op(1109,fx,for).
:-op(1108,xfx,to).
:-op(1107,fx,begin).
:-op(700,xfx,':=').

do1(begin end):-!.
do1(begin X;Y):-!,do1(X),do1(begin Y).
do1(begin X):-!,do1(X).
do1(X):-X.

X := Y :-X is Y.

(for X:= Y to Z do U):-
    for(in(X,Y,Z),do1(U)).

writeln(X):-output(X).
```

Here is the Pascal-like program:

```
runit:-
    for I := 1 to 10 do
       begin
          K := I * I;
          writeln(K);
       end.
?-runit.
1
4
9
16
25
36
49
64
81
100
```

This is still Prolog. However, the reader is warned not to take this example as a serious attempt to implement Pascal. For instance, it is difficult to model the nested program structures such as **begin – end**, because **begin – end** in reality are parenthetical delimiters and not operators.

7.3   Possible implication

Another structured predicate, similar in spirit to the **for** predicate, is the **implies** predicate. It resembles **for**, but is in fact different. While **for** is a predicate for doing actions, **implies** is aimed at testing a possible implication. Consider these facts:

> elephant(lars).
> elephant(nils).
>
> grey(lars).
> grey(nils).
> grey(truls).

It is tempting to state from these facts that, logically, all elephants are grey. However, that is only true if we explicitly state the closed world assumption that **lars** and **nils** are the only elephants in the world. However, the statement can be weakened if it is said that from the knowledge we have, it is *possible* that all elephants are grey. Possible implication is defined by:

> **implies**(X,Y):–not(and(X,not(Y))).

and is true if the predicate Y is true whenever X is, for the same instantiations of variables. A systematic use of this predicate will make many intricate problems appear well-structured and understandable. For example,

%% are all known elephants grey?
?–**implies**(elephant(X),grey(X)).
yes

%% are all known grey things elephants?
?–**implies**(grey(X),elephant(X)).
no

%% have all winged elephants six legs?
?–**implies**(elephant(X) and wings(X),sixlegged(X)).
yes

7.3.1   An application: Mastermind

Some problems are solved by trial and error. An attempt to solve a problem produces feedback which can be used to make a new attempt. The game of Mastermind is a good example.

A player (A) chooses a secret code of four digits while another player (*B*) tries to discover it, guessing four digits at a time. For each guess, the player is told how many digits are correct in the correct place (blacks), and how many are correct, but wrongly placed (whites). Let the following predicate be the score evaluation predicate:

score(Secret,Guess,Blacks,Whites)

where **Secret** and **Guess** are lists of four digits. For example:

score([1,3,5,7],[2,3,4,5],1,1).

In following Shapiro's idea (1983), a Prolog program that plays *B*'s game of guessing is formulated as Figure 7.2.

```
solution(X):-
   try(X),
   consistent(X),
   guess(X,Blacks,Whites),
   Blacks = 4,
   !.
consistent(X):-
   implies(guessed(Y,B,W),        % the previous scores must be
      score(Y,X,B,W)).            % correct if the new guess X
                                  % were the solution.
guess(X,Blacks,Whites):-
   mark(X,Blacks,Whites),
   assert(guessed(X,Blacks,Whites)),
   out('Guess: '),out(X),out(' Mark: '),output((Blacks,Whites)).
try([D1,D2,D3,D4]):-
   digit(D1),
   digit(D2),
   digit(D3),
   digit(D4).
digit(X):-in(X,1,6).              % see library
mark(X,Blacks,Whites):-
   secret(S),
   score(X,S,Blacks,Whites).
score(X,Y,B,W):-
   blacks(X,Y,B,X1,Y1),           % X1, Y1 remaining
   whites(X1,Y1,W).
```
                                                              (cont'd)

Figure 7.2 A Prolog program that plays Mastermind (Shapiro, 1983).

```
blacks([X|Y],[X|Z],B1,Y1,Z1):-    % count and remove
  !,                              % matching pairs
  blacks(Y,Z,B,Y1,Z1),
  B1 is B + 1.
blacks([X|Y],[U|V],B,[X|Y1],[U|V1]):-
  blacks(Y,V,B,Y1,V1).
blacks([],[],0,[],[]).
whites(X,Y,W1):-
  delete(Same,X,X1),
  delete(Same,Y,Y1),
  !,
  whites(X1,Y1,W),
  W1 is W + 1.
whites(U,V,0).
%%%%%%%%
secret([2,3,4,1]).  %
%%%%%%%%
?-solution(X).
Guess: [1,1,1,1] Mark: 1,0
Guess: [1,2,2,2] Mark: 0,2
Guess: [2,1,3,3] Mark: 1,2
Guess: [2,3,1,4] Mark: 2,2
Guess: [2,3,4,1] Mark: 4,0
X = [2,3,4,1]
```

Figure 7.2   (cont'd)

7.4   The cut operator considered harmful

In 1966, the computer scientist E. W. Dijkstra wrote a paper called 'The goto-statement considered harmful'. The goto-statement is a powerful construct in ordinary programming languages that tends to destroy the structure and understandability of algorithms.

The same can be said about the **cut** operator in Prolog. The operator is the principal control mechanism for controlling searches in Prolog. It is a necessity for making predicate logic into a useful programming language – without it not even an inequality could be defined. However, the power of the **cut** operator invalidates symmetrical properties of predicate logic.

It should ideally be used only in a controlled way in standard predicates, and otherwise only when in difficulty. There are some structured uses of the **cut** operator that can be used, but before explaining these, consider the uses of **cut** that can create errors.

7.4.1 Examples of hazardous cuts

Suppose that cut is included in the member predicate to make it more efficient for testing membership:

        testmember(X,[X|Y]):–!.
        testmember(X,[U|V]):–
            testmember(X,V).

Now, if this predicate is used to find all the solutions,

        ?–testmember(X,[1,2,3]),all(X).

will only give one solution:

        1

In the next example, a predicate **noofparents** is intended to find the number of parents of various people:

        noofparents(adam,0):–!.
        noofparents(eve,0):–!.
        noofparents(X,2).   % otherwise

If this predicate is used as a test for the number of parents,

        ?–noofparents(eve,2).

gives the unexpected answer:

        yes

7.4.2 Structured use of cut

The first application of cut is to model negation as failure by the definition of **not**:

        not(X):–X,!,fail.
        not(X).

Another 'legal' application is to model **if then else**.

        :–op(980,fx,if).
        :–op(979,xfy,else).
        :–op(978,xfx,then).

(if X then Y else Z):–X,!,Y.
(if X then Y else Z):–Z.

An example of its use in this way is as follows:

biggest(X,Y,Z):–if $X > Y$ then $Z = X$ else $Z = Y$.
?–biggest(3,4,X)
$X = 4$

Actually, a built-in operator –> is defined in C-Prolog with the same meaning of $X -> Y;Z$ as

if X then Y else Z.

Also, numerous cases of the recognition of patterns in list processing make the use of **cut** natural. Examples are abundant in list processing.

7.5   Resolution preprocessing

The append example given at the start of this chapter gives an excellent opportunity to demonstrate resolution preprocessing again:

append([],List,List).
append([First|Rest],List,Newlist):–
    append(Rest,List,Templist),
    cons(First,Templist,Newlist).
cons($X,Y,[X|Y]$).

Resolution preprocessing is resolution applied bottom up. The effect of the call:

cons(First,Templist,Newlist)

is to set **Newlist** = [First|Templist]. It is perfectly legal in Prolog to carry out such substitutions by hand and eliminate the call for the **cons** predicate. This results in

append([],List,List).
append([First|Rest],List,[First|Templist]):–
    append(Rest,List,Templist).

A more obvious example is calling the equality predicate

$X = Y$

solved by unifying X and Y; this can also be carried out manually before the program is executed. For example:

$p(X):-q(Y),X = Y.$

is equivalent to

$p(Y):-q(Y)$

Sometimes, the preprocessed program is easier to understand than before, but sometimes not. The **quicksort** program contains the conditions

d_convert,d_queue and d_append

which are 'necessary' to understand what is going on, but could be processed away.

Resolution preprocessing must be carried out manually in common Prolog systems, but may well be automatic using sophisticated compilers. In this way, there may not necessarily be a conflict between readability of programs and efficiency of program execution.

7.6 Inversion

Prolog is a logical language that finds solutions to problems posed as conditions. It is, in general, symmetric with respect to input and output parameters. This also applies to list processing, even when the problem is recursive. The following example shows how Prolog can work backwards:

?–append$(X,Y,[a,b,c,d])$,all$(X + Y)$.

$[] + [a,b,c,d]$
$[a] + [b,c,d]$
$[a,b] + [c,d]$
$[a,b,c] + [d]$
$[a,b,c,d] + []$

Another example is the **delete** predicate, which applied backwards can insert elements in a list:

?–delete$(p,Z,[a,b,c])$,all(Z).

$[p,a,b,c]$
$[a,p,b,c]$
$[a,b,p,c]$
$[a,b,c,p]$

An example of a predicate that is not invertible is the standard means of adding of numbers:

X is $Y + Z$

This only works when Y and Z are instantiated numeric expressions. Thus, it is not possible to get a subtraction by

?–5 is $X + 2$.

*** Error in arithmetic expression

This motivates the definition of a symmetric predicate **plus(X,Y,Z)** for the relation $X + Y = Z$. A built-in predicate **var(X)** is used, which is true if X is a variable at the time of call.

plus(X,Y,Z):–not var(X),not var(Y),!,Z is X + Y.
plus(X,Y,Z):–var(X),not var(Y),not var(Z),!,X is Z − Y.
plus(X,Y,Z):–not var(X),var(Y),not var(Z), Y is Z − X.

The definition of **plus(X,Y,Z)** here fails when all three arguments are variables.

With this definition consider a program to compute the length of a list:

numberof([],0).
numberof([X|Y],N):–
   numberof(Y,M),
   plus(M,1,N).

The ordinary use of this predicate is

   :–numberof([a,b,c],N).
$N = 3$

However, if this predicate is inverted as follows:

   :–numberof(L,3).

what should the expected answer be? The answer is any list of 3 elements. The logical solution is a list with three different variables, and this is what is actually achieved when the program is run.

$L = [X\_0,X\_5,X\_10]$

To compute the sum of the elements, the predicate **sumof,**

```
sumof([],0).
sumof([X|Y],S):–
    sumof(Y,R),
    S is R + Y.
```

is not trivially inverted by generalization of the addition, because the **plus** predicate will be called with three variables. However, as soon as this is defined, it should also work. This is left as an exercise.

7.7 Non-Horn logic programming

One point to remember is that resolution is not restricted to Horn clauses; there may be more than one other conclusion. For example:

plane(X) **or bird**(X) **if flying**(X).

The appearance of non-Horn clauses is somewhat unsatisfactory when it comes to problem solving, because it is difficult to exploit vague information as in the following example.

Suppose an unidentified flying object (UFO) is seen. It can be concluded:

plane(UFO) **or bird**(UFO).

However, the same rule can be used in its two versions:

plane(X) **if flying**(X) **and NOT bird**(X).
bird(X) **if flying**(X) **and NOT plane**(X).

In this way the two rules prove a unique conclusion, given that the negation of the other can be proven.

Prolog, which is based on Horn-clause logic, is a powerful language. However, sometimes problems occur that are not ready-made for a Horn-clause solution. One such problem is the Alpine Club problem.

Tony, Mike and John belong to the Alpine club. Every member of the Alpine Club is either a skier or a mountain climber. Mountain climbers do not like rain, and anyone who does not like snow is not a skier. Mike dislikes whatever Tony likes and likes whatever Tony dislikes. Tony likes rain and snow. Is there a member of the Alpine Club who is a mountain climber but not a skier?

The solution is first to transform the problem into a predicate logic formula:

(1) CLUBMEMBER(TONY).
(2) CLUBMEMBER(MIKE).
(3) CLUBMEMBER(JOHN).
(4) $\forall X$ (CLUBMEMBER(X) $\Rightarrow$ SKIER(X) OR CLIMBER(X)).
(5) $\forall X$ (CLIMBER(X) $\Rightarrow$ NOT LIKES(X,RAIN)).
(6) $\forall X$ (NOT LIKES(X,SNOW) $\Rightarrow$ NOT SKIER(X)).
(7) $\forall X$ (LIKES(TONY,X) $\Rightarrow$ NOT LIKES(MIKE,X)).
(8) $\forall X$ (NOT LIKES(TONY,X) $\Rightarrow$ LIKES(MIKE,X)).
(9) LIKES(TONY,RAIN).
(10) LIKES(TONY,SNOW).
(11) $\forall X$(NOT(CLUBMEMBER(X) AND CLIMBER(X) AND NOT SKIER(X))).

To remove the non-Horn clause 4, of the form:

$$A \Rightarrow B \text{ OR } C$$

use standard formula manipulation to yield:

$$B \Leftarrow A \text{ AND NOT } C$$

or alternatively

$$C \Leftarrow A \text{ AND NOT } B$$

The other problem is that the predicate logic operator NOT cannot automatically be transcribed by using the standard **not** operator predicate in Prolog, because this acts as negation as failure. Negation as failure is only equivalent to logical NOT; the predicates to be negated do not have free variables, as exist in this case.

At this point, a new logical operator must be introduced, called **negation**.

```
%%% Prolog version of the Alpine Club problem
:-op(900,fx,negation).  % 'negation' represents logical negation
                        % in contrast to 'not' which is negation as failure
clubmember(tony).
clubmember(mike).
clubmember(john).
climber(X) :- clubmember(X), negation skier(X).
negation likes(X,rain) :-climber(X).
negation skier(X) :-negation likes(X,snow).
negation likes(mike,X) :-likes(tony,X).
```

likes(mike,*X*) :–negation likes(tony,*X*).
likes(tony,rain).
likes(tony,snow).

?–clubmember(*X*),
  climber(*X*),
  negation skier(*X*).

X = mike.

7.8 Meta-programming

A property exclusive to symbolic processing languages is their ability to manipulate their own programs to create more general programming schemes, and Prolog is no exception.

Logic Programming has two aspects: programming and logic. The concept of interpreting programs in a language is called **meta-programming**, while the interpretation of Prolog as a logic deduction mechanism is treated in the next section under the title **meta-logic**.

To manipulate terms and literals, use the built-in operator =..

$T =..L$ % *L* is a list containing the functor and
                    % the arguments of the term

  ?–plus(*a*,*b*,*c*) =..*L*.
L = [plus,*a*,*b*,*c*].

  ?–*X* =..[plus,*d*,*e*].
X = plus(*c*,*d*).

The operator works either way. In meta-programming, it is interesting to create a conditional literal *T*, dynamically, when the functor and its arguments are given separately.

call1(*F*,*X*):– $T =..[F,X],T.$
call2(*F*,*X*,*Y*):– $T =..[F,X,Y],T.$
call3(*F*,*X*,*Y*,*Z*):– $T =..[F,X,Y,Z],T.$

An example of its use is as follows:

  ?–call2(member,*a*,[*a*,*b*,*c*]).
yes

Another similar operation is caused by the built-in predicate **functor**:

functor(*X*,*F*,*N*)

This takes the expression X, and returns the functor in F, and the number of arguments into N.

> ?–functor($p(a,b),F,N$).
> $F = p$
> $N = 2$

An interesting property of functor is that it works both ways:

> ?–functor(T,tab1,3).
> $T = $ tab1($\_1,\_2,\_3$)

i.e. T is assigned a most general functional term with three arguments (uninstantiated variables). Finally, there is the built-in predicate **arg** that indexes an argument of a term. It also is symmetric.

> ?–arg(1,$p(a,b)$,X).
> $X = a$
> ?–arg(2,$p(a,X)$,5).
> $X = 5$

Below are examples of generalized function applications, where a function is applied to sets of data. The first type transforms a list into a new list, while the second type computes an aggregate function of a list.

7.8.1 Element by element application

The copy list example is an example of a generalized application of a function F to a whole list. The scheme is as follows:

> MAPLIST([]) = []
> MAPLIST([$X|Y$]) = [$F(X)$|MAPLIST(Y)]

This is made possible by a general predicate **maplist(F,Inlist,Outlist)** as follows:

```
maplist(F,[],[]):-!.
maplist(F,[X|Y],[U|V]):-
    call2(F,X,U),
    maplist(F,Y,V).
```

If the definition:

```
copy(X,X).
```

is added, the clause becomes:

copylist(*L*1,*L*2):–maplist(copy,*L*1,*L*2).

7.8.2   Aggregate functions

Some predicates describe properties or relations between individual elements. However, some properties are inherent to lists of elements. They are defined as functions of lists, defined recursively. For a list of numbers, the following functions are list functions:

- The number of elements
- The maximum and minimum elements
- The sum of the elements.

A characteristic pattern for defining a list function *F* is the following:

AGGREGATE([]) = some characteristic null element
AGGREGATE([*X*|*Y*]) = *F*(*X*,AGGREGATE(*Y*))
% where *F* is a characteristic composition

For example, the number of elements of a list is defined by the predicate:

numberof([],0).
numberof([*X*|*Y*],*S*):–numberof(*Y*,*R*),*S* is *R* + 1.
?–numberof([3,3,4,47],*N*).
N = 4

In the following example, the sum of a list is defined by the predicate:

sumof([],0).
sumof([*X*|*Y*],*S*):–sumof(*Y*,*R*),*S* is *R* + *X*.
?–sumof([1,2,3],*M*).
M = 6

This list is actually summed backwards, i.e. the tail of the list *Y* is summed before the first element; summation is usually performed forwards. These directions are equivalent for operations which are associative, but not otherwise.

An iterative version of forward summation is easily produced, by inside outwards accumulation, with the help of an extra parameter holding the accumulated value.

itersumof(Acc,[],Acc).

```
itersumof(Acc,[X|Y],Z):–
   Newacc is Acc + X,
   itersumof(Newacc,Y,Z).
```

This recursive scheme can be generalized by a predicate **aggregate**(*C*,**Accum**,**List**,**Result**), where: *C* is a three-place predicate, computing *F* as its third argument. *Accum* is the accumulated value, initially given. **List** is to be processed, while **Result** is the result

```
aggregate(C,Temp,[],Temp).
aggregate(C,Old,[Y|Z],Result):–
   call3(C,Old,Y,Temp),
   aggregate(C,Temp,Z,Result).
```

Example of an aggregate in use:

```
count(X,Y,Z):–Z is X + 1.
numberof(Z,R):–
   aggregate(count,0,Z,R).
sum(X,Y,Z):–Z is X + Y.
sumof(Z,R):–aggregate(sum,0,Z,R).
?–numberof([1,2,3],X).
X = 3
?–sumof([1,2,3],X).
X = 6
```

7.9 Meta-logic

One of the reasons round lists have been described is that the syntax of Prolog itself is built up around round lists. Thus, if programmers are a bit liberal with the syntax, it is possible to implement a meta-interpreter of Prolog in Prolog.

```
% Top-down meta-interpreter
:–op(1199,xfx,‘<–’).
prove(true).
prove((X,Y)):–prove(X),prove(Y).
prove(H):–(H <– B),prove(B).
```

A program in this notation could be:

```
grandmother(X,Z) <– mother(X,Y),parent(Y,Z).
parent(X,Y) <– father(X,Y).
```

```
parent(X,Y) <- mother(X,Y).
mother(helga,catherine) <- true.
mother(catherine,halvard) <- true.
mother(ragnhild,tore) <- true.
father(tore,halvard) <- true.
?-prove(grandmother(X,halvard)),all(X).
helga
ragnhild
```

The idea of making a Prolog interpreter in Prolog may seem funny but of little use, since the self-interpreted program is slower in execution. However, the principle is of paramount importance, because the meta-interpreter can be used to add alternative and extended control functions such as

- other search strategies
- explaining functions
- tracing and debugging facilities

As another example of meta-level logic, consider an interpreter of Horn clauses following a bottom-up strategy.

The strategy is to find conclusions of rules as soon as all their conditions are already established.

```
% Bottom-up meta-interpreter
:-op(1199,xfx,<-).
conclusion(G):-supports(true,G).
supports(X,X).
supports(H,G):-
   (W<-H),
   supports(W,G).
supports(H,G):-
   (W<-H,I),
   supports(W,G),
   conditions(I).
conditions((X,Y)):-!,
   conclusion(X),
   conditions(Y).
conditions(X):-conclusion(X).
?-conclusion(X),all(X).
true
mother(helga,catherine)
```

> parent(helga,catherine)
> grandmother(helga,halvard)
> mother(catherine,halvard)
> parent(catherine,halvard)
> mother(ragnhild,tore)
> parent(ragnhild,tore)
> grandmother(ragnhild,halvard)
> father(tore,halvard)
> parent(tore,halvard)

The example will not be explained further, but it demonstrates that any Prolog program can be interpreted with a different strategy, with some loss of speed. The idea may be applied in language processing, expert systems and many other areas.

The idea of meta-level logic programming stems mainly from Kowalski (1979b). A particularly important paper is Pereira (1982), introducing meta-level logic for alternative control structures. In his thesis, Shapiro (1982) applies it for a system to debug Prolog programs.

Meta-level logic programming is a technique that brings Prolog nearer to fulfilling a fundamental idea of logic programming – to make explicit the logic of the program, and to let the sequence of computations or deductions be determined independently. Or, as Kowalski (1979a) put it:

> Algorithms = Logic + Control

7.9.1   Explaining facility in meta-level logic

By using meta-level logic, it is possible to increase the power of predicate logic. An explaining facility is such a facility. When an ordinary Prolog execution is finished, there is no stored account of how the conclusion or the solutions were found. However, this can easily be done with the help of a meta-interpreter, building up such a history. The principle will have many applications, especially in expert systems.

Instead of :-, define an operator '<-':

> :-op(1199,xfx,'<-').

and replace all the clauses to be incorporated into the explanation facility with this operator. For example:

> grandmother(X,Z) <- mother(X,Y),parent(Y,Z).
> parent(X,Y) <- father(X,Y).
> parent(X,Y) <- mother(X,Y).

```
mother(helga,catherine).
mother(catherine,halvard).
mother(ragnhild,tore).
father(tore,halvard).
```

The purpose is to make the clauses available as referrable facts for the meta-interpreter, which is defined by the predicate **prove(Goal,Explanation)**. The explanation is built up recursively by outside inwards accumulation.

```
% Meta-level interpreter with explanation
prove((X,Y),(ExplX,ExplY)):-
   !,
   prove(X,ExplX),
   prove(Y,ExplY).
prove(X,fact(X)):-
   not(X <- Y),          % X is not determined by any rule
   !,
   X.
prove(X,rule(X,Z)):-
   (X <- Y),
   prove(Y,Z).
show(X):-prove(X,Expl),
   showexplanation(Expl).
```

The last thing that has to be done is to print out the explanation in a readable fashion. As in many cases in programming, the input/output takes some effort. The prettyprinting of the explanation may be carried out at many levels of sophistication, but the program is only needed to print out one explanation, in all details, with indentations:

```
showexplanation(X):-
   output(' I CAN SHOW THAT'),
   nl,
   showhow(0,X),
   nl.
showhow(Indent,fact(X)):-
   tab(Indent),
   out(X),output(' IS TRUE').
showhow(Indent,rule(X,Y)):-
   tab(Indent),out(X),output(' IS TRUE BECAUSE'),
   Nextind is Indent + 4,
   for(element(U,Y),showhow(Nextind,U)).
```

Follow the examples through:

> ?–show(grandmother(*X*,halvard)),
> **fail.** % finds all solutions

I CAN SHOW THAT

grandmother(helga,halvard) IS TRUE BECAUSE
  mother(helga,catherine) IS TRUE
  parent(catherine,halvard) IS TRUE BECAUSE
    mother(catherine,halvard) IS TRUE

I CAN SHOW THAT

grandmother(ragnhild,halvard) IS TRUE BECAUSE
  mother(ragnhild,tore) IS TRUE
  parent(tore,halvard) IS TRUE BECAUSE
    father(tore,halvard) IS TRUE

EXERCISES

7.1   Define a predicate that inverts the predicate which finds the sum of elements in a list of integers.

7.2   Write a program that asserts the elements in a named list as individually numbered facts. For example:

> :–enumerate(tab,[*a*,*b*,p(*c*),*a*]).

should assert the following facts:

> elem(tab,1,*a*).   % '*a*' is the first element in the list tab
>   elem(tab,2,*b*).   % '*b*' is the second
>   elem(tab,3,p(*c*)).
>   elem(tab,4,*a*).

7.3   Make the set operations 'union' and 'intersection' into iterations, using the **aggregate** predicate.

7.4   Implement the Pascal **assignment** statement by using base variables.

7.5   Define a hypothesis vector as a list of individual hypotheses, which itself is a hypothesis-and-percentage pair.
   For example:

> [amsel:5, drossel:0, fink:15, star:30]

Write a Prolog program that normalizes a hypothesis vector, i.e. that removes hypotheses having percentage 0, and scales the percentages so that their sums become 100.
Also try this example:

[amsel:10, fink:30, star:60]

Apply meta-programming techniques as far as possible.

7.6   Combine the bottom-up interpreter with the explanation facility, and apply it to the grandmother example.

7.7   Define a propositional formula to be:

(a)   an atomic truth value (true, false)
(b)   an expression of the form

(not R)
(L Op R)

where **Op** is a Boolean operator (**and, or, impl**) and *L* and *R* are propositional formulae.
    Define the complexity of a formula to be

1   if the expression is an atom
$1 + M$ otherwise, where *M* is the maximum complexity of the operands.

(a)   Write a predicate that computes the complexity of an expression. For example:
?–complexity((true or false),X).
$X = 2$

(b)   Make it reversible, to generate all formulae of a given complexity:
?–complexity(X,1),all(X).

true
false

7.8   In the quicksort definitions, there are some conditions that match unconditional conclusions:

d_queue, d_append, d_convert.

Modify the program by a resolution preprocessing of these conditions to obtain a faster and more condensed version.

Chapter 8
Formula manipulation

> No matter what mind is,
> never mind what matter is!
>
> *Albert Einstein to Sigmund Freud*

8.1 Symbolic differentiation

A popular example of formula manipulation which is not numerical computation is the differentiation of mathematical functions. The rules are simple and directly implemented in Prolog, much more elegantly than in LISP, as anyone with a LISP book at hand will acknowledge.

The example shows strikingly that the pattern matching features of Prolog – a property also shared by SNOBOL (Griswold *et al.*, 1968) – make programs almost as readable as the mathematics itself.

Let all differentiations be with respect to a fixed mathematical variable, x, which is to be treated as a constant identifier by Prolog.

The rules of differentiation are defined by the predicate:

deriv(U,V) $V = dU/dx$

as follows:

```
deriv(x,1).
deriv(N,0):-number(N).        % number(N): See library
deriv(U + V,U1 + V1):-
   deriv(U,U1),
   deriv(V,V1).
deriv(U - V,U1 - V1):-
   deriv(U,U1),
   deriv(V,V1).
deriv(U * V,U1 * V + U * V1):-
   deriv(U,U1),
   deriv(V,V1).
```

deriv(U/V,($V * U1 - V1 * U$)/($V * V$)):–
    deriv($U,U1$),
    deriv($V,V1$).

deriv($U\hat{\ }N$,$N * U\hat{\ }N1 * U1$):–number(N),
    $N1$ is $N - 1$,
    deriv($U,U1$).

deriv(exp(U),exp(U) $* U1$):–
    deriv($U,U1$).

%% skip the other elementary functions

For example:

?–deriv($x * x,Y$).
$Y = 1 * x + x * 1$.

A reader with some calculus background will wonder why the output of the differentiation example is not better, such as $2 * X$, for example. The reason is that Prolog has no inherent algebraic simplification, but that is a task Prolog can implement.

8.2 Manipulation

In a symbolic programming language such as Prolog, programmers are often concerned with the formulae themselves, not only their values. In general, formulae are not just arithmetic, but can be combined arbitrarily by odd operators and operands, according to the recursive **principle of decomposition**: the value of an expression is the result of applying the operator on the value of the operand expressions.

In languages such as Pascal and LISP, this recursive principle is a part of the language semantics. In Prolog, this must be done explicitly, but can be done without difficulties by a recursively defined evaluation predicate.

This scheme is general and is a procedural replica of the recursive principle of decomposition. To evaluate an expression, first evaluate its operands, and then apply the operator on the *values* of the operands.

8.3 Anatomy of operator expressions

To manipulate an expression, programmers must get hold of the subcomponents of that expression. Operator expressions may be written as in Table 8.1, but they are internally stored functional terms, where the operators are functors, e.g.

$X + Y$ is stored as '+'(X,Y)

The built-in operator =.. acts also between an operator expression and a list of components:

$X + Y =..$['+'$,X,Y$]
$+ X =..$['+'$,X$]
X po $=..$[po$,X$]   % if po had been a postfix operator

For example:

?–3 + 2 * 7 $=..[X,Y,Z]$.
$X =$ '+'
$Y = 3$
$Z = 2 * 7$
?–$X =$ ...['–'$,3 + 5,5 * 9$].
$X = 3 + 5 – 5 * 9$

The built-in predicates **functor** and **arg** can be used for expressions as well. For example:

functor(X,F,N)

takes the expression X, and returns the functor, i.e. the operator in F, and the number of arguments into N.

?–**functor**$(1 + 2,F,N)$.
$F = +$
$N = 2$

with the **arg** predicate, however:

arg(N,X,A)

indexes the Nth argument of an expression X, as in these examples:

?–**arg**$(1,$not **true**$,X)$.
$X =$ **true**
?–**arg**$(1,a + b,X)$
$X = a$
?–**arg**$(2,a + X,b)$.
$X = b$

Table 8.1   Examples of binary and unary operators

Binary operations:

$X + Y$	addition
$X - Y$	subtraction
$X * Y$	multiplication
X / Y	division
$X = Y$	equal
$X <> Y$	not equal
$X >= Y$	greater or equal
$X =< Y$	less or equal
$X < Y$	less than
$X > Y$	greater than
X and Y	conjunction
X or Y	disjunction
X impl Y	implication ($=>$)

Unary operations:

$- X$	arithmetic negation
not X	logical negation

8.4 Formula evaluation

The effect of the **is** operator is as follows:

```
?-X is 3 * 7 * 37.
X = 777
?-X is 7 * 11 * 13.
X = 1001
```

This is a built-in operator that evaluates numerical formulae. The evaluation is hidden from the user, although it is definable in Prolog. It may be implemented in Prolog for two reasons: first for teaching the principles of formula evaluation in Prolog; secondly, it may be necessary to include rules of operation that do not strictly accord with the semantics of the **is** operator.

The operator is called **$**, and the expression falls on its left side, with the value on the right.

```
2 + 2 $ 4
```

can be read

'the value of 2 + 2 is 4'.

The $ operator extends **is** by evaluating global variables stored as:

value(*X*,*Y*).

For example:

value(*a*,3).
value(*b*,7).
?–*a* * *b* * 37 $ *X*.
X = 777.

Predicates defining extended evaluation are as follows:

:–op(900,*xfx*,'$').
(*X* $ *X*):–number(*X*),!.   % number see library
(*X* $ *Y*):–value(*X*,*Y*),!.
V $ *U*:0
  V = ..[Op,*X*,*Y*],
  !,
  X $ *X1*,
  Y $ *Y1*,
  W = ..[Op,*X1*,*Y1*],
  U is *W*.
V $ *U*:–
  V = ..[Op,*X*],
  !,
  X $ *X1*,
  W = ..[Op,*X1*],
  U is *W*.

Postfix operators are left as an exercise.

The **is** operator has been left at the bottom level because this is the only way to perform basic arithmetic operations. The $ operator can be used to implement the ordinary assignment of global variables:

:–op(901,*xfx*,':=').
(*V*:=*E*):–*E* $ *T*,
  forget(value(*V*,Any)),
  assert(value(*V*,*T*)).
printx(*X*):–*X* $ *Y*,output(*Y*).

An example of assignments:

```
?-a := 4,
   b := 13,
   c := b * a,
   printx(-c).
-52
```

8.5 Algebraic simplification

Other important applications are formula manipulation, theorem proving in the domain of mathematics, and analysis of programs. Theorem proving is also an integral part of the discipline of program verification, proving that programs are correct.

Theorem proving can be viewed as a special kind of simplification task. A theorem is proven if it can be simplified to the constant **true**. The first part of this section will describe such an algebraic simplifier.

There are a number of rules for various formulae, e.g. associative, commutative and distributive laws. When it comes to algebraic simplification, the rules that reduce the complexity of the formulae are especially interesting. Some of these rules are given below by the predicate **reduce**:

reduce(X + 0,X).	% (X + 0) = X
reduce(0 + X,X).	% similar
reduce(X − X,0).	
reduce(X − 0,X).	
reduce(X * 0,0).	
reduce(0 * X,0).	
reduce(X * 1,X).	
reduce(1 * X,X).	
reduce(0 / X,0).	
reduce(X = X,true).	
reduce(true or X,true).	
reduce(X or true,true).	
reduce(X and false,false).	
reduce(false and X,false).	
reduce(X and true,X).	
reduce(true and X,X).	
reduce(X or false,X).	
reduce(false or X,X).	
reduce(X impl true,true).	
reduce(true impl X,X).	
reduce(false impl X,true).	
reduce(X and X,X).	
reduce(X or X,X).	
reduce(X impl X,true).	

```
reduce(U,V):–
    U = ..[Op,X,Y],
    number(X),
    number(Y),
    !,
    V is U.
```

From these basic reduction axioms, a small simplifier **simplify(F,G)** can be constructed based on the following recursive principle:

- Simplify the operands first, and then the operation itself.
- Repeat until none of the operands are changed.

The algorithm is correct, but not complete. It is not optimally efficient because it may resimplify an operand expression which a more refined algorithm would know had just been simplified. This refinement, however, is left as an exercise.

```
simplify(U,V):–
    simp(U,V,ChangeU).          % The 'simp' predicate
                                % has a third argument
                                % which is true if V <> U
                                % and false otherwise
simp(F,H,true):–
    reduce(F,G),
    !,
    simplify(G,H).
simp(F,Z,true):–
    F = ..[Op,X,Y],
    simp(X,X1,ChangeX),
    simp(Y,Y1,ChangeY),
    member(true,[ChangeX,ChangeY]),
    !,
    G = ..[Op,X1,Y1],
    simplify(G,Z).
simp(F,F,false).
```

Follow these examples:

```
?–simplify(1 * x − x * 1,S).
    S = 0
?–simplify(1 * x + x * 1,S)
    S = x + x
```

The differentiation and the simplification can now be coupled together.

> derivate(U,V):–deriv($U,U1$),
>   simplify($U1,V$).
> ?–derivate($x * x,S$).
> $S = x + x$

8.5.1   Common subexpressions

Simplification is possible when adjacent operations can be found by recognition of fixed patterns. For example:

$$(a + b * j - f) - (a + b * j - f)$$

is recognized by unification of the pattern

$$X - X$$

However, one class of problems is still unsolved, where there are subexpressions that could be moved, according to associative and commutative rules, and be reduced when a unifiable pattern is recognized.

$$(a + b + c + d) - b$$

could be transformed to

$$((a + c) + b) - b$$

which follows a pattern

$$(X + Y) - Y$$

which is reducible to

$$X = a + c$$

In fact, this attraction of common subexpressions is one of the important heuristic principles guiding human experts in algebraic simplification (Bundy, 1983). One problem is covered here but the completion is left as a challenging exercise. The task is to discover if there are common subexpressions.

A subexpression occurring in an expression is easily formulated as:

```
occurs(X,X).
occurs(S,Z):-
    Z = ..[Op,X,Y],
    (occurs(S,X);
    occurs(S,Y)).
```

So the problem of finding out if an expression uses the same subexpression several times is solved by:

```
common(Z,U):-
    Z = ..[Op,X,Y],
    occurs(U,X),
    occurs(U,Y).
```

For example:

```
?-common(w + 1 + 2 * (w + 1),Z),
    all(Z).

w + 1
w
1
```

8.6 Integration

It has been said that differentiation is a craft while symbolic integration is an art. The task of symbolic integration is a subject for knowledge engineering, where human expertise has to be transferred to a computer. In fact, a high quality integration package was implemented in Prolog as early as 1975 (Kanoui, 1975); however, a LISP-based system, MACSYMA, beats most amateur mathematicians in integration. MACSYMA is a program of 300 000 lines of LISP code.

What would happen if the symmetry principle of logic programming were taken literally, and input and output were reversed in the **derivate** predicate? In programming languages other than Prolog, this would be a stupid question. In Prolog, this reversion is exactly the same as integration.

Using this predicate:

```
integrate(Y,Z):-deriv(Z,Y).
?-integrate(1 * x + x * 1,Int).
```

the answer arrived at is in fact:

$$Int = x * x.$$

Unfortunately, Prolog's ability to invert programs is limited. If

?–integrate(0,Int).

is attempted, it eventually calls **number(Int)**. If the built-in predicate **number** had been invertible, the argument **Int** should produce instantiated numbers $(0,1,2,...)$, which are all correct integrations of 0. But instead, only a

no

is generated.

The next problem concerns putting simplification in reverse. On trying:

?–integrate($x + x$,Int)

searching for $x * x$ no answer is achieved, because $x + x$ is only achieved after a simplification. If **simplify** is run in reverse, a recursive trap occurs. However, it is possible to modify the **simplify** predicate to control the depth of recursion. This results in an extremely slow but in theory complete integration package, based on the principle of exhaustive generate and test. This is left as a rather challenging exercise.

8.7 Program verification

Prolog is suitable for proving that programs are correct according to formal specifications; this is officially known as **program verification**. This section assumes some knowledge of the topic, and may be skipped without harm. The book by Backhouse (1986) is recommended as a useful introduction to the subject.

A simple program verifier for Pascal is demonstrated in Prolog as follows. However, before program verification is considered, be warned that logic programming is usually a better specification method by itself, and is of course directly executable.

Find the maximum M of two numbers X and Y. An informal specification of this problem is to say that the maximum M must be equal to one of X and Y, and greater than or equal to both of them. Slightly formalized, this may be written:

$(M = X$ or $M = Y)$ and $M >= X$ and $M >= Y$.

which is in fact a solution in Prolog. However, as a more realistic example, consider a Pascal character array, which contains a number of characters. Write a new array where all sequences of blanks are replaced by one blank.

The sketch of a Pascal solution would be something like this:

```
PROGRAM compress;
CONST blank = ' ';
   n = 24;
VAR s: ARRAY[1...n] OF char;
previousblank:boolean;
i,j:integer;
BEGIN
  s :='THIS     IS  AN EXAMPLE   ';
  previousblank := false;
  i := 0;
  j := 1;
  WHILE j =<n DO
  BEGIN
    IF (s[j] <> blank) OR (NOT previousblank) THEN
    BEGIN
      i := i + 1;
      s[i] := s[j];
    END;
    previousblank := (s[j] = blank);
    j := j + 1;
  END;
  FOR j := i + 1 TO n DO s(j) := blank;
  writeln(s); (*'THIS IS AN EXAMPLE   '*)
END.
```

It is a very difficult task to create a formal non-recursive specification of what this program should and should not do. It should not, for example, permute the non-blank characters. A recursive Prolog program for a similar task, however, is relatively easy to generate, using a recursive predicate **compress(String,Compressed)**. Assume that the string is represented as a string of characters.

```
compress([],[]).          % the compression of an empty string is empty
compress([B,B|R],Y):-     % if it starts with two blanks,
  blank(B),
  compress([B|R],Y).      % then skip the first and recur
compress([C|R],[C|S]):    % otherwise, copy character
  compress(R,S).          % and compress the rest
blank(32).                % ASCII value of blank
:-compress("THIS IS   AN  EXAMPLE  ",X),
```

printstring(X).   % printstring, see library
    X = "THIS IS AN EXAMPLE"

The point is that the Prolog definition is an executable recursive specification of compress that is relatively easy to write and easy to have confidence in. On the other hand, a formal specification of the Pascal program can be difficult to write, and hence would be difficult to trust.

8.7.1 Program verification in Prolog

Given that a user community insists on using ordinary program verification for some legitimate reason, Prolog is a good language in which to implement the program verifier. Ordinary program verification usually follows three steps:

(1) The programmer supplies the program with preconditions, post-conditions and intermittent conditions, such as loop invariants.

(2) Verification conditions are automatically generated from the program text and the conditions, according to the semantics of the language.

(3) The verification conditions are proved by algebraic simplification and theorem proving.

8.7.2 A verification condition generator

This section will sketch a program verification condition generator, and may be skipped without loss by anyone not familiar with program verification. Only partial correctness is considered, correctness on the assumption that the program terminates.

Read **wp(Pre,Statement,Post)** as

Pre is the weakest precondition that must be proved valid when placed before **Statement** in order that **Post** shall be valid after the **Statement** has been executed.

```
:-op(1001,fx,begin).
:-op(1001,fx,invariant).
:-op(1000,xfx,while).
:-op(999,xfx,do).
:-op(700,xfx,':=').
```

```
wp(R,
  (begin end),
  R).
wp(Pre,
  (begin S,REST),
  Post):-
  wp(Inter,(begin REST),Post),
  wp(Pre,S,Inter).
wp((X impl TR) and (not X impl TF),
  (if X then Y else Z)
  ,Post):-
  wp(TR,Y,Post),
  wp(TF,Z,Post).
wp(Pre,
  (X := Y),
  Post):-
  replace(Post,X,Y,Pre).
wp(INV,
  (invariant INV while B do S),
  Post):-
  wp(Q,S,INV),
  theorem((B and INV) impl Q),
  theorem((not B and INV) impl Post).
replace(A,A,B,B):-!.
replace(Z1,A,B,Z2):-
  Z1 =..[Op,X1,Y1],
  !,
  replace(X1,A,B,X2),
  replace(Y1,A,B,Y2),
  Z2 =..[Op,X2,Y2].
replace(Z1,A,B,Z2):-
  Z1 =..[Op,X1],
  !,
  replace(X1,A,B,X2),
  Z2 =..[Op,X2].
replace(X,A,B,X).                % Otherwise
theorem(T):-simplify(T,T1),
  print('*** prove: '),
  output(T1).
verify(Pre,Statement,Post):-
  wp(P,Statement,Post),
  theorem(Pre impl P).
```

```
?-verify(
(b = 5),
(begin a := b,
       x := a,
end),
(x > 4)).
```
*** prove: $(b = 5)$ impl $b > 4$
```
:-verify(
  (a > 2),
  (begin
    (if a > b then c := a
              else c := b),
  end),
  (c > 2)).
```
*** prove: $a > 2$ impl $(a > b$ impl $a > 2)$ and (not $a > b$ impl $b > 2$)
```
:-verify(
  (n >= 0),
  (begin
    (s := 0),
    (i := 0),
    (invariant i =< n and s = i * (i + 1) / 2
      while i < n do
      (begin
        (i := i + 1),
        (s := s + i),
      end)
    ),
  end),
  (s = n * (n + 1) / 2).
```
*** prove: $i < n$ and $i =< n$ and $s = i * (i + 1) / 2$ impl
      $i + 1 =< n$ and $s + (i + 1) = (i + 1) * (i + 1) * (i + 1 + 1) / 2$

*** prove: not $i < n$ and $i =< n$ and $s = i * (i + 1) / 2$ impl
      $s = n * (n + 1) / 2$

*** prove: $n >= 0$ impl $0 =< n$

As the simplifier is not complete, the verification conditions are not proved automatically in this case. However, readers should verify for themselves that these are in fact valid formulae. It is left as an exercise to extend the simplifier to reduce these formulae to true.

EXERCISES

8.1   Write a simplification program that never re-simplifies an expression.

8.2   Extend the differentiation predicate **derivate**, including algebraic simplification, with the following functions:

ln, exp, sin, cos, arctan

and $U^{\wedge}V$, where U and V are general expressions.

8.3   Extend the common subexpression example by taking into account commutative equivalence.

8.4   Find the smallest expression comprising two common subexpressions.

8.5   Write a Prolog program that moves common subexpressions closer to each other, and then makes reductions based on pattern recognition, as before. For example:

$$(a + b + c + d - (a + c))$$

Here, c is a common subexpression that is lifted into the two main operands:

$$(a + b + c + d) \quad ==> \quad ((a + b + d) + c)$$
$$- (a + c) \quad\quad ==> \quad - (a + c)$$

$$\overline{(a + b + d) - a}$$

and then reduced according to the pattern:

$$(X + C) - (Y + C) ==> X - Y$$

Applied recursively, the final result is $(b + d)$.

8.6   Complete the program verifier with rules for simplifying the verification conditions in the program verification examples. Verify manually and automatically the following program:

    begin
       if $x > y$ then $z := x$ **else**
                 $z := y$
    end.

with the following post-condition:

$$\{(z = x \text{ or } z = y) \text{ and } z >= x \text{ and } z >= y\}$$

8.7 Modify the **derivate** predicate to achieve integration by inverted derivation and simplification according to the scheme:

> **integrate$N(U,V,N$levels):–**
> **level(Nlevels),**
> **simplify$N$(Formula,U,Nlevels),**
> **deriv(U,Formula).**
>
> **level(0).**
> **level($N1$):–level(N),$N1$ is $N + 1$.**

where **simplify$N$** simplifies a formula in exactly Nlevels recursive steps (Nlevels $= 0,1,2,...$).

Chapter 9
Logic and Databases

> Everything is expressible in
> first order predicate logic –
> even irony.
>
> *Yu No Hoo*

9.1 Relational databases

A database is a shared collection of inter-related data stored independently of the programs using it, allowing the data to be retrieved,
inserted, deleted and modified in a controlled way. The amount of data
stored is typically large, and the contents change over time. The database
as such may have a longer life-span than any application programs written
to manipulate it.

In Prolog, the database is defined to be the set of facts, even
though this definition does not fulfill all the above characteristics.
However, there is nothing in the language that prohibits it from working
directly on large, permanently-stored relational databases. In any case,
Prolog is well adapted to interface with a relational database.

One of the landmarks in the evolution of the database field was the
introduction of the relational model (Codd, 1970). Here, data are defined
by **relations** over **domains**, and the individual facts are represented as
tuples of values from these domains. A relation with a set of tuples is also
called a table. The relational model is conceptually clean, with a solid
mathematical foundation, and lends itself well to data modelling.

In contrast with ordinary databases, the relational model has no
pointer concept, so the associations between different tables are *via* the
explicit identities of the values of attributes. This principle puts more
strain on the implementors to achieve a high speed, while the gain is
increase in the flexibility and closeness to an easily understandable
model.

The relational model has generated an enormous amount of
research activity, and the interested reader should consult the many good
text books on the topics, e.g. Date (1986). The purpose of mentioning
relational models is that tables are a natural way of storing inter-related
facts in Prolog. Prolog systems of the future will be able to handle larger

relational databases, by letting the programmer think in terms of simple logic, while sophisticated software will take care of the speed and capacity. The Educe System (Bocca, 1985) is an example of that.

The Japanese fifth generation project has planned to make relational databases an integral part of fifth generation computers (Moto-Oka, 1981), each having hundreds of gigabytes of memory.

9.1.1 A relational example

As a little example of relational databases, consider two model relations:

- person – containing name, sex and parents (Table 9.1(a));
- car – containing car number, make, owner and colour (Table 9.1(b)).

Table 9.1(a)   Person relations

name	sex	father	mother
halvard	m	tore	catherine
tore	m	ole	ragnhild
catherine	f	harold	helga
anne	f	tore	catherine
robin	m	harold	helga
ragnhild	f	olaf	alma

Table 9.1(b)   Car relations

number	make	owner	colour
123	fiat	ole	brown
321	volvo	ragnhild	green
314	citröen	tore	blue
111	ferrari	catherine	yellow

A static database of Tables 9.1(a) and (b) would be:

```
%% table person(name,sex,father,mother).
   person(halvard,m,tore,catherine).
   person(tore,m,ole,ragnhild).
   person(catherine,f,harold,helga).
```

```
person(anne,f,tore,catherine).
person(robin,m,harold,helga).
person(ragnhild,f,olaf,alma).
%% table car(number,make,owner,colour)
car(123,fiat,ole,brown).
car(321,volvo,ragnhild,green).
car(314,citröen,tore,blue).
car(111,ferrari,catherine,yellow).
```

One or more of the attributes have a special status of being unique within the table. Such an attribute is called a **key**, and identifies the objects that we store information about. We usually use underscore to tell which attributes are keys. For example:

person
<u>name</u> sex father mother

9.1.2 Binary relations

There exists an even simpler form of relation called a binary relation, with only one attribute for each key. The car relation would then be split into three relations:

number-make	number-owner	number-colour
123 fiat	123 ole	123 brown
....	....	....

However, for convenience, related information is usually collected into one relation as often as possible.

A minor problem occurs when data missing for relational models has to be handled. In a binary representation, the tuple is left out, e.g. for a car without an owner. But if a combined tuple is created, with attributes, then the missing value is represented by a special symbol, e.g. nil. For example:

```
car(222,mercedes,nil,purple).
```

9.1.3 Composite keys

In a simple implementation strategy, it is assumed that there is only one key, which is usually the first argument. For composite keys, we make an *ad hoc* convention to represent the composite key as a list of arguments.

$$(k_1,k_2,k_3)$$

with its own name, but let all the individual attributes k_1,k_2,k_3 appear as separate attributes.

9.2 Database retrieval

Database retrieval means combining and presenting the contents of the database in ways that serves our needs. Databases are used to retrieve information. In ordinary databases, this is carried out by a combination of programs and database. In Prolog, it is done by defining the conditions of the solutions in logic. However, the Prolog variables have no relevance to the attribute names. A few defined general Prolog operators are useful. They were defined earlier, and are also in the library in the Appendix.

> **list** X,Y.   % for all solutions of Y, output X
> **listall** X.   % list all solutions X

Examples:

> 'Who has a Volvo?'
> :–list P,car(N,volvo,P,C).
> **ragnhild**
> 'What make of cars do the women have?'
> :–list MAKE,
> person(P,f,FATHER,MOTHER),
> car(N,MAKE,P,C).
>
> **ferrari**
> **volvo**
>
> List the car relation:
> :–listall car(X,Y,U,V).
>   car(123,fiat,ole,brown)
>   car(321,volvo,ragnhild,green)
>   car(314,citröen,tore,blue)
>   car(111,ferrari,catherine,yellow)

9.2.1 Efficient retrieval

Prolog allows the representation of relational data, and the retrieval of these is easily formulated. However, for larger databases, care must be taken.

All Prolog systems ought to have a mechanism that allows direct lookup in a database when the first argument in a condition is known. The problem becomes more acute when two or more tables are combined, because logically this amounts to looking at all combinations of tuples in two tables. Therefore, a query optimizer is usually involved for serious database applications (Warren, 1981). The query optimizer is usually written in Prolog, handling the query as terms, i.e. it is a meta-interpreter. A possible strategy is first to select the condition with the least number of solutions, assuming all variables are to be instantiated. Query optimization is not discussed in any detail here, but how an efficient Prolog query should be written is covered.

Suppose a crime has been committed, and there is a search for a man in a blue Volvo. The police database has two tables: one with 3000 car tuples, and one with 10 000 suspected persons. Remember that a person may have more than one car.

Suppose there are ten blue Volvos, and that half of the people in the database are men.

There are two ways to formulate the query:

?–car(No,volvo,owner,blue),	% 3000 unifications,
	% 10 successes
person(Owner,m,_,_).	% + 10 checks for male
?–person(Owner,m,_,_),	% 10 000 unifications,
	% 5000 successes.
car(No,volvo,Owner,blue).	% +5000 ∗ 3000 unifications.

Suppose there is a direct lookup when the first argument is known; then the check for persons in the first example is almost free, while in the second example, the program must search through the whole car table for half of the person tuples. The number of unifications is 3010 in the first case, and 15 010 000 in the second case. The lesson to learn is that conditions with the fewest successes should be placed as early as possible.

9.2.2 Virtual tables

The relational model is a subset of Prolog, and it is not necessary to keep within its borders. One of the facilities of Prolog is the possibility to define new tables without creating them, i.e. by logical implication. Such tables are called **virtual tables**. For example, a table **carcolour** can be defined containing only the number and the colour:

carcolour(X,Y):–car(X,_,_,Y).

?–listall carcolour:(X,Y).

   carcolour(123,brown)
   carcolour(321,green)
   carcolour(314,blue)
   carcolour(111,yellow)

The concept of virtual tables is, of course, just an adaptation of the subset of Prolog without function or list symbols, sometimes called Datalog. In addition to the Prolog database, new concepts and rules extend the level of information. The database is then no longer pure, and a more appropriate name is a knowledge base, although that concept is defined later.

Consider the query:

'Who has a grandmother with a green Volvo?'

In Prolog, the rules of grandmother, ownership and car colour are defined if that suits the programmer's purposes:

```
grandmother(X,Z):-mother(X,Y),parent(Y,Z).
parent(X,Y):-father(X,Y).
parent(X,Y):-mother(X,Y).
father(F,X):-person(X,_,F,_).
mother(M,X):-person(X,_,_,M).
make(N,M):-car(N,M,_,_,).
owns(X,N):-car(N,_,X,_).
colour(N,C):-car(N,_,_,C).
```

```
?-list P,
grandmother(X,P),owns(X,C),colour(C,green),make(C,volvo).
```

```
halvard
anne
```

9.2.3 Symbolic naming

When Prolog tables are accessed, the program uses the position in the table of the argument for accessing the column. This becomes awkward when the number of arguments becomes large. Moreover, it ties the program to a concrete realization of the relations. What is needed is a more abstract representation, which allows programs to survive changes in the data model. One solution is to use virtual binary tables, containing the attribute name as an explicit argument. For tables with many attributes, this technique may become a necessity.

A general predicate **tabvalue** can be defined for all the attribute names:

```
tabvalue(car,N,number,N):-car(N,_,_,_).
tabvalue(car,N,make,M):-car(N,M,_,_).
tabvalue(car,N,owner,O):-car(N,_,O,_).
tabvalue(car,N,colour,C):-car(N,_,_,C).
```

The transformation of a general table declaration into a set of predicates that access attributes by name can be automated. This is done in the library with the operator definition **table**, which may be called by

> :–table car(number,make,owner,colour).

For example:

> 'Who has a VOLVO?'
>
> ?–list *P*, tabvalue(car,*N*,make,volvo),
>   tabvalue(car,*N*,owner,*P*).
>
> **ragnhild**

The **table** predicate makes a dictionary of all the tables and their attributes in the form:

> :–table dictionary(tablename,attribute,attributeno)
>
> dictionary(car,number,1).
> dictionary(car,make,2).
> dictionary(car,owner,3).
> dictionary(car,colour,4).

The dictionary table can be accessed as any other table; for example, 'Which attributes does a car have?'

> ?–list *A*, dictionary(car,*A*,*N*).
>
> **number**
> **make**
> **owner**
> **colour**

It is possible to give the symbolic access of tables a more intuitive syntax, by defining the operators:

> :–op(900,*xfx*,has).
> :–op(1,*xfx*,':').
> Tab:Key has Attribute = Value:–
>   tabvalue(Tab,Key,Attribute,Value),
>   not Value = nil.   % The test for nil is to avoid seeing the
>   % missing values.

The same example ('Who has a Volvo?') then becomes:

list *P*, car:*N* **has make** = **volvo,**
   car:*N* **has owner** = *P*.

Alternatively, the soft syntax may be defined slightly differently:

Key has Tab:Attribute = **Value:–**
   tabvalue(Tab,Key,Attribute,Value),
   not Value = **nil.**

Then the same query becomes

?–list *P*,
   N **has car:make** = **volvo,**
   N **has car:owner** = *P*.

9.3 Database updating

The relational model imposes the restriction that certain fields must be key fields, whose values are unique in the table. Thus, **name** is the key in the **PERSON** relation, while **number** is the key in the **CAR** relation. The **table** predicate automatically defines a predicate:

key(Table,Name):–tabvalue(Table,Name,_,_).

so that:

?–key(car,Number)

becomes identical to

:–car(Number,_,_,_).

In Prolog, a system for manipulating relational databases may be implemented very naturally. The basic operations are:

- **forget(tuple)**   % remove tuple
- **remember(tuple)**   % insert a tuple if it is not there
- **update(tuple)**   % forget the old, remember the new tuple

For example:

```
?-forget(car(_,_,tore,_)).          % remove whatever cars Tore has
?-remember(car(555,rolls_royce,tore,pink)).    % new car
```

There is no automatic check whether the key value is unique or not. While the **remember** predicate adds a tuple to the database if it is not already there, the following car tuple is erroneously asserted:

```
?-remember(car(314,citröen,hans,brown)).
```

Now two tuples may end up with the same key, because the tuples are different as a whole, but violate the uniqueness of the key.

```
?-listall car(314,X,Y,Z).
car(314,citröen,tore,blue).
car(314,citröen,hans,brown).
```

This must always be checked beforehand.
   When querying a relational database, the result is usually required as an output. For many purposes, however, there is a need to create and store temporary tables constructed as a composite query, for faster access, or to avoid duplicates. Constructing new tables is greatly facilitated by the **construct** predicate defined as follows:

```
construct(X,Y):-          % create all unique X such that Y
   for(Y,remember(X)).
```

This may be used as in the following example:

```
?-construct(parents(Father,Mother),
   person(N,S,Father,Mother)).      % a temporary table is created
?-listall parents(F,G).
parents(tore,catherine)
parents(ole,ragnhild)
parents(harold,helga)
parents(olaf,alma)
```

The **construct** predicate could, if necessary, be combined with a table declaration to allow symbolic naming.

9.4   Data modelling

A database is not only a collection of data, but also the associations or relationships between the items. The associations between data form a

data model. When building knowledge-based systems, therefore, do not forget that knowledge-based systems are also data-based systems.

Database technology has provided methods and tools for solving complex and large data management problems. The construction of stable and logical data models is a very important task, and research into the use of Prolog in database construction has started (Bouzeghoub *et al.*, 1985). To store information about things and their properties, pure predicate logic is a very strong formalism, capable of representing almost anything, so we often have to restrict the language used for modelling, and revert to predicate logic to explain semantics or to cover non-standard features.

9.4.1 Normal forms

As with all modelling, the only important things to model are the fundamental invariants of a problem domain. The most important invariant property is that objects belong to **classes** that can be stored uniformly as relations.

The evidence that data in a relation are functionally dependent on other data is another such principle. A set of data B is functionally dependent on a set of data A if, for each data element a in A, there exists a unique element b in B, such that b is related to a. The common notations are as follows:

$A \rightarrow B$	B is functionally dependent on A
$A,B \rightarrow C$	means C is dependent on the combination of A,B

For example:

employee $\rightarrow$ employer

From the uniqueness of keys, it follows automatically that all the attributes are functionally dependent on the key.

An important principle behind any good design is to avoid redundancy. The same piece of information should only be stored once. Thus, for any changes of a value, the database needs only to be updated in one place. In relational databases, these principles are taken care of by a process called normalization (Date, 1986). When designing relational databases in Prolog, the merits of normalization are equally valid when the program incorporates a database to be updated at some point.

9.4.2 Relational normal forms

Some principles of good design are embedded in the third normal form (3NF), which is a refinement of second normal form (2NF) and first normal form (1NF). 3NF may be memorized by the motto:

'Every item in a tuple is functionally dependent on the key, the whole key and nothing but the key.'

First normal form – dependent on the key

Avoids repeating groups, as in the example:

EMPLOYER EMPLOYEE1 EMPLOYEE 2 ... EMPLOYEEmax

Not:

employees(su,[wladimir,joseph,nikita,leonid,yuri,konstantin]),

but:

emp(vladimir,su).
emp(joseph,su).
emp(nikita,su).
emp(leonid,su).
emp(yuri,su).
emp(konstantin,su).

Principally, the employees (e.g. nikita) are not functionally dependent on the employer (su). On the contrary, the employer is functionally dependent on the employee, technically speaking. Practically, the benefit appears when Michael is employed, because this fact can be added as follows:

?–remember(emp(michael,su)).

and the programmer does not have to:

- pick up the list of employees of su
- append michael
- make a new list
- delete the old tuple with all employees
- make a new tuple.

A model in the first normal form should therefore be:

EMPLOYEE EMPLOYER

Second normal form – the whole key

This form is relevant for tuples with composite keys:

<u>EMPLOYEE</u> EMPLOYEENAME
<u>EMPLOYEE</u> <u>PROJECT</u> PROJECTNAME HOURS

In this case, each employee has a number (**EMPLOYEE**) and a name (**EMPLOYEENAME**). The employees work on a set of projects with project numbers (**PROJECT**) and names (**PROJECTNAME**). The database is supposed to keep a record of the number of hours each employee has worked on a project.

The anomaly in this representation is that **PROJECTNAME** is not dependent on the whole key (**EMPLOYEE, PROJECT**), but only on a part of it, **PROJECT**. Thus, the **PROJECTNAME** is stored many more times than necessary. If the project name is changed, all the occurrences of the project name must be changed, once for each employee.

A model in Second Normal form would be:

<u>EMPLOYEE</u> EMPLOYEENAME
<u>EMPLOYEE</u> <u>PROJECT</u> HOURS
<u>PROJECT</u> PROJECTNAME

Here, **PROJECTNAME** is stored once for each project, and is changed by one update.

Third normal form – and nothing but the key

A good example of 3NF is when the information about a person, his employer, and the employer's address is stored. If the relation:

<u>EMPLOYEE</u> EMPLOYER EMPLOYERADDRESS

exists, then **EMPLOYERADDRESS** is not functionally dependent on the key **EMPLOYEE** alone ('nothing but the key'), but is actually dependent on **EMPLOYER**, which in turn is dependent on **EMPLOYEE**. As with the earlier case, problems of redundancy and multiple updating arise. Therefore, normalization dictates that this relation is split into two independent relations:

<u>EMPLOYEE</u> EMPLOYER
<u>EMPLOYER</u> EMPLOYERADDRESS

The principles of normalization can be applied manually for small models. However, for larger models, the normalization can be automated by programs. A recent paper by Ceri and Gottlob (1986) describes a routine for normalizing relations in Prolog.

9.5 Beyond the relational model

The pure relational model is not always powerful enough for advanced modelling, because it lacks semantic expressiveness. For one thing, every possible set of tuples in a normalized relational database is allowed. For example, the relational model does not require that, for each employee, the employer attribute corresponds to an existing employer tuple in the database.

In realistic models, there are two kinds of rules that relate the tables to each other.

- generic rules that define new, virtual tables that are not explicitly stored
- constraint rules that set restrictions on what is allowed in the database

An example of constraint rules is given by **functional dependencies** which specify that key attributes are and must be unique. Another example might be a rule that: All elephants are grey, which deduces the colour of an elephant in a database, provided a constraint is imposed on every update that no elephants of any other colour may be stored. Such databases are called **deductive databases**. Gaillare and Minker (1978) is a source of ideas for treating the database field from a logical point of view.

9.6 Semantic nets

Questions of meaning are more important for the design of a knowledge base than methods of encoding data. When database designers add more semantic information their models begin to look like the knowledge representation systems developed by the AI-communities.

One of these knowledge representation systems is the **semantic net**. A semantic net is a formalism for representing facts and relations between facts with binary relations.

For example, in Figure 9.1, 'Tore', '07593016' and 'RUNIT' represent objects, even though the numbers do not necessarily exist in space and time. 'Telephone' represents a relation between the objects 'Tore' and '07593016', while 'Employer' represents a relation between 'Tore' and 'RUNIT'.

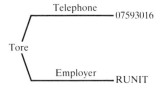

Figure 9.1   A simple semantic net.

The individual relationships are connected into a net by letting the objects, e.g. Tore, be represented only once. For binary relations, semantic nets are an excellent formalism with a simple graphical notation. When moving from binary relations to *n*-ary relations, the semantic net loses some of its appeal, as it forces artificial constructions.

It is believed that much of human reasoning is based on associations along associative links. So the semantic net model is also an interesting model of human thinking.

In Prolog, the binary relations are implemented individually, duplicating the object names, as in the example:

telephone(tore,07593016).
employer(tore,runit).

Storing a semantic net as a network with pointers is one implementation method which gives rapid access in this association process. In Prolog, lacking the pointer concept, the net is stored as individual binary relations. This is a bit slower but very flexible, both for retrieval and update.

9.6.1   The class concept

As soon as an object is classified, a lot is known about it. A **class** is a description of a set of similar objects, specifying attributes and properties common to all its members. Tore, for example, is an object belonging to the class of employees. An **attribute** may be something that can hold a value. Telephone, for example, is an attribute of most employees. A **property** is an attribute together with a **value**. For example, a rose has the property of a colour = red. Tore has the property of a telephone = 07593016. A property may also be an adjective when an attribute name is contrived, e.g. Prolog is exciting.

A class may well be void of elements (e.g. unicorns), and two classes with the same elements may in theory be quite distinct (e.g. the class of research managers and the class of labrador retriever owners).

Examples of classes:
animal

mammal
spermwhale
elephant
shark

Example of attributes:
colour
inhalant
texture
food
bloodtemp
habitat

A class may be a subclass of another class. If *S* is a subclass of *C*, and *x* is a member of *S*, then *x* is also a member of *C*. For example, mammal is a subclass of animal, and elephant is a subclass of mammal. If Clyde is an elephant (i.e. is a member of the class 'elephants'), then Clyde is at the same time a member of the class mammals and thereby a member of the class animals.

If the class has an attribute, it is shared by all its subclasses. Note that a class may have an attribute even if there are currently no members in that class. Values of non-existing attributes, such as the telephone of an elephant, are rejected as meaningless, not by the answer **none**.

In a similar fashion, if an entity has an attribute which is functionally dependent on it – for instance, 'every person has a name' – and this attribute value is missing, the appropriate answer is **unknown**, and not **none**. If, on the other hand, an attribute is not functionally dependent, such as the children of a person, then missing occurrences of children should be answered **none**, and not **unknown**.

For example, all animals have a colour, which varies. Therefore, all mammals have a colour. Elephants therefore have a colour, so Clyde has a colour.

If a class has a property, it is also inherited by all the subclasses and members of the class. For example:

All elephants have colour = grey
    implies that
Clyde has colour = grey.

To store the information of classes in a net together with the information about objects requires a few general relationships (see Figure 9.2).

With the notation in Figure 9.2, a semantic net can be drawn, but bear in mind that some authors prefer the notation **ako** ('a kind of') instead of **are**.

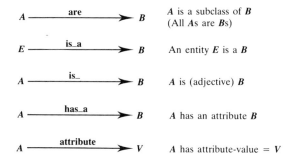

Figure 9.2 Semantic net legend.

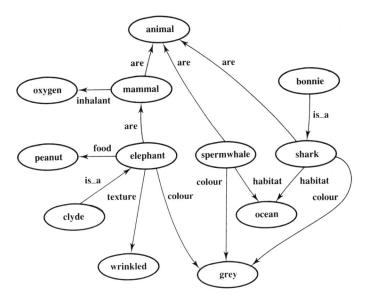

Figure 9.3 A semantic net.

The information in Figure 9.3 may adequately be represented as a set of Prolog clauses: a few infix operator declarations make it more readable:

:–op(900,xfx,[are,is_a,is_,has,has_a]).

animal has_a inhalant.
animal has_a blood_temp.
animal has_a food.
elephant has_a texture.

    mammal has inhalant = oxygen.
    mammal has blood_temp = warm.
    elephant has texture = wrinkled.
    elephant has food = peanuts.
    elephant has colour = grey.
    spermwhale has habitat = ocean.
    spermwhale has colour = grey.
    shark has habitat = ocean.
    shark has colour = grey.
    mammal are animal.
    shark are animal.
    spermwhale are mammal.
    elephant are mammal.

    clyde is_a elephant.
    bonnie is_a shark.

Here are some general axioms defining the class structure

    X is_a Z2:–
        Z1 are Z2, X is_a Z_1.   % transitive closure of is_a
    X has ATT = VAL:–
        X is_a C, C has ATT = VAL.   % transitive closure of has

This can now answer general questions such as:

'Which properties does Clyde have?'

    ?–list (Attr = Value),
        clyde has Attr = Value.

    texture = wrinkled
    food = peanuts
    colour = grey
    inhalant = oxygen
    blood_temp = warm

and

        'What is grey and wrinkled?'
        ?–list OBJ,
            OBJ has X = grey,
            OBJ has Y = wrinkled.
        elephant
        clyde
        'List all the properties'
        ?–listall X has Y = Z.

mammal has inhalant = oxygen
mammal has blood_temp = warm
elephant has texture = wrinkled
elephant has food = peanuts
...

9.7 The course model

We now change topic and build a knowledge base of programming courses which will be able to answer questions pertinent to its content. The knowledge base will not be intelligent in any sense, and will have no expertise, except to have enough additional information to 'understand' certain information.

The definition of relevance is of course a narrow one. Facts such as 'Bergen is a beautiful city' are not usually included, although it is common knowledge in certain parts of Norway.

Prolog will be the language used to query this knowledge base. Chapter 11 on natural language will discuss how to access the contents of the knowledge base in a very restricted, but nevertheless quite useful, natural language subset.

```
% CLASS DESCRIPTION

course_series are thing.        % 'thing' is the universal class
person are thing.
place are thing.
building are thing.
floor are thing.
time are thing.
name are thing.

person has_a full_name.
person has_a last_name.
person has_a first_name.
person has_a occupation.
person has_a phone.
person has_a employer.
person has_a address.
person has_a zip_code.
person has_a post_address.

leader are person.
secretary are person.
participant are person.

date are time.
```

course_series has_a name.
course has_a secretary.
course are course_series.
course has_a start_date.
course has_a exam_date.
course has_a leader.
course are course_series.
course has_a place.

room has_a building.
room has_a floor.

building has_a location.

lp are course_series.
lp has name = 'Logic Programming'.

researcher are participant.
researcher has occupation = 'Researcher'.

% ENTITY DESCRIPTION

lp1 is_a course
lp1 is_a lp.

lp2 is_a course.
lp2 is_a lp.

lp2 has place = 'Room 229'.
lp2 has leader = 'Tore Amble'.
lp2 has secretary = 'Florence Nightingale'.

'Room 229' is_a room.

.
.
.
.

9.7.1 Coupling semantic nets to tables

When facts are stored in tables, the semantic net must be combined with the relational table access at the bottom level. Then the semantic relations can be the attributes, prefixed with the table name to make the relations unambiguous.

X is_a Y :–key(Y,X).
X has Tab:Att = Val :–tabvalue(Tab,X,Att,Val),
   not(Val = nil).

?–table
   participant(full_name,first_name,last_name,
      occupation,phone,employer,address,zip_code,post_address).

%%% Participant database

participant('Mae West','Mae','West',
  'Scientific Assistant','(05)323709','Institute of Science',
  'Kings Street 29','5000','Bergen').

...

The above example automatically simulates the following definitions:

'Mae West' is_a participant.

'Mae West' has participant:full_name='Mae West'.
'Mae West' has participant:first_name='Mae'.
'Mae West' has participant:last_name='West'.

...

'Mae West' has participant:post_address='Bergen'.

9.7.2 Typical questions

The following questions are generic examples that by slight generalizations indicate what the knowledge base must be able to answer. The examples are given with a natural language formulation as initial comment.

(1) 'Who is the leader of the course?'
    ?–list X, L is_a course, L has leader = X.

(2) 'How many participants are there?'
    ?–list N, countall(Y,Y is_a participant,N).

(3) 'Which of the researchers are from Centre of Intelligence?'
    ?–list X, X is_a researcher,
      X has employer = 'Centre of Intelligence'.

(4) 'Which of the participants have no phone?'
    ?–list X, X is_a participant, not X has phone = Y.

(5) 'What is the name and phone of the secretary of the course?'
    ?–list(Name,Phone), L is_a course, L has secretary = S,
      S has name = Name, S has phone = Phone.

(6) 'Who are not participants?'
    ?–list X, X is_a person, not X is_a participant.

(7) 'Where is the course located?'
    ?–list X, L is_a course, L has place = X.

(8) 'Are there any companies with more than one participant?'
    ?–list C, C is_a company,
      countall(X,X has employer C,N), $N > 1$.

EXERCISES

9.1   Define two relations:

emp(Name,Dept,Salary)
dept(Department,Manager).

Write a Prolog query answering 'Which employees have bigger salaries than their managers?'

9.2   Redraft the course example with your class as a case. Discuss the semantic model, with the teacher or lecturer as a moderator. Put information about yourself into a common knowledge base. Try it out, and let it grow.

9.3   Define the following relations:

country(X) X is a country
sea(X) X is a sea
population(X,Y) X has population Y
border(X,Y) X and Y are bordering

Define a Prolog query to answer the question: 'Which country, bordering the Mediterranean, borders a country that is bordered by a country whose population exceeds the population of India?'

9.4   Make a query database of the results of the Winter Olympic Games, from the start in 1924 to the present day. One competition is the ski relay race over various distances. Include the items:

Year;
Place;
Competition;
Men or Women;
The first 6 places in each competition with result;
For team competitions (relay race, games):
the names of the 6 best nations;
and the members of the teams.

Answer the following query: 'Who were team members of the medal winners (1–3) in the ski race relays over any distance at least three times?'

9.5   Modify the predicates for handling relational databases so that multiple keys are stored without redundancies. (Hint: Use virtual tables.)

Chapter 10
Logic Programming and Compiler Writing

I think I am not.
Therefore, I am.

Freely from Descartes

10.1 Language processing

In almost all information systems with a user interface, there is a need for communication between the user and the system in a written language. Prolog is an excellent tool for processing language constructs, from simple command and query processors to algorithmic language compilers and natural language processing. One of the papers that introduced logic programming for compiler writing is Warren (1980). In this chapter, the compilation of a Pascal-like language is used to teach the principles of language processing. The same techniques can be used to process interface languages to knowledge systems, even though Pascal itself is not particularly well suited to that.

Language processing is traditionally divided into at least four stages:

- Lexical analysis   Collecting the input characters into meaningful units
- Syntax analysis   Recognizing the syntactic patterns of the text
- Semantic analysis   Analysing the meaning of the language constructs
- Production   Producing results, actions, code and answers

10.2 Lexical analysis

Lexical analysis is based on simple principles: the characters are collected into symbols which are looked up in the Prolog symbol table. There are three different classes of characters:

- identifier characters   *A–Z, a–z,* **0–9**
- delimiter characters   **(,) . : + − * / < >**
- dummy characters   **<blank> <new line>**

The Prolog library predicate **readsym(Symbol)** that reads one symbol or lexical unit from the current input stream:

(1) skips blank characters until it finds a non-blank character;
(2) if the character is a delimiter, it returns this as a single character identifier;
(3) otherwise, it assembles characters as long as they are identifier characters.

To simplify lexical processing problems, whole text files should be read as a list of symbols in Prolog, and then analysed. Consider the following Pascal program, for example:

```
PROGRAM p;
VAR m,n,x,y,gcd:integer;
BEGIN
  x := m;
  y := n;
  WHILE x <> y DO
  BEGIN
    IF x > y THEN x := x − y else
                      y := y − x
  END;
  gcd := x;
END.
```

This may be read by a predicate **scanner(File,List)**, and put into a list **List**:

[program,*p*,';',
var,*m*,',',*n*,',',*x*,',',*y*,',',gcd,':',integer,';',
begin,*x*,':','=',*m*,';',*y*,':','=',*n*,';',
while *x*,'<','>',do,begin,if,*x*,'>',*y*,then,*x*,':','=',
x,'−',*y*,else,*y*,':','=',*y*,'−',*x*,';',
end,';',gcd,':','=',*x*,';',end,'.']

Single quote marks identify characters that are delimiters. In this example, := is treated as two separate characters, ':', '='.

The predicate **scanner(File,List)**, which reads a file of text and produces the list, is meant to be a utility program, but is in itself a study of low-level text processing. Some comments have been added, but try to run the program in Figure 10.1 and study its behaviour. A brief example of the predicate's use is as follows:

> ?–scanner(user,*K*).
> |:Hello Dolly! (ctrl *Z*)
>
> *K* = [Hello Dolly,!]

```
% Program to scan a file and
% assemble identifiers and delimiters
scanner(File,List):-
   see(File),               % switch to reading File
   reapid(List),
   forget(ch(X)),
   seen.                    % switch back to user
reapid([IX|IY]):-           % produce the list by
   readsym(IX),             % the first symbol
   !,
   reapid(IY).              % and the tail
reapid([]).
readsym(Id):-
   assemble(X),             % assemble characters into a list;
   name(Id,X).              % name converts list X
                           % into an identifier Id

assemble([X|Y]):-
   next(X,idchar(X)),       % read first character X
   !,                      %
   amble(Y).               % read tail
assemble(X):-
   next(Y,dummy(Y)),!,      % skip dummy character
   assemble(X).
assemble([X]):-
   next(X,not idchar(X)),
   !.                      % stop read identifier
amble([X|Y]):-             % read tail of identifier
   next(X,idchar(X)),
   !,
   amble(Y).                                        (cont'd over)
```

Figure 10.1 A utility program for scanning files.

amble([ ]).	% possibly empty
next(*C*,*P*):–	% this is smart
not ch(*C*),	% no buffered character
!,	
get0(*C*),	% physical read character;
savech(*P*,*C*).	% put character in buffer
	% fail if condition *P* fails
next(*C*,*P*):–ch(*C*),	% there is a buffered character
not terminating(*C*),	
P,	% condition *P* is true
retract(ch(*C*)).	% retract buffer
savech(*P*,*C*):–not terminating(*C*),	
P,!.	% *P* is true, accept.
savech(*P*,*C*):–assert(ch(*C*)),	% otherwise, keep character,
fail.	% but fail
%%%Character set%%%%	
terminating(26).	% ASCII end_of_file character
%% terminating(63).	% if user wants return after '?'
dummy(32).	% blank
dummy(10).	% linefeed represents new line
idchar(*C*):–*C* > 65, *C* =< 90;	% capital letters
C >= 97, *C* =< 122;	% small letters
C >= 48, *C* =< 57.	% digits

Figure 10.1 (cont'd)

10.3 Syntax analysis

The purpose of syntax analysis is to recognize the structure of the text. If the text is correct, then the text follows a syntax definition. The simplest form of syntax definition is traditionally carried out using the so-called Backus Naur Form (BNF), which contains definitions of the form:

<program> ::= <declarations> <compound-statement> '.'

The meaning of this definition may be outlined informally as text in the format <program> is composed of text in the format <declarations> followed by text in the format <compound-statement> followed by a '.'. The identifiers in angle brackets are called **meta-variables** and denote **syntactic categories**. The syntactic category of the left hand side is defined in terms of the categories of the right hand side. The right hand side may contain a mixture of syntactic categories and fixed text. The fixed text is defined by **terminal symbols** in the grammar. The syntactic categories to the right are themselves defined in other syntactic definitions. Taken together, they constitute the entire description, which is called a **context-free grammar**. For example:

<declarations> ::= var <list-of-var-type>

A syntactic category may be defined in other ways, or with several equivalent right hand sides, separated by a | (meta-character). A sequence of a syntactic category may be defined as a new category by using recursion:

<list-of-vartype> ::= <var-type> |
  <var-type> <list-of-vartype>

For completeness, some grammar is listed in Table 10.1, sufficient for defining the Pascal program example.

Table 10.1 BNF grammar for a subset of Pascal.

<var-type> ::= <list-of-variables> : <type> ;
<list-of-variables> ::= <variable> |
  <variable> , <list-of-variables>
<type> ::= integer | real | boolean | char
<compound-statement> ::= begin <list-of-statements> end
<list-of-statements> ::= <statement> |
  <statement> ; <list-of-statements>
<statement> ::= <assignment> |
  <if-statement> |
  <while-statement> |
  <compound-statement>
<if-statement> ::= if <expression> then <statement>
  else <statement>
<while-statement> ::= while <expression> do <statement>
<assignment> ::= <variable> <assign-op> <expression>
<expression> ::= <term> | <term> <add-operator> <expression>
<term> ::= <factor> | <factor> <mult-operator> <term>
<factor> ::= <variable> | <constant>
<assign-op> ::= ':' '='   % two separate characters,
                            % due to primitive scanner
<add-operator> ::= + | −
<mult-operator> ::= * | /

The grammar in Table 10.1 is used to recognize a text which is presumably written according to that grammar. The recognition means breaking the text hierarchically into components so that each decomposition step corresponds to a grammatical rule. The grammar is deliberately written without left recursion, to avoid the endless recursion problem. By the explicit drawing of the tree in Figure 10.2, it is shown that the phrase $y := y - x$ conforms to the definition of <assignment>.

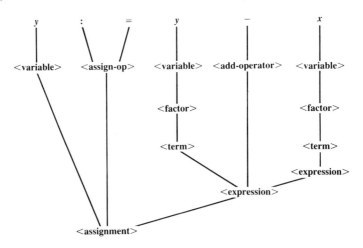

Figure 10.2   A syntax tree.

The purpose of syntax analysis in Prolog may be to build such syntax trees, using list structures which are logically equivalent to the trees. For the time being, to simplify the task, a Prolog program will be written that succeeds if and only if a list is an assignment statement. A good first approximation is to define

assignment(AST):–	% A list AST is an assignment
	% statement if there is a list
variable(V),	% V corresponding to a <variable> and
assign_op(AO),	% AO is an assignment operator;
append(V,AO,LEFT),	% V, AO gives the list LEFT, and
expression(E),	% there is a list E <expression>
append(LEFT,E,AST)	% which appended to LEFT gives AST
expression(E):– ...	

This straightforward use of predicate logic will work perfectly, except that the recursive **append** will give some slow solutions. A faster solution would be to use D-lists. However, a more direct approach can be made with ideas from D-lists applied directly, by maintaining the head and tail as separate arguments.

10.3.1 Clause grammar

The method described at the end of the previous section will be illustrated by a simple example. Consider the grammar:

> <term> ::= <factor> <add-operator> <factor>
> <add-operator> ::= '+'
> <factor> ::= *a*
> <factor> ::= *b*

An input phrase in list form might be:

> [*a*,'+',*b*]

Now define the predicate:

> term(*X*,*Z*)

so that X is a list, starting with symbols which define a <term>, and Z is the list of the remaining symbols. In other words, the difference between X and Z should be a <term>. For example:

> ?–term([*a*,+,*b*],[]).
> yes
> ?–term([*a*,+,*b*,arild],[arild]).
> yes

Then an intermediate list is used:

> term(*X*,*Z*):–
>   factor(*X*,*U*),
>   addoperator(*U*,*V*),
>   factor(*V*,*Z*)

or in words:

> There is a term between X and Z
>   if there is a factor from X to U,
>   an addoperator from U to V
>   and a factor from V to Z.

The predicate **addoperator** is defined by a constant symbol +. So a predicate symbol is defined which 'eats' one symbol, i.e.

> symbol([*S*|*Y*],*Y*,*S*).

Examples are as follows:

> ?–symbol(['+',b],[b],'+').
> yes
> ?–symbol([a,'+',b],X,'+').
> no
> ?–symbol([a,'+',b],Y,Z).
>   Y = ['+',b]
>   Z = a
> ?–symbol([b],X,S).
>   X = []
>   S = b
> addoperator(X,Y):–symbol(X,Y,'+').
> factor(X,Y):–symbol(X,Y,a).
> factor(X,Y):–symbol(X,Y,b).

Finally, consider in detail this analysis of a Prolog problem. The problem is:

> phrase([a,'+',b]).
> ?–phrase(X),term(X,[]).

This generates the following trace, where the quote marks around + are dropped:

> :–phrase(X),term(X,[]).
>   :–term([a,+,b],[]).
>   :–factor([a,+,b],U),addoperator(U,V),factor(V,[]).
>   :–symbol([a,+,b],U,a),addoperator(U,V),factor(V,[]).
>   :–addoperator([+,b],V),factor(V,[]).
>   :–symbol([+,b],V,+),factor(V,[]).
>   :–factor([b],[]).
>   :–symbol([b],[],a).
>   % backtrack
>   :–symbol([b],[],b).
> yes

Returning to the original example, with this notation, the little parser becomes

> assignment(FROM,TO):–
>   variable(FROM,X),
>   assignop(X,Y),

expression(*Y*,TO).

variable(FROM,TO):–symbol(FROM,TO,*S*),
    member(*S*,[*x*,*y*,gcd]).

assignop(FROM,TO):–symbol(FROM,*X*,':'),
    symbol(*X*,TO,'=').

expression(FROM,TO):–term(FROM,TO).
expression(FROM,TO):–term(FROM,*X*),
    addop(*X*,*Y*),
    expression(*Y*,TO).

addop(FROM,TO):–symbol(FROM,TO,*S*),
    member(*S*,['+','−']).

term(FROM,TO):–factor(FROM,TO).
term(FROM,TO):–factor(FROM,*X*),
    multop(*X*,*Y*),
    term(*Y*,TO).

factor(FROM,TO):–variable(FROM,TO).
factor(FROM,TO):–constant(FROM,TO).

symbol([*S*|TO],TO,*S*).

?–assignment([*y*,':','=',*y*,−,*x*],[]).

yes

?–assignment([*y*,−,*x*,':','=',*y*],[]).

no

10.3.2 Table-driven parsing

As in software engineering generally, Prolog programs are often made
table-driven, i.e. the logic initially assigned to the program itself is
replaced by a more general program and a data structure containing the
same information. In this way, the direct connection to explicit logic
thinking is lost, but flexibility is gained, together with security and the
possibility of insight, because the information in the program is available
as data. So, instead of:

assignment(FROM,TO):–
    variable(FROM,*X*),
    assignop(*X*,*Y*),
    expression(*Y*,TO).

write:

syntax(assignment,FROM,TO):–

```
syntax(variable,FROM,X),
syntax(assignop,X,Y),
syntax(expression,Y,TO).
```

Still, the Prolog program with the definitions contains much verbosity – **syntax** appears four times, for example. However, the essence of the information in the definition could be tabulated, in a table called **bnf(Left,Right)**.

bnf(assignment,(variable,assignop,expression)).

bnf(expression,term).

bnf(expression,(term,operator,expression)).

and the syntax analyser could be table-driven. This transformation is another case of meta-level logic. The rules are coded as terms, and interpreted by a meta-interpreter.

The final polishing operation is to make an infix operator ::= instead of **bnf**, so that the content of the table **bnf** is represented more stylishly. Round lists were purposely used for the right hand side, because that makes the parentheses redundant. In addition, square brackets are placed around the terminal symbols, so that Prolog can recognize them:

```
:–op(1100,xfx,::=).
    assignment ::= variable,assignop,expression.
    expression ::= term.
    expression ::= term,addoperator,expression.
    term ::= variable.
    assignop ::= ['='].
    addoperator ::= ['+'].
    addoperator ::= ['-'].
    variable ::= [x].
    variable ::= [y].
```

To avoid repeating almost the same example later, add a fourth argument to the syntax, to hold the syntax tree. This is explained later:

```
%% Prolog parser
syntax([S],FROM,TO,S):–
    !,
    symbol(FROM,TO,S).          % match S identically
syntax(CATEGORY,FROM,TO,[CATEGORY,TREE]):–
    (CATEGORY ::= RHS),
    rightside(RHS,FROM,TO,TREE).
```

```
rightside(FIRST,REST),FROM,TO,[TX|TY]):-
    !,
    syntax(FIRST,FROM,MIDDLE,TX),
    rightside(REST,MIDDLE,TO,TY).
rightside(SINGLE,FROM,TO,[TREE]):-
    syntax(SINGLE,FROM,TO,TREE).
symbol([X|Y],Y,X).
```

10.3.3 Constructing a syntax tree

The final refinement of the table-driven parser has given a predicate that produces a syntax tree. The syntax tree should be constructed from the same components as the symbol list, but with a hierarchical structure of nested lists conforming to the parse tree shown earlier in Section 10.3, and each node in the tree being prefixed with the syntactic category. The modification necessary was to add a fourth argument to the syntax predicate, and the right-hand side predicate, which we have already done.

10.3.4 Prettyprinting a syntax tree

The fourth argument builds a syntax tree, outside inwards. It may be used for further information processing, or for prettyprinting:

```
prettyprint(X):-
    indentprint(0,X).
indentprint(L,[X,Y]):-
    !,
    tab(L),
    output(X),
    M is L + 2,
    for(member(U,Y),indentprint(M,U)).
indentprint(L,X):-
    tab(L),
    output(X).
syntaxtree(S,X):-
    syntax(S,X,[],Tree),
    prettyprint(Tree).
?-syntaxtree(assignment,[y,':','=',y,'-',x]).
assignment
    variable
        y
    assign_op
```

$\vdots$

$=$

    expression

      term

        factor

          variable

            y

      addoperator

        $-$

    expression

      term

        factor

          variable

            x

10.4   Semantics and production

The next step is semantic analysis. This checks the meaning of a program, and finds errors not caught by the syntax check. For smaller systems, it is often possible, and even natural, to do the semantic check together with the production phase.

Below is a sketch of a code generator which takes as input a Pascal-like program in a list format, and generates code for a hypothetical one-accumulator machine NORTH-1. It has the following instruction set:

lda(X)	Load accumulator A with cell X
sta(Y)	Store A in cell Y
add(Z)	Add cell Z to A
sub(U)	Subtract cell U from A
jmp(L)	Jump to cell L
jaz(L)	Jump to L if a = 0
jan(L)	Jump to L if a < 0
jaf(L)	Jump to L if a <> 0
jap(L)	Jump to L if a >= 0

In addition, there is a pseudo-instruction **label(L)** defining the location of a label.

Assume the code is produced from a syntax tree slightly simplified from the earlier example. Instead of a component:

    [Category,List-of-components]

there is only:

    List-of-components

This is because the phrase structure is recognized as a part of the semantic analysis.

There are also some other simplifications made to study the code generation without too much noise. The program is assumed to be represented as follows:

```
program(
[begin,
  [x,':=',m],
  [y,':=',n],
  [while,[x,'<>',y],do,
  [begin,
    [if,[x,'>',y],then,
      [x,':=',[x,'-',y]],
        else,
      [y,':=',[y,'-',x]]
    ],
  end]
  ],
  [gcd,':=',x],
end]
).
```

A code generator may now be defined by printing out the symbolic assembly instructions that will perform the computation specified in the program. With the Pascal program listed above as source code, this compiler should produce assembly code. Logic variables represent temporary labels or locations. Their numbers are not significant, except those which are identical. The elaboration to produce fixed addresses or line numbers is left as an exercise.

```
compile:-program(COMPOUND),
  compound(COMPOUND).              % skip declarations here
compound([begin|STMLIST]):-stmlist(STMLIST).
stmlist([end]):-!.
stmlist([S|L]):-
  statement(S),
  stmlist(L).
statement([if|X]):-!,
  ifstm(X).
```
(cont'd over)

Figure 10.3 A compiler defining a code generation.

```
statement([while|X]):-!,
  whilestm(X).
statement([begin|X]):-!,
  stmlist(X).
statement(V):-assignment(V).
ifstm([TEST,then,S1,else,S2]):-
  iffalse(TEST,ELSELAB),
  statement(S1),
  emit(jmp(OUT)),
  emit(label(ELSELAB)),
  statement(S2),
  emit(label(OUT)).
whilestm([TEST,do,STM]):-
  emit(label(LOOP)),
  iffalse(TEST,OUT),
  statement(STM),
  emit(jmp(LOOP)),
  emit(label(OUT)).
assignment([V,':=',E]):-
  expression(E),                        % constructed to leave value in A
  emit(sta(V)).
iffalse([X,REL,Y],ELSE):-
  expression([X,'-',Y]),
  condjump(REL,ELSE).
condjump('=',ELSE):-emit(jaf(ELSE)).
condjump('<>',ELSE):-emit(jaz(ELSE)).    % jump to ELSE if
                                         % relation is false
condjump('>',ELSE):-emit(jaz(ELSE)),
  emit(jan(ELSE)).
condjump('<',ELSE):-emit(jap(ELSE)).
expression([X,OP,Y]):-!,
  expression(Y),
  emit(sta(TEMP)),
  expression(X),
  operation(OP,TEMP).
expression(X):-
  operand(X).
operand(X):-
  emit(lda(X)).                                         (cont'd)
```

Figure 10.3 (cont'd)

operation('+',TEMP):–emit(add(TEMP)).
operation('–',TEMP):–emit(sub(TEMP)).
emit(X):–output(X).

Figure 10.3 (cont'd)

```
lda(m)
sta(x)              % x := m
lda(n)
sta(y)              % y := n
label(_42)          % label 42 !
lda(y)
sta(_56)
lda(x)
sub(_56)            % A := x − y
jaz(_43)            % if A = 0 then goto label(_43)
lda(y)
sta(_100)
lda(x)
sub(_100)           % A := y − x
jaz(_86)            % if A = 0 then goto _86
jan(_86)            % if A < 0 then goto _86
lda(y)
sta(_124)
lda(x)
sub(_124)
sta(x)              % x := x − y
jmp(_87)
label(_86)          % label 86!
lda(x)
sta(_149)
lda(y)
sub(_149)
sta(y)              % y := y − x
label(_87)          % label 87!
jmp(_42)
label(_43)          % label 43!
lda(x)
sta(gcd)            % gcd := x
```

The compiler expert seeing the non-optimal parts of this code should have no difficulty in making improvements.

10.5   Advanced grammar formalisms

The BNF formalism is an easy to understand and powerful mechanism to express syntax. However, it has shortcomings which resemble those of propositional calculus: it lacks the generalization expressivity that stems from the variable concept of first order logic. There are two different ways to generalize the BNF formalism: these are two-level grammars, and attribute grammars.

10.5.1   Two-level grammars

Two-level grammars can be motivated by the desire to make the grammars shorter. For instance, grammars for defining a list of various categories must be repeated for each category of elements, as in this example:

> <list-of-argument> ::= <argument> |
>   <argument> ',' <list-of-argument>
> <list-of-variable> :: <variable> |
>   <variable> ',' <list-of-variable>

An interesting extension is to parametrize the categories in the BNF-table, to achieve two-level grammars. For example, **list(Category,Delimiter)** could define sequences of texts of the **Category**, separated by **Delimiter**, e.g.:

> listof(argument,',')
> listof(variable,',')

All that is necessary is to define such parametrized definitions in a BNF formalism, without any changes in the grammar interpreter.

> %% Two-level grammar primitives
> **listof(X,Del) ::= X.**
> **listof(X,Del) ::= X,Del,listof(X,Del).**
>
> **X / Y ::= X.**   % defines alternative right hand side
> **X / Y ::= Y.**   % ('|' is illegal as an operator)
>
> **seq(X) ::= X.**   % defines sequence of X
> **seq(X) ::= X,seq(X).**
>
> **opt(X) ::= [].**   % empty right hand side;
> **opt(X) ::= X.**   % an extended analyser will take it

In use this works as follows:

```
var_type ::= [var],listof(variable,[',']),[':'],type.
type ::= [integer].
type ::= [real].
variable ::= [a]/[b]/[c].
```

This covers variable Pascal declarations of the form:

VAR a,b,c. : integer

For example:

?–syntaxtree(var_type,[var,*a*,',',*b*,',',*c*,':',integer]).

gives:

```
var_type
  var
  listof(variable,[,])
    variable
      [a]/[b]/[c]
      [a]/[b]
        a
    ,
    listof(variable,[,])
      variable
        [a]/[b]/[c]
        [a]/[b]
          b
      ,
      listof(variable,[,])
        variable
          [a]/[b]/[c]
            c
  :
  type
    integer
```

This example shows how both the data and text, and the knowledge to understand the text, or grammar, can be treated in a uniform manner, resembling some kind of symmetry between knowledge and data that is typical in logic programming.

10.5.2 Attribute grammars

Attribute grammar is itself a discipline within compiler techniques, with its own formalism and taxonomy. Attribute grammars were introduced by

Knuth (1968) as a direct extension of context-free grammars. The purpose was to formalize part of the semantics in addition to the syntax. The semantics of a text is defined by attributes in each node in the syntax tree. The attributes contain information inherent to the node. This information is related to the nodes higher up and lower down in the tree, by computation rules. Because of the lack of input/output symmetry in languages other than Prolog, these rules may be very complicated regarding the sequence of computation.

For each syntactic class, there may be one or more attributes or values that are extracted from the text. They may be distributed around the syntax tree as a kind of parameter transfer. In Prolog, a kind of uninterpreted attribute grammar is implemented by simply making the syntactic categories parametrized terms instead of identifiers. After the parsing, the instantiation of these variables will be the result of the analysis. The evaluation of the instantiated expression is added as Prolog code in the appropriate places.

It is, in fact, possible to convert the whole code generator into attribute grammar, but a simple example is used to demonstrate the principle, and the code generator is left as an exercise. The demonstration is taken from Knuth (1968).

The syntax of binary floating point numbers can be described by context free-grammar:

s ::= *n*.
n ::= *k*.
n ::= *k*,['.'],*k*.
k ::= *b*.
k ::= *b*,*k*.
b ::= [0].
b ::= [1].

This grammar would accept such strings as:

[1,0,1]
[1,1,0,1,'.',0,1]

but would produce no result. The following parameters are introduced into the grammar:

s(**Result**)	Result is the rational result;
n(**Valueexp**)	Valueexp is the value expression, if evaluated, will be numeric result;
k(**Intvalue,Length**)	Intvalue is the integer value, Length is the length of the bitstring

b(**Bitvalue**)   Bitvalue is the bitvalue

With these attributes, the value expression is created alongside the parsing, and is eventually evaluated.

:–op(1100,*xfx*,::=).

s(Valuexp) ::= *n*(Valuexp).

n(*V*) ::= *k*(*V*).

n(*V*1+*V*2/2^Leng2) ::= *k*(*V*1,Leng1),['.'],*k*(*V*2,Leng2).

K(*V*,1) ::= *b*(*V*).

k(*Ve*1 ∗ 2 + *Ve*2,*L* + 1) ::= *k*(*Ve*1,*L*),*b*(*Ve*2).

b(0) ::= [0].

b(1) ::= [1].

Make two modifications to the earlier Prolog parser. First, allow the symbol [] to allow an empty right side. Secondly, let the term **prolog**(*X*) call the parameter *X* as a Prolog goal, and not represent any part of the text. In addition, let the two-level grammar primitives be a part of the formalism.

%% Attribute-grammar parser in Prolog

syntax((FIRST,REST),FROM,TO):–
  !,
  syntax(FIRST,FROM,MIDDLE),
  syntax(REST,MIDDLE,TO).

syntax(prolog(*P*),*X*,*Y*):–!,*X* = *Y*,*P*.   % activated only if
                                          % empty production;

syntax([],From,To):–!,From = To.   % empty option

syntax([*X*],From,To):–!,From = [*X*|To].   % terminal symbol
                                          % *X* may be a Prolog
                                          % variable

syntax(CATEGORY,FROM,TO):–
  (CATEGORY ::= RHS),
  syntax(RHS,FROM,TO).

analyse(*X*,*Y*):–
  syntax(*X*,*Y*,[]).

%%% End-of-Parser

bitstring([1,1,0,1,'.',0,1]).

test:–bitstring(*X*),
  analyse(*s*(*Z*),*X*),
  output(*Z*),

Num is *Z*,
output(Num).

?–**test**.

$((1 * 2 + 1) * 2 + 0) * 2 + 1 + (0 * 2 + 1) / 2^{(1 + 1)}$

13.25

Such techniques are applied in Chapter 11 on natural language processing.

To gain speed, it may be wise to compile attribute grammars into Prolog clauses. This is left as an exercise.

EXERCISES

10.1 Integrate the following programs:
- the scanner
- the syntax analyser
- the code generator

to make a compiler for the language subset indicated. Extend it as far as it goes.

10.2 The attribute grammar example was actually left recursive, because the ordinary rule for accumulating bit values *B* into numbers *N* is left recursive.

$$N := 2 * N + B$$

Explain, by testing or otherwise, how the parsing is made.

Make a right recursive attribute grammar for the same example, based on the rule

$$N := P * B + N$$
$$P := P * 2$$

where *P* represents the value of the bit position.

10.3 Extend the mini-compiler example to include the Pascal **for** statement.

10.4 Refine the code generator so as to generate the correct line numbers. Extend the code producing predicates with two arguments Line and Lineafter.

For example:

```
stmlist(Line,[end],Line):–!.          % empty statement
stmlist(Line,[S|L],Lineafter):–
   statement(Line,S,Next1),
   stmlist(Next1,L,Lineafter).
```

10.5 Write a program that translates attribute grammar productions such as:

$$n(E_1) ::= k(V_1,L_1),['.'],k(V_2,L_2).$$

into directly executable Prolog code in the following form:

$$n(E1,X0,X3):–k(V1,L1,X0,X1),$$
$$X_1 = ['.'|X2],$$
$$k(V2,L2,X2,X3).$$

The main program may look as follows:

```
compiledcg(Prologfile):–
   tell(Prologfile),
   for((L ::= R),compileproduction(L,R)),
   told.
```

where **compileproduction** makes the compilation of one production as shown.

10.6 If you have a Prolog implementation that can position the cursor on the screen, write a program that prints syntax trees top down:

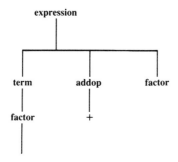

Chapter 11
Natural Language Processing

Time flies faster than light, my son!

Pauline Einstein

11.1 What is natural language?

The industrial societies are slowly entering the so-called information society, where most employees are handling information of some kind. The proliferation of computers in almost all aspects of professional work makes communication with humans and computers in a natural-like language a challenging possibility.

Natural language (NL) is the language people use to communicate with each other. We all use speech and text, and when we communicate, there are other forms of communication, such as body language, and implicit references to common knowledge which is understood without being stated explicitly.

Before going further, consider the phrase 'natural language'. The attitude of many people to artificial intelligence often applies to natural language also. There are two kinds of natural language:

- Pure natural language – language communication indistinguishable from human use of language;
- Applied natural language – the exchange of natural-like language that is understood both by untrained humans and computers.

11.2 Applied natural language

If written language only is considered, there are a number of things that make person–machine communication different from person–person communication. It is acceptable that the computer is a savant idiot which knows about a certain restricted topic, and nothing else. It is acceptable also that the system's understanding is limited to correct and complete sentences. As soon as the NL systems reach an acceptable level, therefore, they will be used more frequently, despite their difference from humans.

Already natural language systems are commercially available for questioning databases with a restricted but useful language subset. Example queries are 'What is the name and salary of the secretaries in New York city?' and 'Are there any women doctors in Boston?' In the next generation of computer systems, natural language processors will be much more advanced, and much more common.

11.3   Natural language systems in Prolog

Natural language processing in Prolog started with Prolog itself, when Colmerauer developed a Prolog-based natural language system called **metamorphosis grammar** in the early 1970s (Colmerauer *et al.*, 1978). The ideas developed here have since been applied in various logic grammar formalisms and systems, e.g. by Dahl (1977), who created a natural language system for Spanish. The most influential formalism, definite clause grammar, was developed by Pereira and Warren (1980) and was applied to make a knowledge-based system CHAT–80 for geography with a natural language interface. CHAT–80 can answer the following question *in extensio*:

'Which country, bordering the Mediterranean, borders a country that is bordered by a country whose population exceeds the population of India.'

The solution, Turkey, is found within 405 milliseconds.

The ORBI expert system for environmental resources (Pereira *et al.*, 1982) is also a Prolog-based system with very advanced language capabilities:

> Which descriptors of the aptitude intensive agriculture
  at point 56,78 are greater than 2 and equal to the
  factor *F*1 of point 12,95?
  ...
> And at point 65,78?
  ...

The system will understand that this is an ellipsis, whose meaning is found by replacing point 56,78 in the question above with point 65,78.

Today, these ideas are available for everyone's personal computers. A system called GEOBASE (Borland, 1986), which is similar to CHAT–80, can answer questions such as:

'Which state borders a state which borders Oregon?'

montana wyoming washington idaho utah
california oregon nevada arizona

Prolog is superbly adapted to the task of natural language
processing in all its main aspects:

- as a grammar formalism
- as a formalism for meaning representation
- as a knowledge-base query language

11.3.1 Definite clause grammars

These systems use a formalism called definite clause grammar (DCG).
DCG was introduced by Pereira and Warren (1980), where it was
presented as an alternative to the LISP-based system called augmented
transition networks or ATN (Woods, 1978). The definition of attribute
grammar used in this book is a simplified version of DCG.

In DCG, this example:

$$s([X,Y]) \longrightarrow np(X), vp(Y).$$

corresponds in this book to:

$$s([X,Y]) ::= np(X), vp(Y).$$

In addition, DCG automatically corrects left recursion in grammars,
making them right recursive. DCG also compiles grammar rules into
Prolog clauses for efficiency. This book will retain its own notation so as
not to confuse the two formalisms.

Earlier a syntax analyser for analysing artificial languages was
demonstrated. Now similar techniques for natural language are applied to
give some idea of how the new problems can be solved.

11.3.2 Natural language is ambiguous

Consider the sentence

'Time flies like an arrow.'

This innocuous little example is sometimes used to show the futility of
trying to analyse natural language sentences, because it has so many

interpretations, including the following:

- Time passes very quickly
- Time is flying with the same speed as an arrow
- Time is flying in a way similar to arrows
- Some time-related flies are fond of arrows (fruit flies like a banana)
- Some flies called 'Time flies' are fond of arrows
- Take the time of flies quickly!
- Take the time of flies as an arrow would do it!
- Take the time of flies with the form of an arrow
- Take the time of flies in the same way as you would take the time of an arrow!

This example is not to solve the natural language problem, but to discuss how Prolog can deal with this kind of ambiguity. A grammar for this may not necessarily be unambiguous. Consider this grammar, which is represented in BNF-form:

```
sentence ::= noun_phrase,verb_phrase.
sentence ::= verb,noun_phrase,comparison.
noun_phrase ::= common_noun.
noun_phrase ::= proper_noun.
noun_phrase ::= article,common_noun.
noun_phrase ::= composite_noun.
verb_phrase ::= verb,complement.
verb_phrase ::= verb,comparison.
complement ::= noun_phrase.
comparison ::= comparator,noun_phrase.
composite_noun ::= proper_noun,common_noun.
verb ::= [time].
verb ::= [flies].
verb ::= [like].
comparator ::= [like].
common_noun ::= [time].
common_noun ::= [flies].
common_noun ::= [arrow].
proper_noun ::= [time].
article ::= [an].
```

Now, by a slight extension of the attribute grammar parser that creates syntax trees, four different trees are generated (see Figure 11.1).

?–syntaxtree(sentence,[time,flies,like,an,arrow]),fail.

```
sentence
  noun_phrase
    common_noun
      time
    verb_phrase
      verb
        flies
      comparison
        comparator
          like
        noun_phrase
          article
            an
          common_noun
            arrow

sentence
  noun_phrase
    proper_noun
      time
    verb_phrase
      verb
        flies
      comparison
        comparator
          like
        noun_phrase
          article
            an
          common_noun
            arrow
```

Figure 11.1   Alternative syntax trees.

While ambiguity in compiler languages is considered an unaccept-
able fault of the language itself, it must be accepted in natural language,
because it is inherently ambiguous at all levels. A later semantic analysis
will show the ambiguity of 'like', and can check in a semantic net what
attributes are meaningful, for example:

- Time can fly in a certain sense
- A fly has no attribute which can have a value 'Time'

sentence
  noun_phrase
    composite_noun
      proper_noun
        time
      common_noun
        flies
  verb_phrase
    verb
      like
    complement
      article
        an
      noun_phrase
        common_noun
          arrow

sentence
  verb
    time
  noun_phrase
    common_noun
      flies
  comparison
    comparator
      like
    noun_phrase
      article
        an
      common_noun
        arrow

Figure 11.1   (cont'd)

- It is not relevant to take the time of flies

Before this grammar is left, it will be used for yet another demonstration of Prolog's ability to invert programs. Instead of analysing sentences for correctness, the parser and the grammar will be used to produce correct sentences, with some minor errors in inflection.

    ?–analyse(noun_phrase,*X*),all(*X*).

produces the following list:

> [time]
> [flies]
> [arrow]
> [time]
> [an,time]
> [an,flies]
> [an,arrow]
> [time,time]
> [time,flies]
> [time,arrow]

which are all noun-phrases according to the grammar. A call for

> ?–analyse(sentence,X),all(X).

produces a list of several hundred lines, too long to be included here, but amusing to read.

11.4 Soft Systems

Soft Systems (Amble *et al.*, 1982) is a Norwegian natural language system for communicating with computer systems, actually with the file handling system of the computer's operating system. The Soft System approach is simple and hopefully instructive. However, the topic has been changed from the operating system to the course knowledge base described earlier.

11.4.1 The Soft Systems language

Most NL applications are characterized as follows by:

- a vocabulary, handled by a lexical module
- a language competence, being the set of language constructs that is recognized. This is the syntactic component
- a semantic knowledge containing what the system knows about the concepts involved
- a knowledge base with knowledge about a specific domain, including interfaces to databases, operating systems

The main function of Soft Systems is to answer questions put to a database, e.g. a file catalogue.

An interesting decision for the language competence of Soft Systems was to orient it around what was called 'de-verbed language', under the motto:

'To be or to have, that is the question.'

In the language only the verbs 'be' and 'have' were taken as semantically primitive, while all other verbs had to be defined in terms of these. Participles such as 'healed' used functionally as adjectives are no exception, as in the example: 'My leg is healed.' Words such as 'does', and participles such as 'got', are considered noise words, as in the phrase 'has got'.

The motto also implies that only questions are analysed for their meaning, while the knowledge is given as a set of exact, unambiguous facts and rules. For example, the statement

'Most people have a car.'

is not representable. What may be represented is a database of cars and people, so that the question:

'Do most people have a car?'

means counting and comparing people with or without cars.

The rationale behind these ideas is that databases store information as factual data, organized by letting the attributes of the database be nouns.

In the table PERSON:

Date of Birth | Department | Address

questions may be reformulated:

- not   'When were you born?'
  but   'What is your date of birth?'
- not   'Where do you live?'
  but   'What is your address?'
- not   'I walked to the course today.'
  but   the explicit formulation of the conclusion of the state of matter you want the listener to draw:

    'I am tired.'
  or   'My house is close to the lecture room.'
  or   'Today my car is broken.'
  or   'My leg is healed.'

However primitive a language this is, it is flexible enough for applications with informed and tolerant users. The semantics is defined by a semantic net model, and is easily portable to other applications. Also, it is simple enough to be implemented by small research groups or even students. Although it is simple enough to understand it is complex enough to be interesting from an engineer's point of view. With respect to questions and answers it is closed, i.e. the information needed to answer a de-verbed question can be defined by de-verbed sentences. The information processing is therefore focused – what a computer can use is expressible in this language subset.

11.4.2   Sample questions

Now, the Soft System approach will be applied to the knowledge base of the logic programming course description. For that case, a Prolog-based query language was developed, and several examples were given. The queries were purposely presented with natural language phrases as informal descriptions of the meaning of the questions. This section describes how to process the natural language queries directly. It is left as a challenging project exercise for advanced students to elaborate it.

The following questions must be answered from the information stored in the semantic net of the course example. However, there may be additional information necessary to capture all the variants of the same questions. Below is also a list of questions, but not all of the questions are correct.

'Who is the leader of the Prolog course?'

'How many participants are there?'

'Which of the researchers are from RUNIT?'

'Which of the participants have got no phone?'

'What is the name and phone number of the secretary of the course?'

'Who are not participants?'

'Where is the course location?'

'Has I got any copanies with with more than one parcitipants?'

11.4.3   The dialogue context

The meanings of all the phrases here are to be understood in the framework of one person communicating by natural language text to a computer. The answers to the questions are presented back to the user.

The answer sets are supposed to be a sequence of factual answers. There are two kinds of questions:

- Context-free questions, having no reference to previous answers. For example: 'What researchers are there?'
- Context-sensitive questions referring to previous answers: 'Which of these are from Bergen?'

Each question/answer in the dialogue represents a theme, which is the class qualifier (e.g. researcher) representing the type of answer. In theory, all the answer sets could be remembered by the computer. However, as it is cumbersome to refer to all of them in natural language, a simplification is understood. If there is more than one answer set for a theme, the system remembers the first and the last answer (set) – any intermediate answers are forgotten. It is a part of an intelligent dialogue handler to find out which answer sets are referred to.

11.4.4 The reference model

In Soft Systems there are four distinct phases (see Figure 11.2). They were chosen because it is considered good engineering practice to separate subproblems into submodules to keep each module manageable. The architecture is reflected in the main Prolog program:

```
soft_system:-
    lexical(user,Wordlist),
    syntax(Wordlist,Syntaxtree),
    semantics(Syntaxtree,Queryexpression),
    query(Queryexpression).
```

The information in the semantic net is available as global information.

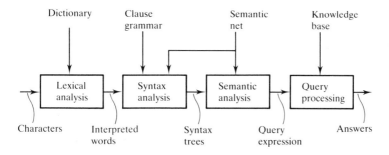

Figure 11.2   The reference model of Soft Systems.

11.4.5 Lexical analysis

The task of the lexical preprocessor for natural language is to scan the characters of the input file, assemble strings into words, analyse each word for morphological inflections, and to perform spelling corrections.

There are many strategies for spelling corrections. From an implementation point of view, as seen from the rest of the system, it is not important which strategy is chosen, the important thing is to live with it and let spelling correction be adapted to new environments when necessary.

An important design criterion is the limit to allowable errors. By using expert system techniques, it is possible to calculate probabilities for typing errors, so that with a combination of statistical calculation involving both lexical, syntactical and even semantical considerations of surrounding fragments, a meaning can be extracted from a very fuzzy text. But, while such techniques are a must for speech understanding, a quite acceptable human reaction to nonsense or complexity is to reject it and ask for a clarification. In Soft Systems, a modest approach is adopted. It represents a plausible sloppy typist. *A priori*, all words could be interpreted as a name, not relying on any capital letter convention, as in the example: 'the book on the Wall by green and wall is Green'. All words could then be presented to the syntax analyser in two forms:

- the exact representation (in case that it is a name),
- the most probable correction.

The most probable correction is chosen according to the following criteria:

- If the word could be transformed from a correct known word by
  - one additional charracter
  - one missing caracter
  - one wrong cjaracter
  - two cahracters interchanged
  then the known word is plausible.

If there is one plausible word, it is taken. If there are several, Soft Systems considers only interpretation of the word as a name. However, a more sophisticated analyser should be able to carry the whole list of plausible words.

Another shortcut in Soft Systems is that only the root form of the known word is used. The actual reason for that derives from the **attitude model** of Soft Systems. There are at least three attitudes generally held in handling erroneous input:

- The post office detective's attitude, to find the correct address at all costs;
- The teacher's attitude, to reject and correct all errors (as teachers do);
- The servant's attitude to understand an order when there is only one plausible interpretation.

Sometimes it suffices to use only the root form to understand the plausible interpretation of a sentence, while the information thereby lost either could only be used for correction of the user, or was redundant information which the system could make no use of.

Output from the lexical analyser is a list of quadruples:

w(word,class,root,found),

where:

word	is the actual word, though in small letters only;
class	is the main word class if found, or 'id' for name;
root	is the root form of the most plausible word;
found	is 1 if the word or a legal inflection was found with perfect match;
	0 if found with imperfect match;
	−1 not found (unknown name).

As an example, take the not quite correct sentence:

'Has I got any copanies with more than 1 parcitipants?'

is represented as a list of quadruples

```
[w(has,verb,have,1),
 w(i,pronoun,i,1),
 w(got,verb,get,1),
 w(any,art,any,1),
 w(copanies,noun,company,0),
 w(with,prep,with,1),
 w(more,adv,more,1),
 w(than,adv,than,1),
 w(1,num,1,1),
 w(parcitipants,noun,participant,0)
]
```

11.4.6 Syntax analysis

The purpose of a natural language system is not to study syntax as such, but to understand and process queries, commands and information. Unless an NL system is based on learning, as in the case of humans, the rules of the syntax must be defined. This is carried out here with a tiny subset, but hopefully the principles are clear, so that students may continue the analysis.

Every complete sentence has a main verb at its root ('has' in this sentence). Sentences are modelled as

subject	who is doing it
verb	what is done
object	what is done to

The subject and object are both described by noun phrases, of which there are two kinds:

classes, expressed by common nouns
entities, expressed by names.

To each class expression a list of properties is attached. These properties are expressed by adjectives or relative phrases. For example:

the	article
dull	adjective
prolog	noun prefix
course	class
which is dull	relative sentence

The semantics of class expressions is to denote the set of members of the class, restricted by the property list. Components in the syntax trees are terms such as:

$ent(X,Y)$	an X such that X is Y
$theof(X,Y)$	an X such that Y has X

11.4.7 A short attribute grammar for de-verbed language

For simplicity, only the root forms occur in the terminals. However, the whole syntax parser operates on the output from the lexical preprocessor, and will know when to use the root form, and when to use the original form.

We will start with the definitions necessary to answer one question. However, all the definitions are generalizations beyond the strictly necessary. The syntax analysis is based on a version of the two-level attribute grammars, as explained in Chapter 10. That is, it builds up an annotated tree of our own design.

Domain independent grammar

sentence(*S*) ::= question(*S*).

question(which(*C*,*V*,*N*)) ::= *wh*1(*C*),verb(*V*),np(*N*).

*wh*1(person) ::= [who].
*wh*1(*C*) ::= [which],class(*C*).

verb(is) ::= [is].
verb(has) ::= [has].

np(ent(id,*X*)) ::= ident(*X*).
np(ent(*C*,(*P*1,*P*2))) ::= prefixes(*P*1),class(*C*),postfixes(*P*2).
np(theof(Att,Ents)) ::= *np*(Att),[of],*np*(Ents).

prefixes((*P*1,*P*2)) ::= opt(art),adjectives(*P*1),nounprefixes(*P*2).

adjectives([]) ::= [].
adjectives([*A*1|*A*2]) ::= adjective(*A*1),opt([and]),adjectives(*A*2).

nounprefixes([]) ::= [].
nounprefixes(*N*1) ::= ident(*N*1).

postfixes([]) ::= [].
postfixes(*A*) ::= postfix(*A*).
postfixes([*A*|*B*]) ::= postfix(*A*),[and],postfixes(*B*).

postfix(*A*) ::= *wh*,[is],adjectives(*A*).

wh ::= [who].
wh ::= [which].
wh ::= [that].

art ::= [the].
art ::= [a].

hasgot ::= [has].

ident([*A*]) ::= idword(*A*).
ident([*A*|*B*]) ::= idword(*A*),ident(*B*).

Domain dependent words

The following definitions are in practice gathered from the semantic net of the application domain. The definitions needed for the questions are as follows:

idword(prolog) ::= [prolog].
idword(bergen) ::= [bergen].

idword(runit) ::= [runit].
adjective(dull) ::= [dull].

class(leader) ::= [leader].
class(course) ::= [course].
class(researcher) ::= [researcher].
class(secretary) ::= [secretary].

Who is the leader of the dull Prolog course

The parser is naturally connected to the scanner predicate of the previous chapter. Assume ".","?" and "!" are defined as terminating characters, so that the scanner program make the parser stop scanning and start analysing.

?–scanner(user,*P*),
   analyse(sentence(*S*),*P*).

|: who is the leader of the dull prolog course?

S = which(person,is,theof(ent(leader,(([],[]),[])),
   ent(course,(([dull],[prolog]),[]))))

11.4.8 Semantic analysis with semantic nets

The purpose of selecting the de-verbing restriction on the language is that the semantics of de-verbed language is approximated by the content of a semantic net, as explained. The semantic analysis should end with a check on the meaning of the sentences. There are many definitions of the meaning of 'meaning'. This book will follow the very pragmatic thinking of axiomatic semantics implicit in logic, that a word has no meaning in itself except for relations it bears to other words. Therefore, the semantic analysis will be a check for the coherence of the words in the question, compared with the definition in the semantic net. To illustrate this, one test is whether or not an attribute 'belongs' to a class (see Figure 11.3). Consider the following sentences.

'What is the address of the course?'

The sentence is syntactically correct, and should be recognized as a question which deserves an answer. However, the question is seman tically wrong, because an address is not defined for a course, so the answer should be an indication of the error.

'What is the address of the participants?'

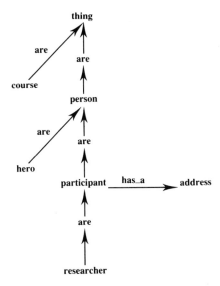

Figure 11.3   A semantic net for researchers.

Here address is defined as an attribute of participant, so there is no problem.

'What is the address of the researchers?'

Now, address is not directly defined for researchers, but researchers are a kind of participant, and as such inherit the address attribute.

'What is the address of the persons?'

Unfortunately, persons have no address attribute, and do not inherit any from a super class. So, the query implicitly contains a qualification that can be formulated as:

'What is the address of the kind of persons that have an address?'

These kinds of persons are the participants, and there may be others.

11.4.9 Query processing

After the semantic analysis of a syntax tree, and a transformation of the tree to a suitable form, where all semantic ambiguities and discrepancies have been removed, a query processor is called. If there is a larger database at the bottom, a query optimization is needed. The problems involved therein are described in Warren (1981), where the queries are translated into efficient executable Prolog code.

A query can be processed in an interpretive way, using the semantic net as a knowledge base. In this way, the following query is generated:

```
answer(Z) <-
    X is_a course,
    X has Someattribute = prolog,
    X is_ dull,
    X has leader = Z.
```

11.5 Pure natural language

Prolog can be applied to person–machine communication. The natural language text is parsed and given a formal representation. It is fair to say that natural language processing is a knowledge-intensive problem, while the parsing problems are technically soluble. In the example following, they are trivial, but in general they may be computationally demanding. Our example is carried out on a logical level, however, some infix operators are defined to make the logic more readable.

The following scenario outlines how a situation is described in logic:

> In a room, there are two people, she and he.
> She says: 'It is cold in here.'
> He closes the window.

He interprets the utterance as the request: 'Shut the window.' The following paraphrase is an attempt to fill the gap between the original and the interpreted sentence by logic. If a human should do such a detailed reasoning explicitly, it would be a symptom of insanity. The purpose of the example is to show how much knowledge humans process unconsciously.

11.5.1 A logic for commonsense knowledge

Commonsense knowledge is modelled as logical rules, even if they cannot be proven. The main predicate for this model is:

knows(A,K,S)   *A* knows that *K* is true in situation *S*

There could also be an alternative predicate:

believes(*A*,*K*,*S*)

if it was necessary to distinguish belief from reality. Truth could be modelled with a predicate:

holds(*K*,*S*)

Alternatively, truth could be modelled as the knowledge of a postulated omniscient being, 'god', say, i.e. **knows(god,*K*,*S*))**. The following rule would then be adequate:

knows(*A*,*K*,*S*) :– believes(*A*,*K*,*S*),holds(*K*,*S*).

However, this distinction is not needed in this example. This example can be solved by using only one global state, so the state variable can be left out. The **knows** relation becomes binary, and can be represented by an infix operator:

X **knows** *Y*

This and several other operators are defined as right associative operators so that parentheses to the right are unnecessary.

X **knows** *Y* **knows** *Z* = (*X* **knows** (*Y* **knows** *Z*))

11.5.2 Why do we do what we do?

The rationales behind our actions are as manifold as life itself. A certain class of rational actions is characterized by

- the actions are good for someone
- the actions are non-redundant.

In a more egocentric interpretation, an action is rational if it improves the welfare of the actor, directly or indirectly. In the following example, an action is defined as rational if:

- it solves the problem directly (the manual approach)
- it is a request for someone to solve it (the procedural approach)
- it indicates enough information from which another person is able to deduce a wish for a solution (the declarative approach)

For the Prolog program below, the call

   ?–rational(*X*).

will give three answers:

   X = she does perform(shut(window))
   X = she does request(shut(window))
   X = she does indicate(she is cold)

11.5.3   A Prolog program for a room situation

:–op(999,*xfy*,[knows,likes,dislikes,does,wants,is_attending,
   can_hear,inside,causes,implies,initiates,obeys]).

% :–op(700,*xfx*,is) is predefined and used here without evaluation

rational(*X* does *Y*):–
   situation(*S*),
   X knows *S* implies *X* is uncomfortable,
   X knows *T* implies *X* is comfortable,
   X knows Action causes *T*,
   (*X* does *Y*) initiates Action.

(*Y* does perform(*Z*)) initiates *Z*.   % the direct solution
                                          is to do it oneself

(*S* does request(*Y*)) initiates *Y*:–   % the more indirect way is
   H can_hear *S*,   % to request it
   S knows *H* obeys *S*.

(*S* does indicate(*C*)) initiates *Z*:–   % the most indirect way is
   H can_hear *S*,   % to indicate it
   S knows *H* wants *S* is comfortable,
   S knows *H* knows *C* implies *S* is uncomfortable,
   S knows *H* knows *D* implies *S* is comfortable,
   S knows *H* knows *Z* causes *D*.

Y knows *X* wants *Y* is comfortable:–
   Y knows *X* is_attending *Y*.

Y knows *X* obeys *Y*:–
   Y knows *X* is_attending *Y*.

X knows *Y* causes *Z*:–
   X knows *U* implies *Z*,
   X knows *Y* causes *U*.

H can_hear *S*:–
   situation(*S* inside *R*),

```
        situation(H inside R),
        not(S = H).
```

situation(she inside room).
situation(he inside room).
situation(she is cold).

she knows he is_attending she.

she knows (she is cold) implies (she is uncomfortable).
she knows shut(window) causes (she is warm).
she knows (she is warm) implies (she is comfortable).

she knows he knows X:–   % by no means obvious
    she knows X.

he knows she knows X:–   % by no means obvious
    he knows X.

11.6   Natural language processing in the future

Natural language communication should have many applications; access to databases is only one. Conversing with computers in a network is another, where the need for asking questions is urgent because of unfamiliar environments at remote computers. The most important application, however, will be in connection with an intelligent knowledge-based system that can understand the questions using knowledge-based techniques, and may itself access less intelligent data processors when necessary.

Natural language is knowledge intensive, and a common world knowledge system will be a large, shared component of many intelligent knowledge-based systems of the future. It is certain that a proper understanding of natural English will require a large program, and a large software engineering project. It seems obvious that such a program must have the language capabilities and general knowledge to be able to read new knowledge by itself from natural language sources that can be prepared to be read by both humans and computers. Such a program will exist in several layers, incorporating expert systems technology just to handle its own knowledge base. Such a program will also require special hardware for efficiency reasons.

On the other hand, intensive research is being carried out in the USA, the UK and Japan, large programs are within the capabilities of software engineering, and appropriate hardware will be with us in a couple of years.

EXERCISES

11.1 Write a Prolog program to understand the following type of dialogue:

> All boys are something.
> Some boys are good.
> Some boys are bad.
> Magnus is a boy.
> Magnus is good.
> Is Magnus good?
>   yes
> Who is good?
> Magnus

11.2 Write a Prolog program that will recognize names and addresses from a name list, with the same competence as yourself regarding background information, misspelling, truncation and other distortions.

11.3 Write an attribute grammar clause to capture the sentence: 'Which country, bordering the Mediterranean, borders a country that is bordered by a country whose population exceeds the population of India?'

11.4 Write a natural language system to analyse sentences in naturally readable logic, and translate them into Prolog. For example:

> a man is the grandfather of a person if
>   this man is the father of another person and
>   this other person is the parent of the person.

> a man is the parent of a person if
>   this man is the father of the person.

> a woman is the parent of a person if
>   this woman is the mother of the person.

> Olav is the father of Harald.
> Harald is the father of Haakon
> Harald is the father of Martha

Chapter 12
Logic for Problem Solving

To understand something
is to understand
how little there
is to understand
from it.

Freely from Piet Hein

12.1 What is the problem?

The ability to solve problems, where the solution can be found by
deduction from the evidence, is an integral part of human intelligence,
and is necessary in knowledge-based systems to be called expert systems.
The problem-solving capability of expert systems is not necessarily of a
deep or complicated nature. Human expertise, for example, usually comes
from applying a large number of fragments of knowledge adequately.

The problems that appear may be of different kinds with respect to
how well defined they are. Many human problems in everyday life are not
well defined at all, and their solution implicitly defines the criteria by
which they are solved. In knowledge processing environments, however,
programmers are forced to handle well-defined problems, because the
definitions of what problems are cannot be left to the computer.

A problem is well defined if it is not a problem in itself to check
how good the solution is when it is found. However, finding optimal
solutions may still be a computational challenge. Readers with some
background in complexity theory (Garey and Johnson, 1980) should
compare this with the definition of the hardness of problems. In
complexity theory, the computing model that measures complexity is an
infinitely parellel computer that finds all the solutions. This process is
comparable with the task of a single processor to check one solution.

12.2 Generalized function application

Many problems are implicitly well defined by generalized function
application (see Figure 12.1). The specification is the information that

governs the behaviour of the function. It may be empty, i.e. the specification is compiled with the function, which is interpreted by the interpreter. However, in symbolic processing, the specification is usually explicitly represented, and the function is a high-level interpreter of this information.

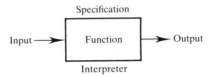

Figure 12.1   Generalized function application.

The usual way to implement a function is to fix the interpreter and specification to give input, and wait for the output. This is called **function application**. Many problems are defined by **function inversion**. That is, keeping the interpreter and specification fixed, giving the output, and then trying to find an input that would give that output. A good example of this is symbolic integration.

A more advanced problem is **function induction**, where the interpreter is fixed, a **set** of input/output pairs is given. The problem is to find the specification of a function that, when applied to all the inputs, gives the outputs. For instance let the input set be phrases of a language, and the output be approval or disapproval; the function would be a table-driven parser, and the specification would be produced as a grammar for the language.

The most advanced problem in this framework would be to find an interpreter that fits specifications, inputs and outputs.

12.3   Algorithmic versus search problems

The most important classifications of problem solving are:

- there is an algorithmic solution,
- the solution must be found by search.

To start with a problem which has an algorithmic solution, consider the well-known Tower of Hanoi problem in Figure 12.2. On peg A, there is a heap of discs of decreasing size. The problem is to find a sequence of moves so that all the discs can be moved one at a time from A to C, using any peg for temporary storage, but at no time is a larger disc allowed to be put upon a smaller disc.

The solution to this problem lies in inductive thinking and a recursive formulation. To move a stack of N consecutive discs from X via Y to Z:

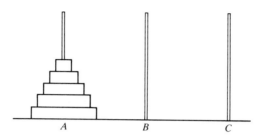

Figure 12.2   The Tower of Hanoi.

> move the stack of the uppermost $N - 1$ discs from X via Z to Y
> move the disc (stack of size 1) from X to Z
> move the stack of $N - 1$ discs from Y via X to Z

The solution in Prolog begs itself:

```
move(1,X,_,Z):-!,
   out('move disc from '),out(X),out(to),output(Z).
move(N,X,Y,Z):-N1 is N - 1,
   move(N1,X,Z,Y),
   move(1,X,_,Z),
   move(N1,Y,X,Z).
:-move(3,a,b,c).
```

move disc from *a* to *c*
move disc from *a* to *b*
move disc from *c* to *b*
move disc from *a* to *c*
move disc from *b* to *a*
move disc from *b* to *c*
move disc from *a* to *c*

Apart from the elegance of the solution, the length of the solution increases exponentially with the number of pegs, actually $2^N - 1$. If there were no algorithm, and the sequence had to be found by trial and error, the amount of search to find a sequence of moves would be super-exponential: $3^{(2^N - 1)}$. The gain by the knowledge of the algorithm is enormous, so the maxim is: 'If you have an algorithm, use it!'

12.4   Knowledge for problem solving

Knowledge is often classified into three categories:

Facts, corresponding to a database,
Rules, giving relations between facts,
Heuristics, how and when to apply the rules.

Whereas the facts and rules define the solution space, heuristics must be used to guide the search to solve practical problems. To illustrate the problem solving of well-defined problems in Prolog, consider some simple problems. The simplest of all problems is when the solution lies explicitly in the question, for example:

Find an X such that $X = 6$.

What colour do red roses have?

Even if such problems do not always occur, it is only a small step to problems of finding a solution such that a constraint is fulfilled, such as:

Find an X that is mortal.

Such **constraint-satisfaction problems** are automatically solved by Prolog by a program that checks the correctness of a formally described problem. This is, in any case, the least to be done to define the problem properly. For small problems, not to mention countless intermediate problems, this is sufficient, and the user has been relieved from the error-prone programming task.

To be more precise, Prolog reduces constraint-satisfaction problems to automatic search. The set of possible solutions is called the **search-** or **solution space**. If this is small, the solutions are generated automatically, otherwise more control information must be included in the programs. In the worst case, this control problem causes so many *ad hoc* control constructions that Prolog loses the benefits of automatic search, and becomes inferior to other languages.

Prolog's search strategy is goal oriented. This means that it starts with a more or less instantiated conclusion, and reasons backwards until it matches known evidence. The solution often comes as the instantiation of the variables in the conclusion. This strategy is usually adequate, but sometimes the search must be controlled in specific ways by means of meta-level programming techniques, to model other search strategies, e.g.:

- forward reasoning,
- reasoning with delaying undecidable conditions,
- heuristic search.

12.4.1 Generate-and-test

A combination of algorithm and search is applicable to the so-called nine-digit problem.

Find a nine-digit number:

$$D1,D2,D3,D4,D5,D6,D7,D8,D9$$

so that all digits are different, none of them is 0, and for each n, the number composed of the first n digits is divisible by n.

If the solution were proposed to be:

987654321

this fails, because the seven-digit number 9876543 is not divisible by seven.

The problem is exponential in nature, i.e. the solution space increases exponentially with the length of the number. Without knowing the answer and without an infinite number of programs attempting the problem in parallel, the only thing to be done is to search for a candidate, applying as much knowledge as is known, and then test if a candidate really is a solution. This **generate-and-test** paradigm is fundamental to mechanized problem solving, but the way it is carried out can make a great difference to its success.

The generate-and-test paradigm is illustrated in Figure 12.3. The constraint knowledge is the rules for the correctness of the solution, while the heuristic knowledge is the knowledge of how to search intelligently. If the amount of heuristic knowledge is small, there will be many candidates for the solution, which may take a long time to arrive at. In the nine-digit problem, there are $9! = 362\ 880$ permutations of the nine digits that *a priori* could be solutions.

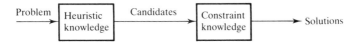

Figure 12.3   Generate and test principles.

If knowledge of number theory is applied, however, the heuristic knowledge-base is greater, but the number of candidates is much smaller. For instance, finding that the fifth digit must be five reduces the search space by a factor of nine.

A skilled mathematician can solve this problem with few actual tests for divisibility – try it yourself. But, more importantly, unskilled mathematicians can formulate the problem in Prolog, put in as much knowledge as they have, and leave the rest to the automatic search. This co-operation between available expertise and automatic search for a solution is at the core of knowledge engineering.

The problem in this form is given as an exercise. The number is to be represented as a list of integers, e.g.:

[9,8,7,6,5,4,3,2,1]

so the exercise is also a perfect one for list processing.

12.4.2 Generate-or-test

Prolog is symmetric, in principle, between generating a solution, and testing if a solution is acceptable. This **generate-or-test** feature is an extremely useful property, if used with care. It helps creative thinking, because the programmer may concentrate on the task of writing a complete program for testing a solution. This definition represents the least of what a programmer has to specify, and, if done with skill, the same program will also be able to generate the solution.

However, if used uncritically, the program may be grossly inefficient. It may not terminate at all, and, if combined with cut operations, will usually be wrong in its suggested solution. Prolog searches for solutions to combined constraints in the order that the conditions are given. So there is a responsibility on the programmer to arrange the conditions in such a manner as to minimize the search. Generate-or-test symmetry can be used here, in which each predicate will instantiate the free variables occurring in a condition to all possible solutions. However, there are certain predicates that are not of this kind:

- inequality tests
- predicates involving numerical operations

Suppose there are a number of boxes and pyramids. The problem is to find two boxes that are different.

```
box(a). box(b). box(c).
pyramid(d). pyramid(e).
?- box(B1),box(B2),
   ne(B1,B2),
   all([B1,B2]).
[a,b]
[a,c]
[b,a]
[b,c]
[c,a]
[c,b]
```

With the definition

> ne(X,Y):–not $X = Y$.

this works well, because the two box predicates assure that both X and Y are instantiated. However, if the sequence were reordered:

> ?–box($B1$),
>   ne($B1,B2$),
>   box($B2$),
>   all([$B1,B2$]).

it would call ne($B1,B2$) with the last variable $B2$ free, but ne($B1,B2$) would fail because it is defined by

> not $X = Y$

which fails when X and Y are unifiable. It is impossible to decide correctly whether two terms are different if they are not both fully instantiated. X is substituted for a in the first clause, causing the condition ne(X,a) to be rejected. However, X may very well be instantiated to b later, which would let ne(X,a) succeed if the test could be postponed.

If ne($B1,B2$) were test-symmetric, the program would generate all possible pairs of objects that were different. For demonstration, we will make such a test-symmetric predicate ne (not equal), but since inequality is in fact an infinite relation, it must be demonstrated restricted to a closed world, with only the objects a, b, c, d and e.

> object(a). object(b). object(c).
> object(c). object(d).
> ne(X,Y):–object(X),
>   object(Y),
>   not $X = Y$.

With this definition of ne, the following:

> ?–box($B1$),
>   ne($B1,B2$),
>   box($B2$),
>   all([$B1,B2$]).

gives the correct answers:

> [a,b]
> [a,c]

$[b,a]$
$[b,c]$
$[c,a]$
$[c,b]$

The point is that the price paid for making the **ne** test symmetric was an exhaustive search through the 'whole world', which fortunately was small in this example.

The intelligence of the Prolog mechanism lies in the instantiation of variables as solutions to local problems. If programmers are forced to instantiate the variable to something just to make the inequality test consistent, they thereby make **redundant instantiations**, which have nothing to do with the problem. There are no ideal solutions to this problem in Prolog, but some other logic programming languages, such as Prolog-II (Giannesini *et al.*, 1986), have implemented various extensions to Prolog, allowing uninstantiated goals to be postponed as long as necessary.

A small extension to the Prolog search mechanism is implemented here in Prolog, to defer undecidable tests. The extension is yet another example of meta-level logic; the price paid is speed.

12.5   A meta-problem solver

The key to the meta-problem solver is the predicate:

   prove(Goal,Oldunless,Newunless)

where:

- **Goal**   is a Prolog goal to be solved,
- **Oldunless**   is a set of undecided conditions in negated form,
- **Newunless**   is the new set of undecided negated conditions still not resolved during the proof of **Goal**.

The undecided conditions in this case are restricted to conditions of the type

   not $X = Y$

Ideally, these conditions should be tested as soon as any substitutions instantiate some parts of the terms X or Y. However, this is not feasible in sequential Prolog and a less satisfactory solution must be accepted. The list **Oldunless** is checked each time the meta-interpreter matches a condition to a fact. The list, which is logically a conjunct of inequalities, is kept in a negated form as a disjunction (';') of identities ('=='), so that it can be tested as a Prolog goal itself in one call:

:–not U.

Using the negated form saves time and space.

This strategy guarantees that the **Oldunless** list is checked regularly, because the branch on the extreme left of the Prolog search tree regularly ends in a fact.

```
% Meta-problem solver
:–op(1199,xfx,'<–').
solve(Y):–prove(Y,false,C).
prove((P,Q),U,W):–
    !,
    prove(P,U,V),
    prove(Q,V,W).
prove(not X = Y,P,C):–
    X == Y,!,fail.                    % since X == Y,
                                      % not X = Y will always fail

prove(not X = Y,P,P):–
    not X = Y,!.                      % not X = Y succeeds because
                                      % X = Y is impossible at present.
                                      % Hence, X = Y will also be
                                      % impossible later.

prove(not X = Y,P,(X == Y;P)):–!.    % X = Y is not decidable.
                                      % X == Y is added to the list of
                                      % constraints that can be tested
                                      % as a Prolog goal.

prove(X,U,U):–
    not((X <– Any)),                  % X is not determined by a rule
    !,
    X,
    not U.                            % The test for admissibility is
                                      % only performed at leaf level

prove(Y,U,V):–
    (Y <– Z),
    prove(Z,U,V).
% End of meta-problem solver
```

Applied to the box example:

box(*a*). box(*b*). box(*c*).
?–solve((not *X* = *Y*,box(*X*),box(*Y*))),
  all([*X*,*Y*]).
[*a*,*b*]
[*a*,*c*]
[*b*,*a*]
[*b*,*c*]
[*c*,*a*]
[*c*,*b*]

12.6   Robot planning

An interesting problem is **robot plan formation**, where the meta-problem solving techniques are applicable. The method adopted solves all possible planning problems, but also leads to an explosion in the number of combinations generated. This is known as a combinatorial explosion (see Section 12.7.2). Another method is also mentioned – this solves a restricted kind of 'good-tempered' problems called **linear problems**.

12.6.1   Kowalski's formulation

Consider a box world, with boxes *a*, *b* and *c* positioned initially as in Figure 12.4. (The scenario is taken from Kowalski, 1979b.) The situation can be modelled in Prolog, by the predicate

holds(CONDITION, SITUATION)

where **CONDITION** is a term denoting a condition to hold, and **SITUATION** is a term identifying a certain system state. If **start** is the initial system state, and **on** and **clear** are terms, then a meta-predicate **holds** states that a predicate represented as a term in the first argument is true in the situation represented as a term in the second argument.

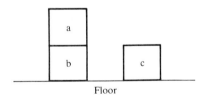

Figure 12.4   Initial box situation (Kowalski, 1979b).

holds(on(*a*,*b*),start).
holds(on(*b*,floor),start).

holds(on(c,floor),start).

holds(clear(floor),S).   % floor is always clear
holds(clear(a),start).
holds(clear(c),start).

The robot is required to move the boxes one by one until the situation in
Figure 12.5 occurs. This is achieved in an unknown state **FINAL** defined
by:

holds(on(a,b),FINAL),
holds(on(b,c),FINAL),
holds(on(c,floor),FINAL).

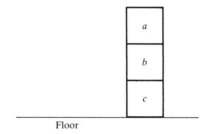

Figure 12.5   Final box situation.

The solutions should be a term with the operations in the form:

FINAL =
do(do(do(start,move(a,b,floor)),move(b,floor,c)),move(a,floor,b))

This term, which contains the initial state **start**, and a sequence of actions,
move(x,y,z), is called a composite state.

The whole system of boxes and places is a **SYSTEM**. It may be in
different states according to different actions made on it. However, the
state is uniquely determined by an initial state, and the sequences of
actions. In this case, the actions are defined by using the term
move(x,y,z).

The problem solver is divided into three different levels:

(1) the problem-solving mechanism;
(2) problem-domain rules;
(3) the actual problem setting and solution constraints.

The problem-solving mechanism

It is sometimes impossible to predict the right sequence of conditions that makes negations correctly. For that purpose, the whole problem solver is put under the control of the meta-problem solver. The problem-solving strategy due to Kowalski (1979b) (see also Nilsson, 1982) is to axiomatize the rules for:

holds(CONDITION,do(STATE,ACTION))

(1) EITHER a condition is true in a STATE, AND the condition is INVARIANT to the action
(2) OR the condition is a CONSEQUENCE of the ACTION, AND the action is legal in the STATE.

Translated into Prolog this becomes:

```
holds(Condition,do(State,Action)) <-
    holds(Condition,State),
    invariant(Condition,Action).
holds(Condition,do(State,Action)) <-
    consequence(Condition,Action),
    legal(Action,State).
```

To force the problem solver to find the shortest possible solution, and at the same time to avoid an infinite number of trials, the solution space is controlled according to the principle of stepwise increased solution length. The set of all possible *a priori* general states is defined recursively by the predicate **try(X)**.

```
try(start).
try(do(State,Action)):-
    try(State).
```

The main predicate is

```
solve(G,S):-
    try(S),
    prove(G,false,_),
    !.
```

where **prove** is the problem solver, *G* is the goal, and *S* is the solution.

Problem-domain rules

These are the rules of the tiny box world

> invariant(on(U,V),move(X,Y,Z)) <–
>   not $U = X$.
> invariant(clear(U),move(X,Y,Z)) <–
>   not $U = Y$, not $U = Z$.
> consequence(on(X,Z),move(X,Y,Z)).
> consequence(clear(Y),move(X,Y,Z)).
> legal(move(X,Y,Z),S) <–
>   holds(clear(X),S),
>   holds(on(X,Y),S),
>   holds(clear(Z),S),
>   not $X =$ floor, not $X = Y$, not $Y = Z$, not $X = Z$.
> holds(X,start) <– given(X).
> holds(X,ANY) <– fact(X).

The actual problem

This information concerns an actual case, and may alternatively be given by interactive sessions.

> fact(clear(floor)).
>
> given(on(a,b)).
> given(on(b,floor)).
> given(on(c,floor)).
>
> given(clear(a)).
> given(clear(c)).
>
> answer(S) <–
>   holds(on(a,b),S),
>   holds(on(b,c),S),
>   holds(on(c,floor),S).
>
> ?–solve(answer(S),S).
>
> $S =$
> do(do(do(start,move(a,b,floor)),move(b,floor,c)),move(a,floor,b))

The example gives another opportunity to use generate-or-test symmetry in Prolog. If you put in a complete solution instead of a variable, you will get a consistency check on the solution. For example:

```
try(do(do(do(start,
    move(a,b,floor)),
    move(b,floor,c)),
    move(a,floor,b))).
?–try(S),solve(answer(S),S).
```

Also, if a part of this solution is uninstantiated, it will be instantiated consistently. If used to find a solution from scratch, the method of solution is a blind-search method without any heuristics guiding it. Therefore, it will run into combinatorial explosions very soon. But it is adequately efficient for local problem solving, and for a final consistency check on the solution, no matter how it was generated. However, the method is also open to a more intelligent generation strategy:

```
solve(G,S):–
    plausible(G,S),
    prove(G,false,_).
```

where plausible makes intelligent guesses for S.

12.6.2   Linear planning

Linear planning is based on the assumption that the solution of one subproblem is not destroyed by the solution of other subproblems. The box problem happens to be non-linear, because a solution to the subgoal of having box a on box b is solved initially. However, even though the attempt to move b on c must cause a to be moved away from b. So, a naive linear planner would present the solution

```
do(do(start,move(a,b,floor)),move(b,floor,c))
```

12.7   Using estimates to guide searches

In problem-solving situations, the set of solutions to be found may vary.

- one solution to be found
- all solutions to be found
- the best solution to be found
- one acceptable solution to be found

Finding all solutions is easy in Prolog, given a program for finding one solution: the mechanism is forced backtracking. However, if the solution space is infinite, there may be infinitely many false candidates, and all these must not be attempted initially.

When it comes to finding the best solution, there are two main strategies:

(1) to formulate the search strategy so that the best solution is found first;

(2) to search for all solutions by forced backtracking, but remembering the best solution so far (otherwise they are forgotten by backtracking), and always cutting off the search when new candidates are not significantly better.

12.7.1 Stepwise increasing length of solution

One way of finding the shortest path, through a number of cities, for example, is to preset the solution to a list of steps, with a unique variable representing each step, letting the list be increased systematically at the top level, and filled in by the search program.

try([]).
try([$X|Y$]):–try(Y).

Applied to the connection problem described in Chapter 7, the following is generated:

stepconnect(X,Y,Z):–
    try(Z),
    connection(X,Y,Z).

This scheme forces Prolog to try all possible solutions of length N before it tries solutions of length $N + 1$. It causes a de-memorizing backtracking when it steps up the level. However, the strategy is not as bad as it sounds. First, it saves space, because backtracking regains storage. Secondly, it can be argued (Stickel and Tyson, 1985) that a blind search in a graph is an exponential problem, so that the number of nodes to search is a power of the length. (The root of the power R is the average number of successors to each node.) Suppose the actual length of the solution is L. If that were known exactly, the search work would be

$$S = R^L$$

If not, the stepwise increase strategy causes a search:

$$1 + R + R^2 + R^3 + ... + R^L = (R^{L+1} - 1)/(R - 1) \approx S * (R/(R - 1))$$

i.e. not much longer than the search with the longest path.

12.7.2 Finding short paths

The exponential increases in searches are called **combinatorial explosions**, which leave theoretically solved problems still unsolved in practice. This is illustrated by the generic mouse-king problem: see Figure 12.6. A mouse (*M*) is placed on a chess board, on a square (e.g. A4). In another position (e.g. H1), there is a piece of cheese (*C*), which the mouse can see. The mouse can move, one step at a time, in all directions (just as a king in chess).

The mouse will remember where it has been and can use that information by making an estimate of the length of the shortest path from a node to the goal node, and the shortest path from the start node to the node. How does the mouse use its information to find the cheese in a minimum number of steps?

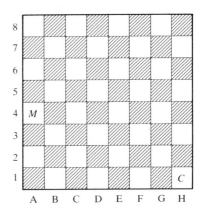

Figure 12.6 The mouse-king problem.

The problem may seem too trivial to be interesting, but study this small problem domain and evaluate the various strategies against larger search spaces, where combinatorially explosive solutions will show their devastating effect. It demonstrates the necessity of applying knowledge to solve even simple problems in an acceptable time. Knowledge to aid the discovery of solutions is called **heuristics**.

The relation relating neighbouring nodes or squares is defined as follows:

```
leg([X1,Y1],[X2,Y2]):–
  onestep(DX,DY),
  plus(X1,DX,X2),
  plus(Y1,DY,Y2),
  legal([X1,Y1]),
  legal([X2,Y2]).
```

```
onestep(-1,+1).                  % NW
onestep(0,+1).                   % N
onestep(+1,+1).                  % NE
onestep(+1,0).                   % E
onestep(+1,-1).                  % SE
onestep(0,-1).                   % S
onestep(-1,-1).                  % SW
onestep(-1,0).                   % W
legal([X,Y]):-oct(X),oct(Y).     % no barriers
oct(X):-X >= 1, X =< 8.
```

Using the connection example of Chapter 7, the connection matrix is defined as follows, where the definition of input/output is purposely made symmetric by using the **plus** predicate. Let the letters A, B, ... be represented as 1, 2, ..., and board positions be two-element lists, e.g. [1,4]. With the connection algorithm (CA), the mouse could find a way in an extremely odd manner. This is left as an exercise.

The point is that even a stupid mouse, providing it were hungry, would move in a direction that is diminishing the distance to the cheese, according to its own estimate. Suppose that that estimate is exact. Then, the estimate, H, of the distance in number of steps between the mouse and the cheese is:

```
estimate([X1,Y1],[X2,Y2],H):-
    abs(X1 - X2,DX),
    abs(Y1 - Y2,DY),
    max(DX,DY,H).
```

So, instead of trying out the neighbours in a fixed order, the mouse should order them according to their estimates, and try them out in that order, depth first. That would lead directly to the goal in this case, because the experimenter has not set up any barriers. There is a cheaper solution that avoids sorting at each node, but looks for successors that reduce the remaining distance before looking for successors that do not.

```
goal([8,1]).                                        % H1
remains(Pos,R):-goal(Z),estimate(Pos,Z,R).
search(Atpos):-goal(Atpos),!.
search(Atpos):-
    bestway(Atpos,Nextpos),
    output(Atpos-Nextpos),
    search(Nextpos).
bestway(Atpos,Nextpos):-
    remains(Atpos,A),
```

```
    leg(Atpos,Nextpos),
    remains(Nextpos,N),
    N < A.
bestway(Atpos,Nextpos):–
    remains(Atpos,A),
    leg(Atpos,Nextpos),
    remains(Nextpos,N),
    N >= A.
?–search([1,4]).
[1,4]–[2,5]
[2,5]–[3,6]
[3,6]–[4,5]
[4,5]–[5,4]
[5,4]–[6,3]
[6,3]–[7,2]
[7,2]–[8,1]
```

(Note that though the path is not straight, this does not mean it is not minimal.)

12.7.3   Making a plan before execution

The search method could be imagined as a search being done in parallel with the execution of the plan. The mouse, for example, thinks while it runs. For this setting, backtracking in Prolog literally corresponds to the mouse following its tracks back to a point with alternatives. However, imagine a search process that finds a short path done in the brain of the mouse, before the plan was executed. When thinking, the planning process could have several parallel paths to pursue, trying out the most promising by expanding the node at the end of each path.

An important problem area that is studied in AI research is **heuristic searches**. The problems are then represented as general graphs, with a known start node and a known end node, having complete knowledge of how to reach from one node to the next, but with incomplete or heuristic knowledge of how to estimate how far a node is from the goal node.

A well-known method of general graph search is the A* algorithm which is a best-first method. It means that the algorithm simultaneously contains several paths which may all be candidates for the shortest path. At any time, it selects the most promising node (best first) at a time for expansion, and incorporates the successor nodes into the search graph. The criterion for evaluation is the length of the path from start to the node plus the estimate of the remaining distance (cost). The theory says that if the remaining estimate is an underestimate, the first found solution will be optimal.

Such general search strategies are optimal with respect to time, but space consuming because of all the memorizing. Interested students should refer to Nilsson (1982) and Bratko (1986) who goes further into solving search problems in Prolog.

EXERCISES

12.1 A kind of puzzle called a cryptarithmetic problem is to assign unique digits to letters, so that a certain calculation expressed by letters becomes correct. Some examples are:

	ONE	
SEND	+ TWO	CROSS
+ MORE	+ FIVE	+ ROADS
= MONEY	= EIGHT	= DANGER

Solve the following problem in Prolog
(Hint: make a predicate.

   addigit(C,D,E,F,G)

   where C is the old carry,
     D and E are digits
     F is the new digit and
     G is the new carry.)

12.2 Find the route that the mouse-king uses from A4 to H1, with the fixed order selection algorithm.

12.3 The eight-queens problem is as follows: Place eight queens on a chessboard so that they do not threaten each other. The queen can move in any direction, any number of squares.

12.4 A monkey is situated at place A. At place B, there is a box, and a banana is hanging from the ceiling at place C. The banana can be reached only by climbing the box underneath the banana. Formulate the problem as a plan formation problem in Prolog, and solve it.

12.5 Solve the nickel-and-dime problem. The board consists of 5 squares as follows:

with two nickels (*N*) and two dimes (*D*) placed as shown. Using legal moves, the nickels and dimes are to switch places:

The legal moves are as follows:

- A dime can move one to the left if free.
- A dime can jump over a nickel, if adjacent, and the place behind is free.
- A nickel can move one to the right if free.
- A nickel can jump over a dime, if adjacent, and the place behind is free.

12.6 The number 777 (three sevens) has the mystical property of being composed of 3 * 7 * 37. A number which is not mystical is 6666.

$$6666 <> 4 * 6 * 46$$

Are there other mystical numbers in the ten-digit system? What about other number systems? (If not, is this the reason why we have 10 fingers?)

12.7 The following problem is called the Impossible Problem.

Two numbers, *A* and *B*, are given but not known to two mathematicians, *P* and *S*. However, *P* knows the product (*A* * *B*) of the numbers, while *S* knows the sum (*A* + *B*). They both know that both numbers are greater than 1 and not greater than 100.

The following diaglogue is heard:

P: I don't know the numbers.
S: I knew that; I don't know them either.
P: Now I know the numbers!
S: Now I know them too!

What are the numbers?

In fact, the limit of 100 could be replaced by a bigger number; how big is still open.

Chapter 13
Expert Systems

> If you had to decide by using
> one question whether you were
> communicating with a machine or a man,
> would you choose this question?
>
> *Freely from Turing*

13.1 Expert systems

Advanced programs that can solve a variety of new problems based on stored knowledge without being reprogrammed are called knowledge-based systems or just knowledge systems. If their level of competence approaches that of human experts, they become expert systems, which is the popular name for all knowledge systems, even if they do not deserve the name.

The archetypal expert system is MYCIN (Shortliffe, 1976), which is an expert system to guide doctors in diagnosing blood infections. MYCIN is a **rule-based expert system**, i.e. the knowledge of MYCIN was mostly composed of rules of the kind:

'If the morphology of the organism is coccus, and the stain of the organism is not known then there is suggestive evidence (0.6) that the stain of the organism is Grampos.'

The number 0.6 is called a certainty factor, and the conclusion gets a certainty value which is the minimum of the certainty values of the conditions, multiplied by 0.6.

Analysis of this system led to the discovery that certain parts were of a general kind that could be made as a separate expert system **shell**, EMYCIN (for Essential MYCIN or Empty MYCIN), while the domain specific part could be separated as a knowledge base on blood diseases. The expert system shell performs the following functions:

- inference engine,
- search processing,
- dialogue handling.

while the knowledge base contains facts, rules and heuristics, that is, advises how to use the facts and rules.

EMYCIN's inference engine is based on **backward chaining**, similar to Prolog, which means that the rules are applied top down, starting with the goal. An alternative strategy is **forward chaining**, which corresponds to bottom-up processing, i.e. starting with facts, and using the rules to derive new facts. An expert system shell using forward chaining is OPS5 (Forgy, 1981).

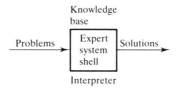

Figure 13.1   A schematic expert system.

13.2   Expert systems in Prolog

One of the first expert systems implemented in Prolog was a system for prediction and retrieval of drug interactions developed in Hungary (Futo *et al.*, 1978). This system is reported not only to find the interactions that were obvious to the doctors, but also to have found interactions that were confirmed later.

Another milestone was the development of the APES expert system shell at Imperial College London (Hammond, 1980). APES stands for Augmenting Prolog for Expert Systems and it reasons with logical rules of the form:

> X should take Y if
> X complains of Z and
> Y suppresses Z and
> not Y may harm X.

APES epitomizes the content and message of this book, namely to apply logic programming for knowledge engineering, by using meta-level logic programming techniques.

This chapter describes the methodology of APES adapted to the logic programming framework. This includes almost all of the techniques explained in previous chapters. It demonstrates how these features can be realized in Prolog by giving the details of how to build and use an expert system shell. The shell will be 'analytical', as opposed to synthetical, where the solution is a complex data-structure, e.g. a plan. In addition, it will be based on backward chaining, i.e. it has goal-oriented, top-down inference. The rules have 'free variables'. This feature, lacking in EMYCIN, makes backward chaining much more flexible.

The system will also apply 'exact reasoning', which means that it is not concerned with uncertainties, but regards all information as true or false.

13.3   Principles of the EXPLAIN expert system shell

An expert system shell called EXPLAIN will be based on the ideas of meta-level logic as explained in Chapter 7. However, the more usual syntactic conventions will be introduced. Rules will put the conditions first, for example, followed by the conclusion in an if-then-else fashion. In addition, the logical operators **and** and **or** will be used instead of ',' and ';' in Prolog. For instance:

grandmother(X,Z) $<-$ mother(X,Y),parent(Y,Z).

is written:

if mother(X,Y) **and** parent(Y,Z) **then** grandmother(X,Z).

The change is only syntactic, and does not imply that the language moves from backward reasoning to forward reasoning.

First there is an example of how EXPLAIN is used. Then you will see how the expert system shell is constructed and works, by studying a simplified version. Later in this chapter is a listing of a complete version that should be studied properly. Also in this chapter are descriptions of how to create knowledge bases in EXPLAIN, and how to use the expert system. These explanations are important parts of the documentation of the EXPLAIN shell.

13.3.1   Why and how – explanation

Explanation facilities are a crucial part of knowledge systems. They make the program trustworthy because it will on request explain its reasoning in sufficient detail for the user to agree with the conclusion, or to be given exact references to rules that are given by experts. Without 'explaining' facilities, the system becomes a black box that is uncontrollable.

In Chapter 7, meta-level logic explains how to make Prolog explain how a conclusion was derived. This explanation facility can be improved in various ways:

- the users can be asked at each level of rule if they want to see the explanation;

- the users will be asked if they want to see more solutions;
- if an input is requested from users, it may explain why the data is needed.

13.4   An example of use of EXPLAIN: television repair

The first example is taken from the domain of television repair. At Brundalen technical college in Trondheim, a teacher is responsible for teaching television repair. He has been a practising television serviceman for several years before he entered into teaching, but feels he is starting to forget his expert knowledge. So the school buys a personal computer with Prolog software, and with some help from a knowledge engineer, he starts building up an expert system to guide the students in television fault diagnosis and repair.

The knowledge that has to be represented is not of a theoretical kind, but is based on his experience. It consists of:

- general knowledge of the blocks that constitute the modules of a typical television set;
- knowledge of each television type;
- knowledge of the manual procedures that are developed to guide the service engineer;
- experience of frequently reported errors from other sources.

The expert system can operate in two modes. The first and obvious mode is that the expert system asks the student to answer questions, make observations and perform measurements, so that the expert system can conclude what the error is. The second mode uses the same rule base, but the expert system is used to test the student on a simulated error. An error is announced to the student, and 'planted' in the knowledge base. However, the student is obliged to know the consequences of this error, and has to answer the questions without consulting an actual television. If

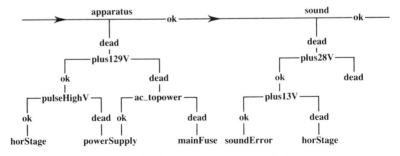

Figure 13.2   An error tree for a television.

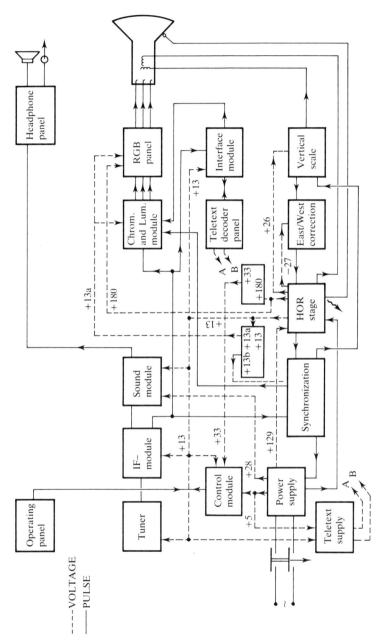

Figure 13.3 Block diagram of a colour television.

the student is successful, the system will confirm the announced error.

Consider the first problem type: manual procedures have been devised to guide service engineers into the initial phases of error detection in the form of an 'error-tree' (see Figure 13.2). The way to represent this in EXPLAIN is to regard the tip nodes as conclusions, and all the intermediate nodes as conditions. Compare the error-tree with the following rule base!

%%%%%EXPLAIN knowledge base for television repair %%%%%%%

if dead(apparatus) and ok(plus129V) and ok(pulseHighV)
then error(horStage).

if dead(apparatus) and ok(plus129V) and dead(pulseHighV)
then error(powerSupply).

if dead(apparatus) and dead(plus129V) and ok(ac_topower)
then error(powerSupply).

if dead(apparatus) and dead(plus129V) and dead(ac_topower)
then error(mainFuse).

if ok(apparatus) and dead(sound) and ok(plus28V) and ok(plus13V)
then error(soundError).

if ok(apparatus) and dead(sound) and ok(plus28V) and
    dead(plus13V)
then error(horStage).

if ok(apparatus) and
    dead(sound) and
    dead(plus28V)
then error(powerSupply).

if ok(apparatus) and
    black_hvltg_sound and dead(plus190V)
then error(horStage).

if ok(apparatus) and black_hvltg_sound and
    ok(plus190V) and dead(plus13A)
then error(horStage).

if ok(apparatus) and black_hvltg_sound and
    ok(plus190V) and ok(plus13A)
then error(chrom_lum).

if ok(sound) and
    black_screen and high_voltage
then black_hvltg_sound.

if not dead(X) then ok(X).

askable dead(X).
askable black_screen.
askable high_voltage.

Sample dialogue

```
?–show error(X).
dead(apparatus) ? >n.
dead(sound) ? >why.
BECAUSE
if ok(apparatus) and
   dead(sound) and
   ok(plus28V) and
   ok(plus13V)
then error(soundError)

dead(sound) ? >y.
dead(plus28V) ? >y.

error(powerSupply) is PROVED >how.
   BECAUSE
   ok(apparatus) is PROVED >ok.
   dead(sound) is GIVEN
   dead(plus28V) is GIVEN
OTHER SOLUTIONS ? >y.

NO OTHER SOLUTIONS
?–show not error(soundError).

error(soundError) is NOT PROVED >how.
BECAUSE
   ok(apparatus) is PROVED >ok.
   dead(sound) is GIVEN
   ok(plus28V) is NOT PROVED >ok.
OTHER SOLUTIONS ? >y.

NO OTHER SOLUTIONS
?–
```

13.5   The structure of EXPLAIN

13.5.1   Important predicates

The key predicates of EXPLAIN are:

(1) prove(Goal,Why,How)
(2) askabout(X,Why)
(3) showhow(How)

In (1), **Goal** is the Prolog goal to be proved and **Why** is a structure containing the search tree so far. **How** is a term building the final proof.

The **Why** term is different from the **How** term principally because **Why** contains the history of the search, which is built up inside outwards, whilst **How** is developed outside inwards and contains the final proof when a goal is solved. The purpose of **How** is the final explanation, whilst **Why** is relevant when the user is asked for input. Then the **Why** contains a nested set of all the goals that the expert system is trying to solve, which justifies why the question was asked. The shell will ask the user for all conditions that are declared as askable.

In **askabout(X,Why)**, the **Why** variable will keep a nested list of rules that comprises the input request. If the user types a **why**, he or she will be shown the innermost rule. By typing **why** successively, the rules are stripped off successively, until the system prints the original outermost rule.

In **showhow(How)** the **How** variable contains the final proof. This will be shown at the next detail level, for each **how**, otherwise it will continue.

13.5.2   EXPLAIN **program skeleton**

```
prove((X and Y),Why,(HowX,HowY)):-
  !,
  prove(X,Why,HowX),
  prove(Y,Why,HowY).

prove(X,Why,given(X)):-
  askable(X),
  !,
  askabout(X,Why),
  ...

prove(X,Why,fact(X)):-
  not(if Y then X),              % X is not determined
  !,                             % by an if-rule
  X.

prove(X,Why,rule(X,Y)):-
  if Y then X,                   % new Why – structure
  prove(Y,(rule(X,Y),Why),rule(X,Y)).   % includes rule(X,Y).

show X:-prove(X,true,How),
  showhow(How).
```

13.5.3   Handling of negation

The system is able to both handle and explain negation-as-failure. The main principle is that

not(A and B)

is not treated as

not(A) or not(B)

because that would cut the connection that lies in the shared variables in A and B. Instead, it is based on the following scheme (given in quasi-Prolog):

PROVE NOT A IF   % NOT A fails if A succeeds
   PROVE A,
   !,
   FAIL
% hence, assume that the whole goal cannot be proven

PROVE NOT (A AND B) IF   % if we know that A and B cannot be
   PROVE NOT A.   % proven and A cannot be proven,
                                 % that is the reason

PROVE NOT (A AND B) IF
   PROVE A AND   % otherwise, the failure lies
   PROVE NOT B.   % in the next condition

Since the sequence of conjunctions

A and B and C is stored as
A and (B and C)

the quasi-Prolog scheme is applied recursively.

13.5.4   Opening the closed world

The closed world assumption is taken for granted. The system will regard any goal which cannot be proven as false. However, by **declaring** conditions as **askable**, the system will allow the user to give the answer, thereby opening up the closed world. Conditions with base variables $(b = X)$ will automatically be open. This method of handling the user dialogue is called **querying the user** (Clark and McCabe, 1984) and replaces ordinary reading from the user.

The benefits of goal-oriented reasoning appear in connection with dialogue handling, because the user is only asked relevant questions, whose purpose is to arrive at a conclusion. The rule with conclusion is itself the reason for asking, and may on request be presented to the user. In contrast, dialogue handling in forward-chained systems may easily become random and unmotivated.

It is fair to mention a slight anomaly here, because the user may be asked some irrelevant questions. For example:

> **if** (*a* **or** *b*) **and** *c* **then** *d*.
> **askable** *a*.
> **askable** *b*.
> **askable** *c*.

The user will be asked

> *a*?
> > y
> *c*?
> > n
> *b*?
> >

Here, the question *b*? is redundant, because the conclusion *d* is blocked by the failure of *c*. A more advanced scheme would not ask questions if the conclusion would fail regardless of the answer to the current question. Another possible refinement is to let the system ask for the conclusion directly, if one of the conditions is unknown.

13.5.5 Storage versus recomputation

The expert system shell operates with global base variables. A value given by the user will be stored and used until explicitly changed or forgotten. Otherwise, all conclusions will be re-evaluated. By not storing any intermediate conclusion, the consistency of the final conclusion is guaranteed, because it follows logically from the given facts and the rules. By manipulating the values of the base variable by explicit commands, the user may create hypothetical consultations to answer 'what if?' questions.

This implementation decision is time consuming, and is not the only possible strategy, but the alternative would be a very advanced truth-maintenance system.

13.6   EXPLAIN reference manual

13.6.1   Rules

EXPLAIN is a Prolog-based expert system shell made explicitly for teaching expert system principles. It is simple and should not be compared with commercial systems such as APES. This section is written as a reference manual for writing knowledge bases to be run by the EXPLAIN shell.

The most important thing to understand is that EXPLAIN is in fact a Prolog program itself, with some extensions. It is possible to give guidelines of how to make knowledge bases for the shell without going too deeply into Prolog, except for the parts that fall outside the rule paradigm, and have to be programmed in Prolog. For the student it is instructive to compare the external descriptions with the listing.

The rules are written in the form:

if Cond1 and Cond2 and ... and Cond*n* then Conclusion.

For example:

```
if      method = smaw
and     bm_unalloyed
and     req_yeld_strength = Yield and Yield < 440
and     req_tensile_strength = Tensile and Tensile < 510
and     pos_is_one_of([1,2,3,4,5,6])
then    filler_material = 'Norweld Supra'.
```

The next most important point is that the knowledge base is divided into two levels:

(1) the rule level which uses the specified form;
(2) the Prolog level, which is Prolog programs.

The system starts at the rule level, and will interpret on the rule level all conditions matching the conclusion of a rule. However, if a condition is not covered by a rule, then it is interpreted as a Prolog goal, and evaluated accordingly as an arbitrarily complex Prolog program. However, as seen from the rule interpreter, such a condition will appear to be satisfied by facts.

It is a consequence of the two-level subdivision, that a Prolog goal may itself call the meta-level rule interpreter recursively. The challenging possibilities that follow from this idea are left as an interesting exercise for students to explore.

The division into levels is a feature of this expert system, and must not be compromised by conditions that match both rule conclusions and Prolog conclusions. If a Prolog rule happens to be unconditional, it must be written as a rule with condition **true**. Instead of

> if *a* then *b*(5).
> *b*(4).

the Prolog fact must be given as a conclusion of an alternative rule:

> if *a* then *b*(5).
> if true then *b*(4).

13.6.2   Base variables and equality

The system distinguishes between

base variable names	starting with lower case
data values	numbers, identifiers and quotes
Prolog variables	starting with upper case letters

The general form is **basevariable = 'data value'** or **basevariable = 'Prolog variable'**. For example:

> if weld = butt or weld = fillet then
>   buttorfillet.

Prolog code can be inserted, but Prolog does not operate on the base variable names, only on their values, which must be picked up directly using an equation:

> basevariable = Prologvariable.

as follows:

> if weld = *W* and member(*W*,[butt,fillet]) then
>   buttorfillet.

or:

> if num = *N* and *N* > 5 then   % if num > 5 is not allowed
>   sufficient.

The semantics of the equality relation (=) differs at the rule level from the Prolog level, which might cause some confusion. In fact, the = at the rule level corresponds to the $ ('value is') operator introduced in Chapter 8.

In Prolog, the condition $X = Y$ means a unification of the terms X and Y. On the rule level, equality is used to access the values of global base variables. The condition:

basevariable $= X$

has several effects:

(1) if **basevariable** $= Y$ is a conclusion of a rule, then this value will be evaluated by that rule, but not stored;

(2) otherwise, if the **basevariable** is not stored as a fact

value(basevariable,val),

then the system will ask the user for a value. This value will be remembered as a value tuple;

(3) assuming the basevariable is stored as

value(basevariable,val),

if the condition is

basevariable $= X$,

then the unification of X with **val** will be attempted. If X is a Prolog variable, an instantiation occurs. Otherwise, if X is a value, it must be equal to **val**.

13.6.3 Coupling to relational tables

The expert system is connected to relational tables *via* an operator definition. The principles are described in Chapter 9 on Prolog and databases, but here is a summary:

Data are stored in normalized tables:

person(halvard,tore,catherine).
person(anne,tore,catherine).

A table declaration command is given to each table:

:–table person(name,father,mother).

and this makes a system-defined predicate meaningful. For example:

'Which person *K* has tore as father?'

  ?–list *K*, **person:*K* has father** = **tore.**

halvard
anne

This form will fail and backtrack when the value returned is nil, because this is used to model a missing value. Thus the knowledge-base programmer is freed from having dummy values of data that are logically non-existent.

13.7   EXPLAIN **user guide**

13.7.1   **Expert system components**

This section explains how to use an expert system written in EXPLAIN. An expert system based on EXPLAIN consists of the following components, in addition to the Prolog system itself:

- The EXPLAIN expert system shell ('explain')
- The domain-specific knowledge base (e.g. 'welding')

Behind this simple structure a further decomposition is hidden. The EXPLAIN expert system is augmented with the general predicate library as present in this book. The Prolog code of EXPLAIN dynamically includes it from the file ('booklib').

The knowledge base is mainly composed of a rule base as described. In addition, there may or may not be Prolog programs to support the low-level programming of the rule base. It is the responsibility of the code file for the knowledge base to make the necessary inclusion. For example, the knowledge base is called **welding**, consulting a file with an application library called **weldlib**, and a rule base called **weldrule**. Also, table declarations and tuples may occur anywhere. In this chapter they are gathered into one file, **weld-table**.

The expert system shell is stored as a text on a file **explain**, and compiled or transformed to internal form by calling the Prolog interpreter. After the Prolog interpreter is invoked, the user asks to consult the EXPLAIN expert system shell, and then the file containing the knowledge base. Just remember, all input to Prolog is ended with a '.'.

13.7.2 Calling EXPLAIN

```
?–[explain,welding].
booklib is included          (included by explain)
explain is included
weldlib is included          (included by welding)
weldrule is included         ...
weldtable is included        ...
welding is included
?–
```

When all files have been read, the user may give Prolog commands or queries.

13.7.3 Summary of commands

A set of Prolog commands is defined in the expert system shell that activates the expert system:

?–explain.	Resets the expert system shell, forgets status, and lists the problems;
?–problems.	Lists the solvable problems, i.e. the conclusions of the rules;
?–show Goal.	Goal is a Prolog goal that is solved under the regime of EXPLAIN. The solution will be presented with an option for detailed explanations of the proof or alternative solutions;
?–showall Goal.	All solutions are found and listed, without user interrogation(except for input/output);
?–eval Basevar.	Same as show Basevar $= X$.
?–give $X = Y$.	X is a so-called base variable, typically a Prolog identifier. Y is the given value of the base variable. The old value of X is listed, if any;
?–take X.	X is a base variable. The value is listed and taken away;
?–status.	Lists all the values of the base variables.

13.7.4   The EXPLAIN dialogue explained

Query the user

The system may ask the user when it needs more information. There are two ways to make the system ask, both explained in the reference manual.

(1) by declaring the condition as askable. When the rule interpreter comes to a condition the user is asked:

   some-Prolog-condition condition?>

   and the user types 'y.' or 'n.'

(2) when an equation is activated, and no value exists:

   give some-base-variable = X ?>

   where X is the internal representation of the Prolog variable (in the form **_142** or another number) that will be instantiated to the value.

WHY explanation

Every time users are asked for a value by the prompt '>', they may ask

   >why.

whereupon the system will output current rule activation applying where the input request occurred. Then it will repeat the request. The rule activation is an instance of the rule with all current instantiations of the Prolog variables shown. In fact, EXPLAIN will keep a chain of embracing rule activations, so that if the user repeats **why.**, the next outer rule is listed. The chain stops at the outermost rule which is the rule that was called by the show command. Here, the system states:

   THAT WAS YOUR ORIGINAL PROBLEM!

and repeats the question.

HOW explanation

When a solution is found, the system prints:

-so-and-so is PROVED>

Here, the user may type **how.** or **ok.**. If it is **ok.**, the system continues, but if **how.** is typed, the system prints the following explanations of each of the conditions that were premises for this conclusion, and how those conditions were established:

-so-and-so is GIVEN	when the user has given the answer;
-so-and-so is TRUE	when the fact is established by Prolog;
-so-and-so is PROVED>	a conclusion of a new rule. Here, the user responds 'ok.' or 'how.' as before;
-so-and-so is NOT PROVED>	This answer will only occur when a goal is called that starts with a 'not'. The user responds 'ok.' or 'how.'

When a solution is found, and presented in this fashion, the user is asked:

OTHER SOLUTIONS?

The user replies 'y.' or 'n.'. If 'y.', the next solution is given, until the system prints:

NO MORE SOLUTIONS.

13.8 Another example of EXPLAIN: pollution detection

This example is taken from the domain of pollution detection at a chemical plant (see Figure 13.4). The task is to create an expert system to assist the security officer in charge of leading the search for a possible source of pollution, as soon as evidence of it is reported. The problem is taken from Hayes-Roth *et al.* (1983), where it is used as a touchstone example for a number of other expert systems such as EMYCIN, KAS, EXPERT, OPS5, ROSIE and RLL (see Hayes-Roth for references).

13.8.1 The pollution detection knowledge base

% One drainage basin at Oak Ridge National Laboratory

bldg(3550). bldg(3515). bldg(3024). bldg(3025).
bldg(3508). bldg(3026).
bldg(3517). bldg(3525). bldg(2503). bldg(3023).

bldg(3518). bldg(3504). bldg(3505).

pond(3513).

storage(oil,X):–member(X,

[$s1,s2,s4,s6,s7,s12,s13,s14,s15,s23,s25,s29,s30,s37,s38,s39,s40$,
$s47,s50,s51,s52,s53,s54,s55,s56,s61,s62,s63,s68,s69$]
).

storage(base,X):–member(X,

[$s17,s18,s24,s32,s33,s34,s59,s60,s64,s65,s66,s67,s70$]
).

storage(acid,X):–member(X,

[$s3,s5,s8,s9,s10,s11,s16,s19,s20,s21,s22,s26,s27,s28,s31$,
$s35,s36,s41,s42,s43,s44,s45,s46,s48,s49,s57,s58$]
).

manholes([$m1,m2,m3,m4,m5,m6,m7,m8,m9,m10,m11,m12,m13$,
$m14,m15,m16,m17,m18,m19,m20,m21,m22,m23,m24$,
$m25,m26,m27,m28,m29,m30,m31,m32,m33,m34,m35$,
$m36,m37,m38,m39,m40,m41,m42,m43,m44,m45,m46$]).

manhole(X):–manholes(Y),member(X,Y).

drainholes([$d1,d2,d3,d4,d5,d6,d7,d8,d9,d10,d11,d12,d13,d14,d15$]).

drainhole(X):–drainholes(Z),member(X,Z).

leg($m2,m1$).

leg($m3,m2$). leg($m4,m2$).

leg($s64,m3$). leg($s63,m3$). leg($s65,m3$). leg($s66,m3$).

leg($m5,m4$).

leg($m6,m5$). leg($m8,m5$). leg($m11,m5$). leg($d7,m5$).
  leg($d8,m5$). leg($d9,m5$). leg($d10,m5$).

leg($m7,m6$). leg($s67,m6$).

leg($s68,m7$).

leg($m9,m8$). leg($m10,m8$).

leg($s70,m9$).

leg($s59,m10$). leg($s61,m10$). leg($s62,m10$).

leg($m12,m11$). leg($m13,m11$).

leg($m14,m13$).

leg($m15,m14$). leg($d11,m14$). leg($s53,m14$). leg($s54,m14$).

leg($m16,m15$). leg($m21,m15$).

leg($s49,m16$). leg($s50,m16$). leg($m17,m16$).

leg($s51,m17$). leg($s52,m17$).

leg($s47,m18$). leg($s48,m18$). leg($m19,m18$).

leg($d14,m21$). leg($m29,m21$). leg($m22,m21$).

leg($m24,m22$). leg($m23,m22$).

leg($s23,m23$). leg($s24,m23$). leg($s25,m23$).

leg(*m*33,*m*29).
leg(*m*34,*m*33).
leg(*m*35,*m*34). leg(*m*40,*m*34). leg(*m*45,*m*34).
leg(*m*38,*m*35).
leg(*s*43,*m*38). leg(*s*44,*m*38).
leg(*m*46,*m*45). leg(*d*15,*m*45).
leg(*s*38,*m*46). leg(*s*37,*m*46).

leg(*s*1,*d*1). leg(*s*2,*d*1).
leg(*s*3,*d*2).
leg(*s*4,*d*3).
leg(*s*5,*d*4).
leg(*s*6,*d*5). leg(*s*7,*d*5).

leg(*s*8,*d*6). leg(*s*9,*d*6).
leg(*s*10,*d*7). leg(*s*11,*d*7).
leg(*s*12,*d*8). leg(*s*13,*d*8).
leg(*s*14,*d*9). leg(*s*15,*d*9).
leg(*s*16,*d*10). leg(*s*17,*d*10).
leg(*s*18,*d*11). leg(*s*19,*d*11). leg(*s*20,*d*11).
leg(*s*21,*d*12). leg(*s*22,*d*12).
leg(*m*23,*d*13).
leg(*s*26,*d*14). leg(*s*27,*d*14). leg(*s*28,*d*14).
leg(*s*29,*d*15). leg(*s*30,*d*15). leg(*s*31,*d*15).

leg(*m*1,woc_6).

%% COMPUTABLE FACTS %%

connection(X,Y):–leg(X,Y).
connection(X,Y):–leg(X,U),connection(U,Y).

inspectable(X):–not(storage(ANY,X)).

%% RULE BASE %%%%%%

if whatisobserved = WHAT and
  whereisitobserved = WHERE and
  storage(WHAT,FROM) and
  flowing(WHAT,FROM,WHERE)
then polluting(FROM).

if leg(FROM,LOC) and
  storage(WHAT,FROM)
then flowing(WHAT,FROM,LOC).

if leg(ABOVE,LOC) and
  connection(FROM,ABOVE) and
  present(WHAT,ABOVE) and
  flowing(WHAT,FROM,ABOVE)
then flowing(WHAT,FROM,LOC).

if storage(WHAT,LOC)
then present(WHAT,LOC).

if inspectable(LOC) and
   isobservedat(WHAT,LOC) then
   present(WHAT,LOC).

askable isobservedat(WHAT,LOC).

13.8.2 Sample dialogue

% Find a possible source of pollution!
?–show polluting(X).
give whatisobserved = _41? >oil.
give whereisitobserved = _69? >woc_6.
isobservedat(oil,$m1$) ? >y.
isobservedat(oil,$m2$) ? >why.
BECAUSE
if inspectable($m2$) and
   isobservedat(oil,$m2$)
then present(oil,$m2$)

isobservedat(oil,$m2$) ? >y.
isobservedat(oil,$m4$) ? >n.
isobservedat(oil,$m3$) ? >y.

polluting($s63$) is PROVED >how.
  BECAUSE
  whatisobserved = oil is GIVEN
  whereisitobserved = woc_6 is GIVEN
  storage(oil,$s63$) is TRUE
  flowing(oil,$s63$,woc_6) is PROVED >how.
    BECAUSE
    leg($m1$,woc_6) is TRUE
    connection($s63$,$m1$) is TRUE
    present(oil,$m1$) is PROVED >ok.
    flowing(oil,$s63$,$m1$) is PROVED >how.
      BECAUSE
      leg($m2$,$m1$) is TRUE
      connection($s63$,$m2$) is TRUE
      present(oil,$m2$) is PROVED >ok.
      flowing(oil,$s63$,$m2$) is PROVED >ok.
OTHER SOLUTIONS ? >n.
?–

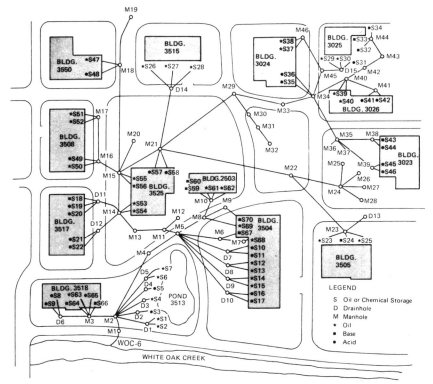

Figure 13.4 One drainage basin at Oak Ridge National Laboratory.

13.8.3 The structure of the pollution knowledge base

This example gives a clear indication of the benefits of having a two-level rule base. The **connection** predicate is a so-called computable fact that is evaluated as a Prolog predicate outside the scope of the explanation facilities, so that the explanation is not overloaded with details. The purpose of the **connection** predicate is to ensure that only plausible routes are pursued from a pollution source to the place of discovery. Without it, many questions as to whether something is detected at certain places, involving time consuming inspection, would be redundant.

The components of the plants are given by relational facts of the buildings, ponds, storages and inspectable holes. The topology of the drain system is given by a relation leg describing the connection between the components. For simplicity, the coordinates of the components have not been included. However, this is essential information to the user, presumably the security officer on duty. The knowledge of the coordinates should direct the search in an efficient way, as described under the section heuristic search. However, the program also works without this information.

13.9   EXPLAIN expert system shell listing

%%%%%% EXPLAIN EXPERT SYSTEM SHELL %%%%%%%%%%

```
:–consult(booklib).                    % includes the library predicates

:–op(1100,fx,show).                    % operator definitions
:–op(1100,fx,showall).                 % for the user interface
:–op(1100,fx,eval).
:–op(1050,xfx,then).
:–op(1040,fy,if).

% :–op(1000,xfy,','). Below, operators with 1 arg

:–op(950,fx,give).
:–op(950,fx,take).
:op(950,fx,askable).

explain:–                              % Main entry.
  output('EXPLAIN EXPERT SYSTEM'),
  forget(value(ANY,BODY)),             % reset status
  problems.                            % list conclusions

problems:–                             % list all the terms
  output('LIST OF PROBLEMS'),          % which are conclusions.
  for(if Y then X),output(X)).

status:–for(value(X,Y),output(X = Y)). % list the values of
                                       % the base variables

give X = Y :–take X,                   % removes the old value of
  remember(value(X,Y)).                % the base variable X and
                                       % remembers the new value Y

take X:–value(X,Y),                    % find the old value of X,
  out('Old value'),output(X = Y),      % print it and
  retract(value(X,Y)).                 % forget it

show X:–showhow(X),                    % user dialogue entry.
  fail.                                % avoid standard response.

showall X:–prove(X,true,ANY),          % find all solutions
  output(X),                           % without explanations
  fail.

eval X:–show X = ANY.                   % evaluate a base variable X,
                                       % defined by the condition X = ANY.

showhow(X):–                           % prove X with explanation dialogue
  prove(X,true,HOW),                   % prove X with empty WHY
                                       % explanation

  nl,nl,                               % and generate the HOW explanation
  askhow(HOW,0),                       % user may want to see explanation
  request('OTHER SOLUTIONS ? >',Y),
```

```
      Y = n,
      !.                                    % stop explanation dialogue
   showhow(X):–output('NO
      OTHER SOLUTIONS').                    % otherwise
   controlled(not(X)).                      % if a condition is not 'controlled',
   controlled(X):–                          % it will be called as an ordinary
      (askable X);                          % Prolog condition
      (if Y then X).
   askable X = Y:–
      value(X,ANY),!.                       % conditions with basevariables are
                                            % askable if there is a value

   askable X = Y:–
      not(if Z then X = ANY).               % otherwise, they are askable if
                                            % not governed by a rule.
%%%%%%%%%%%%%% Inference engine %%%%%%%%%%%%%%%
%
% prove(C,WHY,HOW) is the key predicate
%
% C is the condition to prove;
% WHY at any time contains a nested set
% of rules that are attempted;
% HOW at any time contains the proof tree so far.
%
%%%%%%%%%%%%%%%%%%%%%%%%%%%%%%%%%%%%
   prove((X and Y),WHY,
      (HOWX,HOWY)):–!,                      % to prove a conjunction,
      prove(X,WHY,HOWX),                    % prove each of the conjuncts.
      prove(Y,WHY,HOWY).                    % (HOWX,HOWY) is the combined
                                            % explanation

   prove(X,WHY,proof(X,is,'TRUE')):–        % single condition.
      not(controlled(X)),                   % proof() is just a node term.
      !,                                    % If not controlled, then
      X.                                    % called as a Prolog condition
   prove(not(X),WHY,
      proof(X,is,'DENIED')):–               % proof of negation
      value(X,N),                           % yes no answer
      !,                                    %
      N = n.                                % answer was no
   prove(not(X),WHY,ANY):–                  % proof of negation of X.
      prove(X,WHY,ANY),                     % if X succeeds,
      !,                                    % then
      fail.                                 % not(X) fails
```

```
prove(not((X and Y)),WHY,HOWX):-          % (X and Y) fails if
    prove(not(X),WHY,HOWX),               % X fails
    !.
prove(not((X and Y)),WHY,(HOWX,HOWNOTY)):-
    !,                                    % (X and Y) fails if
    prove(X,WHY,HOWX),                    % X succeeds but
    prove(not(Y),WHY,HOWNOTY).            % Y fails
prove(not(X),WHY,proof(X,is,'NOT PROVED')):-
                                          % as we know, X fails
    not (if Y then X),                    % so not(X) succeeds if
    !.                                    % X is not a conclusion
prove(not(X),WHY,proof(not(X),because,HOWNOTY)):-
                                          % to prove X fails
    (if Y then X),                        % if X is a conclusion
    prove(not(Y),((if Y then X),WHY),HOWNOTY).
                                          % prove that the
                                          % conditions Y fail

prove(X,WHY,proof(X,is,'GIVEN')):-        % proof stops if
    askable X,                            % X is an askable
    !,                                    % condition
    askabout(X,WHY).                      % If n, conclusion fails.
prove(X,WHY,proof(X,because,HOWY)):-
                                          % This is the normal case
    (if Y then X),                        % If X matches a conclusion
    prove(Y,((if Y then X),WHY),HOWY).
                                          % prove the conditions.

%%%%%%%%%%%%%%%% Dialogue %%%%%%%%%%%%%%%%
askabout(X = Y,WHY):-
    value(X,Z),                           % X has a value Z
    !,                                    % if Y is a variable,
    Y = Z.                                % then Y is assigned by unification
askabout(X = Y,WHY):-                     % X has no value,
    !,
    getresponse(give(X = Z),ANS),         % ask for a value
    handleresponse(give(X = Z),ANS,WHY),
                                          % and get it into Z
    Y = Z.                                % assign the value
askabout(C,WHY):-                         % C is an askable condition
    value(C,Y),                           % already stored together with
    !,                                    % a y/n answer
    Y = y.                                % askabout fails if not y.
askabout(C,WHY):-                         % C is askable, but no answer yet
```

```
getresponse(C,ANS),                          % get an answer into ANS and
handleresponse(C,ANS,WHY).                   % handle the ANS response

getresponse(C,ANS):-                         % get a response to C
  out(C),                                    % present it
  request('? >',ANS).                        % prompt an answer

handleresponse(C,why,(U,T)):-                % if user types why, and the
  !,                                         % why explanation term is a chain (U,T)
  reasonwhy(U),                              % present the most recent rule,
  askabout(C,T).                             % call askabout with the remaining
                                             % chain T.

handleresponse(C,why,true):-                 % if the chain is empty
  !,                                         % the user has reached the
                                             % outermost rule
output('THAT WAS YOUR ORIGINAL PROBLEM!'),
askabout(C,true).

handleresponse(give(Y = X),X,ANY):-          % if not why, X gets value
  !,                                         % by unification
  remember(value(Y,X)).                      % store value

handleresponse(C,Z,WHY):-                     % y/n condition
  remember(value(C,Z)),                      % remember answer anyhow,
  !,                                         % but
  Z = y.                                     % fail if response is not y

reasonwhy(U):-                               % explains one rule
  output('BECAUSE'),                         % that is attempted
  outrule(U),                                % print out rule with
  nl.                                        % instantiations
```

%%% Explanation of final proof (HOW explanations)

```
askhow(X,Y),LEVEL):-                         % X and Y is a combined explanation
  !,
  howprove((X,Y),LEVEL).          ˙          % handled by howprove

askhow(proof(C,because,D),LEVEL):-
  !,                                         % C is the conclusion of a rule
  tab(LEVEL),outn(C),                        % C is printed out with indentation
  input(H),                                  % the user may
  respondhow(H,D,LEVEL).                     % get the details

askhow(proof(X,is,Y),LEVEL):-                % X is not found by conclusion
  tab(LEVEL),
  out(X),out(is),output(Y).                  % present how

outn(not(X)):-!,
  out(X),out('is NOT PROVED').               % embellishment
outn(X):-out(X),out('is PROVED').            % for presenting negation

respondhow(how,D,LEVEL):-                     % the user typed 'how' to
```

```
    !,                              % get explanations
    NEXTLEVEL is LEVEL + 4,         % increase indentation by
    tabout(NEXTLEVEL,'BECAUSE'),    % four columns
    howprove(D,NEXTLEVEL).          % give conditions on next level
respondhow(ANY,D,LEVEL):–!.         % no further details are wanted
howprove(CONDS,LEV):–               % prints out explanations
    for (element(X,CONDS),askhow(X,LEV)).
                                    % on next level, with
                                    % options for further recursion
outrule((if Y then X)):–            % prettyprint a rule
    !,
    out('if '),
    outconditions(Y),
    out('then'),output(X).
outconditions((X and Y)):–          % prettyprint the
    !,                              % conditions of a conjunction
    out(X),output(and),
    tab(5),outconditions(Y).
outconditions(X):–                  % prettyprints a single rule
    !,
    output(X).
tabout(N,X):–                       % idented output
    tab(N),
    output(X).
% GENERAL RULES
if X then (X or Y).                 % no special treatment
if Y then (X or Y).                 % for the or operator
%%%%% END OF EXPLAIN EXPERT SYSTEM SHELL %%%%%%%
```

13.10   Non-exact reasoning

13.10.1   Multivalued logic

Multivalued logic is logic with more than two logical values (**TRUE**, **FALSE**). To start with a special case; introduce a logical value U (**UNKNOWN**), which is either T (**TRUE**) or $Få$(**FALSE**), where the result of a logical operation including U, may be F, U or T. For example:

$$U \text{ OR } T = T \qquad \text{\% regardless of } U$$
$$U \text{ AND } T = U \qquad \text{\% result is unknown}$$

U AND $F = F$ % always F
U OR $F = U$ % unknown
NOT $U = U$ % unknown
U AND NOT $U = U$ % corollary
U OR NOT $U = U$ % corollary

A truth table for this logic coincides with a logic of half-truths, where we assign

0 to F,
½ to U and
1 to T,

and interpret

AND   as minimum,
OR   as maximum
NOT X as $1 - X$

The next generalization is to allow any real number in the interval **[0...1]**, but with the same interpretations of **AND**, **OR** and **NOT** as above. This is known as **fuzzy logic** (Zadeh, 1974).

The idea carries over from propositional to predicate logic, so that formulae containing logical variables become functions of the variables to the truth continuum [0,1]. The generalized truth value is called a **certainty level**, with **TRUE = 1.0** (absolutely certainty), and **FALSE = 0.0** (certainty of negation). The name fuzzy logic was also used by Zadeh to denote a set of linguistic truth values including 'very old' and 'more or less false'.

Because the name fuzzy logic is so closely connected with Zadeh's logic, the term **uncertain logic** should perhaps be used to denote logic with levels of certainties or uncertainties. Uncertain logic plays a very important part in expert systems, because in the real world there is no such thing as truth.

13.10.2 Uncertain logic

The real-valued logic plays an important role in expert systems. In uncertain logic, a degree of certainty may be assigned to a conclusion. For instance, 'a man of age X is old to the degree of Y', where Y is a function of X, ranging from 0 at age 0, and 1.0 at age 100.

The combination of such predicates may follow the rules of uncertain logic, as described, but a snag with uncertain logic is that well-known logical laws, such as the exclusive law, are no longer valid. If a

man of 40 is 'old' with certainty 0.4, then he is 'not old' with certainty
0.6 = 1 − 0.4. Conclusively, he is 'old and not old' with certainty
0.4 = min(0.6,0.4). However, in classical logic, a man is never 'old and
not old' so the logical value is F, corresponding to certainty value = 0.

There is another interpretation of a real logical value, namely a
probability for a positive answer to the question:

Is a man of age X old? (yes or no).

The curves in Figure 13.5 go from 0 probability at age 0, to 1.0 at age
100, but can have different shapes.

A man of age X is old to degree Y (xxx)
A man of age (above) X is (regarded as) old with probability Y (ooo)

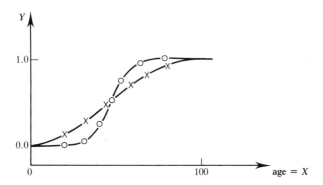

Figure 13.5   Probabilities versus certainties.

The combination of such predicates is subject to the laws of
probability calculus often related to Bayes theorem for updating *a
posteriori* probabilities from *a priori* probabilities and new evidence.

$$P(\text{Hyp}|\text{Ev}) = P(\text{Hyp}) * P(\text{Ev}|\text{Hyp}) / P(\text{Ev})$$

A unifying view of various applications of real-valued logic is
appropriate here. The unifying idea for these examples, and many others,
is that all the literals in a rule are assigned a value called a **certainty
value**. Certainty values of the conclusion are computed from the certainty values
of the conditions by conventions, and by other modifying parameters. For
two good reasons, one psychological and one arithmetical, it is sometimes
preferred to let the certainty be between −1 and +1,

$$[-1,+1]$$

or any other interval symmetric about 0. **NOT** X is denoted by $-X$.

Now, uncertainties can be combined using a multiplying factor to scale-down certainty values to values closer to 0, i.e. less certain, more uncertain. For example, if X has a certainty value of 0.7, then the multiplication of X by 0.6 gives a certainty value $= 0.42$.

The expert system MYCIN/EMYCIN adopts this kind of uncertain reasoning. In the MYCIN rule given initially, the number 0.6 is called a certainty factor, and the conclusion has a certainty value, which (somewhat simplified) is the minimum of the certainty values of the conditions, multiplied by 0.6. If two rules C1, C2 confirm the same conclusion, then the combined certainty is

$$C1 + C2 - C1 * C2$$

13.10.3 Uncertainties in EXPLAIN

Syntactically, in the EXPLAIN framework, the certainty factor in front of the conclusion can be attached to an operator (certainty):

    if morphology(organism,coccus)
    and stain(organism,unknown)
    then 0.6 certainty stain(organism,grampos).

Semantically, the expert system shell is modified to incorporate uncertain reasoning. In doing so, this will not be faithful to EMYCIN, but make another rule of combination of certainties. The explanation facility and other features are omitted. Try their inclusion as an exercise.

```
:-op(978,xfx,then).
:-op(980,fy,if ).
:-op(100,xfx,certainty).
prove(Goal1 and Goal2,Certainty):-
  !,
  prove(Goal1,C1),
  prove(Goal2,C2),
  min(C1,C2,Certainty).
prove(Goal1 or Goal2,Certainty):-
  !,
  prove(Goal1,C1),
  prove(Goal2,C2),
  max(C1,C2,Certainty).
prove(not Goal1,Certainty):-
  !,
```

    prove(Goal1,*C*),
    Certainty is −*C*.

prove(Goal,Certainty):−
    (if Conditions then Factor Certainty Goal),
    prove(Conditions,*C*), *C*>*O*
    Certainty is *C* ∗ Factor.

prove(Fact,1):−
    not (if *C* then Cert certainty Fact),
    !,
    Fact.

show(*X*):−prove(*X*,*C*),
    listelements((*X*,is,proved,with,certainty,*C*)).

listelements(*X*):−for(element(*U*,*X*),out(*U*)),nl.

%%%%% Example of knowledge base

if dayafter(Day,Daz) and
    weather(Day,*X*)
then 0.65 certainty weather(Daz,*X*).

if reported(*X*,*Y*)
then 1 certainty weather(*X*,*Y*).

dayafter(monday,tuesday).
dayafter(tuesday,wednesday).

reported(monday,terrible).

% Sample forecast

?−show(weather(wednesday,*X*)).

weather(wednesday,terrible) is proved with certainty 0.422499

(to be exact).

EXERCISES

13.1 Write an expert system for classifying animals according to the
following knowledge:

    all carnivores are mammals
    all ungulates are mammals
    all birds are animals
    cheetahs and tigers are carnivores
    giraffes and zebras are ungulates
    ostriches, penguins and albatrosses are birds.

giraffes and ostriches have long necks
giraffes and ostriches have long legs
tigers and cheetahs have tawny colour
cheetahs and giraffes have dark spots
tigers and zebras have black stripes
all birds except penguins and ostriches can fly
no bird except penguins can swim
ostriches have black-and-white colour

all mammals have hair
all mammals give milk
all birds have feathers
all birds lay eggs
all carnivores eat meat
all carnivores have pointed teeth and claws
all ungulates have hooves

The expert system is to find which animal is present based on its characteristics.

13.2 Convert the following medical advice (LBS 1985) into the EXPLAIN language.

If a person complains of a symptom and
    a medicine suppresses this symptom and
    this medicine does not harm this person then
this person should take this medicine.

Aspirin suppresses pain.
Lomotil suppresses diarrhoea.
Alcohol suppresses everything.

If a medicine aggravates a symptom and
    a person suffers from this symptom then
    this medicine may harm this person.

If a person has an age and
    this age is less than 18 then
    alcohol may harm this person.

Aspirin aggravates peptic ulcer.
Lomotil aggravates impaired liver function.

13.3 The EXPLAIN rules are in the form:

if a and b then c.

However, it may be necessary to use the form

c if a and b

Change the EXPLAIN shell to accept this new rule syntax.

13.4 Both EXPLAIN in its original form, and the modification in Exercise 13.3 use top-down (backward chaining). However, by using ideas from the bottom-up Prolog interpreter of Prolog, it is possible to implement a kind of forward chaining. Explore these ideas within the EXPLAIN framework.

13.5 Explore the possibilities of calling EXPLAIN from a condition in the rule base.

Chapter 14
Knowledge Engineering

Make a Prolog program
that automatically solves
Prolog programming problems
formulated in natural language.

The last exercise

The process of creating an expert system is considered to be a task for three groups of people, or rather people having three roles:

- real **experts** on a subject domain;
- **knowledge engineers**, who design systems and can choose expert system shells and knowledge representation methods and tools. Their task is **knowledge acquisition**, that is, transferring knowledge from experts and other sources to the expert systems' knowledge base;
- **expert system programmers** who solve problems associated with expert system implementation.

Typical expert systems are developed with the following characteristics:

- human expertise already exists;
- the kinds of problems for the system can be solved over the telephone;
- there is a set of experts willing to share their knowledge;
- there are knowledge engineers responsible for the knowledge transfer;
- there are expert system programmers available if necessary.

14.1 A knowledge engineering example

The final treatment of this book will be of a practical knowledge engineering prototype project developed at the Technical University of

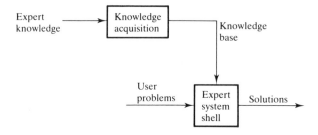

Figure 14.1   Knowledge engineering schema.

Trondheim. The task was to make a prototype expert system for planning a welding process. The purpose was to gain experience in many aspects of expert systems without making too many investments in advanced and expensive equipment at an early stage. However modest this approach was, it answered the questions of what an expert system should be, how it should be made, and how it should work.

The welding expert system was one of a few research projects at the university using different approaches. Prolog was chosen as the implementation tool for this particular project, to give the programmers a wider experience. Another reason for the choice was that Prolog is a tool that had produced fast and impressive prototypes on a number of advanced problems, and that there was reasonably competent Prolog expertise available. Prolog was the only implementation language. However, the kernel of an expert system shell in Prolog existed at the start of the project.

Students of knowledge engineering will probably be in a similar situation when they begin making expert systems of their own. The expert system shell described here will hopefully provide a good starting point.

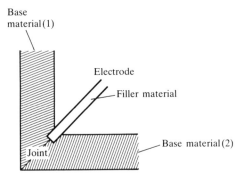

Figure 14.2   Welding taxonomy.

14.1.1 The problem

The welding expert system described in this chapter is meant to be a decision support tool for planners. Most of them are not experts on welding, but they often have to decide how a welding job should be done.

The task of designing a welding process is quite complicated . In many cases, all the passes in a joint are specified in detail (see Figure 14.2), and for heavy constructions, there can be many passes. Another typical problem in welding is the uncertainty connected with the parameters. At the same time, a number of the parameters depend on each other. This often leads to deadlock situations; before a joint type can be found, the method must be known, and the method often depends on the joint type.

In industry, the specification work is often carried out as a trial and error process. A specification is worked out, the joint is welded, and afterwards the joint is tested for quality. If the joint fails, the welding procedure is refined, and the testing carried out again. If the tests prove the joint to hold the required quality, the parent company has a welding procedure specification (WPS) which qualifies for that actual set of constraints. The specification is used for actual construction, and is also saved in a library of qualified procedures.

When a new procedure is being developed, an older one with similarities is often used as a base for the specification. But when the constraints are different, and the quality requirement is strong, the new specification must be tried out in a test. Whether a welding procedure is good or not depends on the fulfillment of the quality requirement, but it must also be economical. This makes the procedure specification an expert's job: a trade-off between quality and economy is crucial. Good welding procedures give an important competitive edge, so their importance is unquestioned.

The information in welding procedure specifications differs from company to company. In this project, carried out in co-operation with a Norwegian company, we concentrated on some critical parameters: joint types, welding method, filler material and heat treatment.

14.1.2 The project

To perform the project work, two experts from the company were brought together with three researchers from the Technical University of Trondheim. The researchers came from different fields, namely welding, mechanical engineering and computer science. The project started in the spring of 1985, and a prototype was finished in October after approximately 18 man-months.

There were two principal tasks to be performed: the acquisition of knowledge from the experts, and the development of an expert system shell to accommodate that knowledge. The project work was distributed in the following way: the knowledge engineering group consisted of a scientist in mechanical engineering as the project leader, and a research scientist on welding. The expert group consisted of two domain experts from the company. The computer scientist acted as the expert system programmer, and was responsible for adapting the expert system shell to the application.

The role of expert system programmer is often combined with the role of the knowledge engineer. There is a large gap in technology between the experts and the knowledge processor, however, and this case proved that the gap may not necessarily be filled by a single person.

14.1.3 Knowledge acquisition

The knowledge engineer worked together with two experts from the company. This work dealt firstly with knowledge acquisition: the experts explained how they specified welding procedures. Step by step, the parameters in the specification were worked out for several examples. All the rules that the experts used were written down in prose, and they were constantly interrupted by questions from the knowledge engineer looking for explanations. This work resulted in a set of rules which were edited by the welding scientist.

The rules were converted into the syntax of the expert system shell:

if Condition1 and Condition2 and ... then Conclusion.

For example:

> **if method = smaw**
> **and bm_unalloyed**
> **and req_yield_strength = Yield and Yield < 440**
> **and req_tensile_strength = Tensile and Tensile < 510**
> **and pos_is_one_of([1,2,3,4,5,6])**
> **then filler_material = 'Norweld Supra'.**

This format was natural for the knowledge engineers, and was chosen among other alternatives.

Besides the rules, a significant number of data tables were necessary in the system. It was clear that much of the information in the knowledge base should be packed into tables, and not written out as rules. The tables were declared by table declarations, followed by the tuples. They were all represented in text form initially, manipulatable by ordinary text editors.

% First a table declaration defining the attribute names:
% then, the tuples in sequence

:–table
filler('Name','Method','Position','Cover','Curr','Pol','No').

filler('OK 48.30',smaw,'123456','BASIC','DC','+',1).
filler('185 T',smaw,'123','RUTIL','DC/AC','+/−',2).

...

filler('Norweld Supra','smaw','123456','BASIC','DC','+',22).

The data in the tables are very company specific. They contain data of the filler materials used by the company, the base materials used in the welded constructions, and the default joint data for different joints. All this information was provided by the company but edited and converted to table form by the knowledge engineer. The tables that were created contained information about materials to be welded (base materials), materials of the electrodes (filler materials), and quality properties as well as chemical analysis.

The tables were found in various reference manuals. To conform with the relational model philosophy, some of them had to be normalized so that all the information was identified by unique keys. This amounted to splitting up repeating groups, and making new tables when necessary.

The first example of a knowledge base was made by the expert system programmer, but after a while, this was taken over by the knowledge engineer. However, the former was consulted several times for assistance as difficulties appeared during installation.

14.1.4 Knowledge base statistics

The welding knowledge base grew to 544 clauses, including rules, table entries and Prolog clauses (see Table 14.1), when the projected was halted for an evaluation phase. This is quite a small expert system. However, if the data in the tables were formulated as rules, several thousand rules would be created, which would make it a medium-sized system.

Table 14.1 Expert system statistics

Standard library	(Prolog clauses)	54
Expert system shell	(Prolog clauses)	60
Welding library	(Prolog clauses)	10
Table entries	(tuples)	303
Rule base	(rules)	117
Number of clauses		544

A complete listing of the knowledge base will not be given, as the example is too large, but no techniques were used that are not covered already in this book.

14.1.5 Performance

It is clear, from the way the prototype performs, that it requires a lot of computer resources. Whilst most problems were answered within seconds, the worst cases took two to three minutes to answer on a VAX11/780. This is too slow for industrial use, where a response time exceeding 20–30 seconds is not acceptable. At the same time, however, it must be stated that some response time is required as a cosmetic to convince the user that an expert was consulted!

The expert system shell was not tuned or optimized for larger bases, and the search for rules to match, and the database retrieval mechanism, were inherently slow in the interpreted Prolog version used. However, there are optimization techniques and language features that were not exploited. These could cut the response time to acceptable limits. But, of equal importance, Prolog compilers an order of magnitude faster are now available, which could do away with considerably larger knowledge bases than ours.

14.1.6 User reactions

The explanation facilities in the expert system shell could:

- explain how conclusions were reached;
- explain why a conclusion was not proven;
- explain why questions were asked.

The company experts liked these features very much. Some of their natural scepticism was dissipated when they found their own rules, specified earlier, as the reason for 'doubted' conclusions. The reaction of the users was typically sceptical. Artificial intelligence and expert systems were far beyond their day to day problems. But when the system was demonstrated, most found it interesting and wanted to try it out.

To make this expert system work in industrial environments, more effort is needed to achieve a high-quality user interface and integration with other systems. An expert system used as a decision-support tool should be available behind, or alongside a system for the storage and retrieval of welding procedures.

A traditional view is that this may be solved by a final reprogramming of the expert system in C or even FORTRAN. However,

knowledge processor technology is rapidly progressing to give systems
with sufficient speed at acceptable costs without reprogramming.

14.1.7   Sample dialogue for a welding consultation

```
| ?–give method = smaw.
yes
| ?–eval electrode.
same_base_material ? >y.
give base_material = _142 ? >'St 52–3'.
give req_yield_strength = _397 ? >400.
give req_duct_temperature = _620 ? >10.
give position = _828 ? >4.
electrode = Norweld Supra is PROVED >how.
  BECAUSE
  method = smaw is GIVEN
  filler_material = Norweld Supra is PROVED >how.
    BECAUSE method = smaw is GIVEN
    bm_unalloyed is PROVED >how.
      BECAUSE
      base_mat = St 52–3 is PROVED >how.
        BECAUSE
        same_base_material is GIVEN
        base_material = St 52–3 is GIVEN
      to_base_mat = St 52–3 is PROVED >how.
        BECAUSE
        same_base_material is GIVEN
        base_material = St 52–3 is GIVEN
      basematr:St 52–3 has Type = STRUCTURAL STEEL is
        TRUE
      STRUCTURAL STEEL <> STAINLESS STEEL is TRUE
  quality_ok(Norweld Supra) is PROVED >how.
    BECAUSE
    yield_strength_ok(Norweld Supra) is PROVED >how.
      BECAUSE
      req_yield_strength = 400 is GIVEN
      filler:Norweld Supra has No = 22 is TRUE
      fip:22 has Yield = 440 is TRUE
      400<440 is TRUE
    duct_temp_ok(Norweld Supra) is PROVED >how.
      BECAUSE
      req_duct_temperature = 10 is GIVEN
      filler:Norweld Supra has No = 22 is TRUE
      fip:22 has SSt = 0 is TRUE
```

```
        10 > 0 is TRUE
     position_ok(Norweld Supra) is PROVED >how.
        BECAUSE
        position = 4 is GIVEN
        filler:Norweld Supra has Position = 123456 is TRUE
        index(123456,4) is TRUE
OTHER SOLUTIONS ? >y.

electrode = OK 48.30 is PROVED >ok.
OTHER SOLUTIONS ? >y.

root_clipping_possible ? >y.
electrode = Comet 56 LH is PROVED
OTHER SOLUTIONS ? >no.
 | ?–
```

14.2   Comparison with traditional system development

Developing expert systems is not very different from designing ordinary systems, except that: it is important to get a preliminary prototype running at an early date to keep the experts interested. In addition, the user requirement specification is typically rough. It is difficult to make the prospective users work out a detailed specification. However, always bear in mind that the knowledge acquisition needs more effort than you may imagine when the project starts. For example, you may have to go through more cycles than standard system design and testing, due to the fact that rules will never be complete.

As knowledge technology becomes more widespread, it will certainly have a big impact on professional life. Expert systems will make expertise available to more people than ever before. The economic considerations will eventually be the decisive factors for their widespread use, but hopefully they will be made interesting and instructive to use, so that the professional level of use will be increased together with the profit.

Appendix
Predicate Library

The predicates are listed in alphabetic order for quick reference. This organization is highly recommended for larger programs. Built-in predicates are mingled with the library predicates, also in alphabetical order. These are listed as comments here, so that the whole test is a valid Prolog program.

```
%%%% GENERAL PREDICATE LIBRARY
%%%% This text contains a list of defined
%%%% operators in alphabetical order, and then
%%%% a list of the Prolog library predicates
%%%% that are used frequently.
%%%% Intermingled are the built-in predicates
%%%% as comments, so that a lookup will
%%%% show them together.
%%%   OPERATOR DEFINITIONS
:-op(1100,fx,[list,listall]).

:-op(980,fx,if ).
:-op(979,xfy,else).
:-op(978,xfx,then).
:-op(960,xfx,impl).          % implication
;-op(950,fx,table).
:-op(950,xfy,or).            % same as ';' but higher priority
:-op(940,xfy,and).           % same as ',' but higher priority
:-op(900,xfx,has).

:-op(1,xfx,':').
%%% OPERATOR BODIES
%%% Operator-declared predicates are defined
and(X,Y):-X,Y.               % Same as (X,Y)

list X,Y:-nl,nl,
   for(Y,output(X)),nl,
   fail.                     % avoid standard response

listall X:-list,X,X.

(if X then Y else Z):-X,!,Y.
(if X then Y else Z):-Z.
```

```
or(X,Y):-X.                          % Same as (X;Y)
or(X,Y):-Y.
```

% not(X). built-in, X is not provable

%%% ALPHABETIC LIST OF PREDICATES

```
abs(X,Z):-                           % Z is the absolute value of X
  Y is X,
  (if Y > 0 then Z is Y else Z is -Y).
```

```
all(X):-output(X),fail.              % output all X by forced backtracking
```

% append(X,Y,Z) Z is a new list of the members of X and Y

```
append([],X,X).
append([X|Y],U,[X|V]):-
  append(Y,U,V).
```

% arg(N,F,X) built-in argument no N of term F is X

```
cons(X,Y,[X|Y]).                     % relational definition of cons
```

```
construct(X,Y):-                     % create tuples of form X for all solutions
  for(Y,remember(X)).                % of the predicate Y
```

```
countall(X,Y,N):-                    % N is number of unique X such that Y
  findall(X,Y,Z),                    % Z is the set of them
  numberof(Z,N).                     % N is the length of this list
```

% delete(X,Y,Z) Z is the list where X is taken out of Y

```
delete(X,[X|Y],Y).
delete(X,[U|V],[U|Y]):-
  delete(X,V,Y).
```

% element is the membership predicate for innermost
% elements in a round list.

```
element(X,Y):-
  var(Y),                            % Y is a variable
  !,                                 % avoid trap
  X = Y.
element(X,(U,V)):-!,
  (element(X,U);
  element(X,V)).
element(X,X):-not X = nil.
```

```
expect(X,Y):-X,!.                    % if X is true, ok
expect(X,Y):-output(Y),              % otherwise, print message Y
  fail.                              % and fail.
```

% fail. built-in, always fail.

% findall(X,Y,Z) Z becomes set of unique X such that Y

```
findall(X,Y,Z):-
  construct(new(X),Y),
```

```
    reap(Z).
for(X,Y):-X,Y,fail.                    % iteration by backtracking
for(X,Y).                              % do Y for all solutions of X

forget(X):-for(X,retract(X)).          % forgets all facts unifiable with X
% functor(FX,F,N) FX is a term
%                 F is the function name of FX,
%                 N is number of arguments
% works both ways

% get0(X) built-in. Reads one ASCII character (value)

% in(I,L,H) instantiates by demand I to integers between L and H
in(I,I,H):-H >= I.
in(I,L,H):-L < H,
    N is L + 1,
    in(I,N,H).

implies(X,Y):-not((X,not(Y))).         % X possibly implies Y if there
                                       % are no contradictions

input(X):-request('>',X).              % standard prompt

listelements(L):-                      % list elements in round list
    for(element(E,L),out(E)),nl.

listof(X,Y,Z):-                        % find list of X so that
    for(Y,assert(new(X))),             % Y is true, and put them into Z
    reap(Z).

max(X,Y,Z):-                           % Z is the maximum of the
    XX is X,                           % values of X and Y
    YY is Y,
    (if XX > YY then Z = XX else Z = YY).

member(X,[X|_]).                       % standard membership in square lists
member(X,[_|V]):-
    member(X,V).

min(X,Y,Z):-                           % Z is minimum of X and Y values
    XX is X,
    YY is Y,
    (if XX > YY then Z = YY else Z = XX).
% name(Atom,ASCIIlist) built-in, convert Atom to ASCIIlist
% nl. built-in, prints new line
% not(X). built-in, succeeds if X is impossible.
% number(N). built-in, N is a number.
% numberin(X,L,N). X occurs as element number N in the list L
numberin(Symbarg,[Symbarg|R],1):-!.
numberin(Symbarg,[R|B],N):-
```

```
    numberin(Symbarg,B,BN),!,
    N is BN + 1.
```

% numberof(X,N). N is the number of elements in the list X

```
numberof([],0).
numberof([X|Y],N):-
    numberof(Y,M),
    N is M + 1.
```

```
out(X):-                          % prints a term with a space
    print(X),
    print(' ').
```

```
output(X):-                       % prints a term with a new line
    print(X),
    nl.
```

% plus is a symmetric predicate which solves
% the equation X + Y = Z, provided not more than
% one variable

```
plus(X,Y,Z):-not var(X),not var(Y),!,Z is X + Y.
plus(X,Y,Z):-var(X),not var(Y),not var(Z),!,X is Z - Y.
plus(X,Y,Z):-not var(X),var(Y),not var(Z),Y is Z - K.
```

```
printstring(X):-                  % prints list of ASCII values as a string
    name(I,X),output(I).
```

% reap is an auxiliary predicate to make
% the solution of the predicate 'new' into a list

```
reap([X|Y]):-
    retract(new(X)),
    !,
    reap(Y).
reap([]).
```

```
remember(X):-X,!.                 % asserts a fact if it is not
remember(X):-assert(X).           % already known
```

```
request(TEXT,VALUE):-             % get input from user with an
    print(TEXT),                  % explaining text (prompt)
    read(VALUE).
```

% see(F). built-in, switch to input file F
% seen. built-in, switch back to user input
% tell(F). built-in, switch output file to F
% told. built-in, switch back to user output
% var(X). built-in X is an unbound variable
%%%%%%%%%% END OF STANDARD LIBRARY %%%%%%%%%%

%%% RELATIONAL LIBRARY
%%% makes relations accessible by symbolic names.

% table is declared accessible by symbolic names

```
table T:- listelements(('TABLE',T)),
    T = ..[F|L],
    functor(T,G,N),
    functor(TX,G,N),
    assert(template(F,TX)),
    assertallargs(F,L,1).
```

% has is the important operator for access

```
Rel:Key has Att = Value:-
    tabvalue(Rel,Key,Att,Value),
    not Value = nil.
```

```
key(Tab,Keyv):-
    template(Tab,TX),
    arg(1,TX,Keyv),
    !,
    TX.
```

```
tabvalue(Table,Key,Neim,Value):-% predicate to access table
    dictionary(Table,Neim,N),        % Neim is argument number N
    template(Table,T),               % T is a tuple template
    arg(1,T,Key),                    % key is inserted as first argument
    arg(N,T,Value),                  % value becomes Nth argument
    !,
    T.                               % this tuple is searched for
```

```
assertallargs(Tab,[X|Y],M):-!,
    assert(dictionary(Tab,X,M)),
    N is M + 1,
    assertallargs(Tab,Y,N).
```

```
assertallargs(Tab,[],_).
```

%%% END OF RELATIONAL LIBRARY

Bibliography

Amble, T. (1984). *Logic Programming – An Introduction with NTH-Prolog.* Trondheim: TAPIR (out of print)

Amble, T., Stalhane, T. and Wessel, T. (1982). 'Soft Systems progress report', *Sintef report STF1482010*

Aristotle. *Organon*

Backhouse, R. C. (1986). *Program Construction and Verification.* Prentice-Hall International

Backus, J. (1958). 'The FORTRAN automatic coding system' in *Programming Systems and Languages*; S. Rosen; Ed.

Bocca, J. (1985). *Educe – A Marriage of Convenience: Prolog and a Relational DBMS.* Munich: European Computer Industry GmbH

Bolc, E.; Ed. (1978). *Natural Language Communication with Computers.* Berlin: Springer-Verlag

Boole, G. (1854). *Investigations of the Law of Thought.*

Borland International (1986). *Turbo-Prolog: The Natural Language of AI.* Borland

Bouzeghoub, M., Gardarin, G. and Metais, E. (1985). 'Database design tools: an expert systems approach', *Proceedings of the VLD8.* Stockholm

Boyer, R. S. and Moore, J. S. (1972). 'The sharing of structure in theorem-proving programs', *Machine Intelligence*, 7

Bratko, I. (1986). *Prolog Programming for Artificial Intelligence.* Wokingham: Addison-Wesley

Buchanan, B. G. and Shortliffe, E. H. (1984). *Rule-based Expert Systems: The MYCIN Experiments of the Stanford Heuristic Programming Project.* Reading, Mass.: Addison-Wesley

Bundy, A. (1983). *The Computer Modelling of Mathematical Reasoning.* Academic Press

Ceri, S. and Gottlob, G. (1986). 'Normalization of relations and Prolog', *Communications of the ACM*, **29**(6)

Chang, C. L. and Lee, R. C. T. (1973). *Symbolic Logic and Mechanical Theorem Proving.* New York: Academic Press

Clark, K. L. (1978). 'Negation as failure', *Logic and Databases.* Plenum, H. Gaillare and J. Minker; Eds.
274

Clark, K. L. and McCabe, F. G. (1982). 'Prolog: a language for implementing expert systems', *Machine Intelligence*, **10**

Clark, K. L. and McCabe, F. G. (1984). *Micro-Prolog Programming in Logic*. Prentice-Hall International

Clark, K. L. and Tarnlund, S. A. (1982). *Logic Programming*. Academic Press

Clocksin, W. and Mellish, C. (1982). *Programming in Prolog*. Berlin: Springer-Verlag

Codd, E. (1970). *Communications of the ACM*

Coelho, H., *et. al.* (1982). *How to Solve it with Prolog*. Laboratoria Nacional di Engenhara Civil

Colmerauer, A., *et. al.* (1971). *TAUM–71*. Group TAUM; Université de Montréal

Colmerauer, A. *et. al.* (1978). 'Metamorphosis grammars', *Natural Language Communication with Computers*. Springer-Verlag, E. Bolc; Ed.

Dahl, V. (1977). *Un Système Déductif d'interrogation de Banques de Données en Espagnol*. Université d'Aix-Marseille

Dahl, V.; Ed. (1985). *Natural Language Understanding and Logic Programming*. North-Holland

Date, C. J. (1986). *An Introduction to Database Systems*. Reading, Mass.: Addison-Wesley, 4th edn

Dijkstra, E. W. (1966). 'The goto statement considered harmful', *Communications of the ACM*, **11**(3), pp. 147–8

Feigenbaum, E. A. and McCorduck, P. (1984). *The Fifth Generation: AI and Japan's Computer Challenge to the World*. Reading, Mass.: Addison-Wesley

Forgy, C. L. (1981). *OPS5 User's Manual*. Carnegie-Mellon University

Frege, G. (1879). *Begriffschrift eine der Arithmetischen Nachgebildete Formelsprache des reinen Denkens*. Halle: Louis Nebert

Futo, I., Darvas, F. and Szeredi, P. (1978). 'The application of Prolog to the query answering of QA and DBM systems', *Logic and Databases*. Plenum, H. Gaillare and J. Minker; Eds.

Gaillare, H. and Minker, J.; Eds. (1978). *Logic and Databases*. Plenum

Garey, M. R. and Johnson, D. S. (1980). *Computers and Intractability*. W. H. Freeman

Genesereth, M. R. and Ginsberg, M. L. (1985). 'Logic programming', *Communications of the ACM*. September

Giannesini, F., Kanoui, H. Pasero, R. and van Caneghem, M. (1986). *Prolog*. Wokingham: Addison-Wesley

Green, C. (1969). 'Theorem proving by resolution as a basis for question answering', *Machine Intelligence*, **4**

Griswold, R. (1968). *The SNOBOL 4 Programming Language*. Prentice-Hall International

Hamilton, A. G. (1978). *Logic for Mathematicians*. Cambridge: Cambridge University Press

Hammond, P. (1980) in Clark and McCabe (1982)

Harmon, P. and King, D. (1985). *Expert Systems: Artificial Intelligence in Business*. Chichester: John Wiley and Sons

Hayes, P. (1973). 'Computation and deduction', *Proceedings of the Second MCFS Symposium*. Czechoslovak Academy of Sciences

Hayes-Roth, F., Waterman, D. A. and Lenat, D. B.; Eds. (1983). *Building Expert Systems*. Reading, Mass.: Addison-Wesley

Herbrand, J. (1930) 'Recherche sur la theorie de la demonstration'. Thèse, U. de Paris. In *Escrits logiques de Jacques Herbrand*. PUF, Paris (1968)

Hoare, C. A. R. (1962). 'Quicksort', *Computer Journal*, **5**(1) pp. 10–15

Hoare, C. A. R. (1972). 'An axiomatic definition of the programming language PASCAL', *Report (6)*, Zurich: Fachgruppe C–W ETH

Holberg, L. (1730). *Erasmus Montanus*.

Horn, A. (1951). 'On sentences which are true for direct unions of algebras', *Journal of Symbolic Logic*, **16**

Jackson, P. (1986). *Introduction to Expert Systems*. Wokingham: Addison-Wesley

Kanoui, H. and Bergman, M. (1973) Application of mechanical theorem-proving to symbolic calculus. *Third International Symposium of Advanced Computer Methods*. VNRS, Marseilles

Knuth, D. (1968). 'Semantics of context-free languages', *Mathematical Systems Theory*, **2**(2), Springer-Verlag

Kowalski, R. A. (1974a). 'Predicate logic as a programming language', *Proceedings of the IFIP Congress*.

Kowalski, R. A. (1974b). 'A proof procedure based on connection graphs', *Journal of the ACM*, **22**

Kowalski, R. A. (1979a). 'Algorithm = logic + control', *Communications of the ACM*, August, **22**, pp. 424–43

Kowalski, R. A. (1979b). *Logic for Problem Solving*. North-Holland

Kowalski, R. A. and Kuehner, D. (1971). 'Linear resolution with selection function', *Artificial Intelligence*, **2**

Lloyd, J. W. (1984). *Foundations of Logic Programming*. Springer-Verlag

Logic Based Systems Ltd (1985). *Augmented Prolog for Expert Systems*. LBS

Moto-Oka, T. (1981). 'Fifth generation computer systems', *Proceedings of the*

International Conference on Fifth Generation Computer Systems

Nilsson, N. J. (1982). *Principles of Artificial Intelligence*. Springer-Verlag

O'Keefe, R. (1982). 'A smooth applicative merge-sort', *D.A.I. Research Paper* (1982) *Information Processing Letters*

Pereira, F.; Ed. (1984). *C-Prolog User's Manual, Version 1.5*. EdCAAD, University of Edinburgh

Pereira, F. C. N. and Warren, D. H. D. (1980). 'Definite clause grammars for language analysis', *Artificial Intelligence*

Pereira, L. M.; Ed. (1982). *Logic Programming Newsletter*

Pereira, L. M. (1982). 'Logic control with logic', *First International Logic Programming Conference*, Marseille

Pereira, L. M., Sabatier, P. S. and Oliveira, E. (1982). 'ORBI: an expert system for environmental resource evaluation', *First International Logic Programming Conference*, Marseille

Reiter, R. (1978). 'On closed world data bases, *Logic and Databases*. Plenum. H. Gaillare and J. Minker; Eds.

Robinson, J. A. (1965), 'A machine-oriented logic based on the resolution principle', *Journal of the ACM*

Roussel, P. (1975). Prolog: *Manuel de Référence et d'Utilisation*. Groupe d'Intelligence Artificielle, Université d'Aix-Marseille

Shapiro, E. Y. (1982). *Algorithmic Program Debugging*. The MIT Press

Shapiro, E. Y. (1983). 'Logic programs with uncertainties: a tool for implementing rule-based systems', *IJCAI 83*, Karlsrühe

Shortliffe, E. H. (1976). *MYCIN: Computer-based Medical Consultation*. Elsevier

Siekmann, J. and Stephan, W. (1976). 'Completeness and soundness of the connection graph proof procedure', *Interner Bericht*, (7/76) Institut für Informatik Universität Karlsrühe

Stickel, M. E. and Tyson, W. M. (1985). 'An analysis of consecutively bounded depth-first search with applications in automated deduction', *International Joint Conference on AI*

Wall, R. (1972). *Introduction to Mathematical Linguistics*. Prentice-Hall International

Warren, D. H. D. (1974). 'WARPLAN: a system for generating plans', *Memo 75 DCL*, University of Edinburgh

Warren, D. H. D. (1977). 'Implementing Prolog – compiling predicate logic programs', *D.A.I. Research Report*, (39) University of Edinburgh

Warren, D. H. D. (1980). *Logic programming and compiler writing: software practice and experience*.

Warren, D. H. D. (1981). *Efficient processing of interactive relational database queries expressed in logic.* IEEE

Warren, D. H. D. (1982). 'Higher-order extensions to Prolog – are they needed?', *Machine Intelligence*, **10**

Warren, D. H. D. and Pereira, F. C. N. (1981). 'An efficient and easily adaptable system for interpreting natural language queries', *D.A.I. Research Report*, (155), University of Edinburgh

Warren, D. H. D., Pereira, F. C. N. and Pereira, L. M. (1977). 'Prolog – the language and its implementation compared with LISP', *SIGPLAN Notices* **12**(8)

Warren, D. H. D., *et. al.* (1979). 'User's guide to DEC System-10 Prolog', *D.A.I. Research Report.* University of Edinburgh

Waterman, D. A. (1985). *A Guide to Expert Systems.* Reading, Mass.: Addison-Wesley

Whitney, R. *et. al.* (1985). 'A predicate connection graph-based logic with flexible control', *IJCAI*

Winston, P. H. and Horn, B. K. P. (1981). *LISP.* Reading, Mass.: Addison-Wesley

Wirth, N. and Jensen, K. (1974). *Pascal User Manual and Report.* Springer-Verlag

Woods, W. (1978). 'Augmented transition networks', *Natural Language Communication with Computers.* Berlin: Springer-Verlag, E. Bolc; Ed.

Zadeh, L. A. (1974). 'Fuzzy logic and its application to approximate reasoning', *IFIP Congress.* North-Holland

Index

A* algorithm   226
abduction   13
APES   230
append   86
arg   132
Aristotle   4
arity   25
artificial expertise   10
artificial intelligence   8
assert   69
atom   76
attribute grammar   183

backtracking   47
backward chaining   230
basevariable   240
Bayes theorem   256
best-first search   226
Boole, George   5
Boolean algebra   13
bottom up   24
bottom-up interpreter   125
built-in operator   66
built-in predicate   62

certainty factor   229
class   159
clausal form   16
clause   16
clause grammar   173
clause normalization   36
closed world assumption   57
Colmerauer, A.   7
combinatorial explosion   224
comment   46
compiler   167
complete   30
conclusion   17
condition   17
conjunction   16
conjunctive normal form   37

connection graphs   42
cons   84
consistent   29
constant identifier   22
constant in Prolog   45
consult   63
cut   54

database   146
decidable   31
declarative semantics   46
definite clause   17
definite clause grammar   190
delete   87
difference list   95
differentiation   130
disjunction   16
D-list   95
dotted pair   79

elimination rule   15
empty list   81
EMYCIN   229
end_of_file   63
expert system   10, 229
EXPLAIN   231
extralogical   75

fact   45
factoring   40
fail   57
fifth generation computers   3
file   66
findall   92
first order predicate logic   20
for   109
forget   70
formula manipulation   132
forward chaining   230
Frege, G.   5
function   25

functional term   25
functor   25, 132
functor   122
fuzzy logic   255

generate-and-test   213
generate-or-test   214
get0   170
goal   47

Herbrand, J.   6
heuristic search   226
heuristics   224
Horn clause   17
how explanation   231

inconsistent   30
input resolution   41
inside outwards accumulation   106
instantiate   21
integration   138
interpretation   29
is   67

knowledge acquisition   264
knowledge-based system   9
knowledge engineer   11
knowledge engineering   11
knowledge system   10
Kowalski, R.   7

left-recursive   49
Leibniz, G.   5
lexical analysis   167, 198
library   62
linear resolution   41
LISP   78
list   80
list (empty)   81
literal   17
logic programming   7, 26
logical implication   30
logical negation   120

member   85
mergesort   97
meta-logic   124
meta-programming   121

model   30
MYCIN   229

naive reverse   88
name   99
natural language   11
negation as failure   56
nl   65
not   59
number   76

occur check   52
op   72
operator   71
outside inwards accumulation   106

possible implication   112
predicate   21
predicate calculus   33
predicate library   62
predicate logic   20
print   65
priority of operators   71
procedural semantics   46
program verification   139
Prolog   2
proof   17, 30
proof strategy   24, 41
propositional calculus   13
propositional logic   13

quantifier   22, 31
query-the-user   237
quicksort   98

read   65
recursion   48
refutation   17
relational database   146
remember   70
repeat   109
resolution   23, 39
resolve   23
resolvent   23, 39
retract   70
right-recursive   49
Robinson, J.A.   6
round list   100

rule   45
rule-based expert system   229

satisfiable   29
second order logic   32
see   66
seen   66
semantic net   158
semantics of Prolog   46
set   89
set of support   41
setof   92
S-expression   78
shell   229
Skolem, T.   34
Skolem constant   35
Skolem function   34
smart reverse   88
string   99
syllogism   4
symmetry   53
syntax analysis   170
syntax of Prolog   44

tab   65
table   152

tell   66
term   25
told   66
top down   24
top-down interpreter   124
Tower of Hanoi   77, 210
transitive closure   107
truth table   13
Turing test   8
two-level grammar   182

uncertain logic   255
unification   26, 38
unique name assumption   22
user   63

var   76
variable condition   59
variable in logic   21
variable in Prolog   44
virtual table   150

Warren, D.H.D.   7
well-formed formula (WFF)   33
why explanation   231